The Least of These

THE LEAST OF THESE

BY

CURT YOUNG

MOODY PRESS
CHICAGO

Library of Congress Cataloging in Publication Data

Young, Curt, 1952-
  The least of these.

  Bibliography: p.
  1. Abortion—Religious aspects—Christianity. 2. Abortion—United States. 3. Abortion—Law and legislation—United States. 4. Pro-life movement—United States. I. Title.
HQ767.3.Y68 1983   363.4'6'0973   84-9096
ISBN 0-8024-0355-7

2 3 4 5 6 7 Printing/AF/Year 89 88 87 86 85 84

Printed in the United States of America

Contents

To Mrs. Anne V. Higgins,
the most courageous pro-lifer I'll ever know,
and a very fine lady

Acknowledgments

This book would not have been written except for the persistent encouragement of the fine people at Moody Press. Special thanks to Ella Lindvall, who initially approached me about the project, and to Jerry Jenkins, a long-time ally and friend. Lynn Ekblad's cheerful support and enthusiasm for the book stirred me up. She patiently entertained my ideas and with equal patience endured my groanings.

My gratitude to the Christian Action Council runs deep as well. The board permitted me time to write the book, and my colleagues on staff filled in during my absences. To the extent this book makes a contribution to solving the abortion problem, it is their book.

Last, and most important, I thank my bride, Diane. In this as in all facets of my life, she proved a helpmate in every sense. Her love inspires me.

Introduction

Dear Sir,

I agree with you 100% on abortion, but I had one. It was the hardest thing I ever had to do in my life. I'm gonna tell you straight out how I feel. My boyfriend and I fell in love, we made love, and I got pregnant. . . . My mom had noticed I had skipped my period. I was taken to the doctor. He said I was about six weeks pregnant. So she said I had to have an abortion. . . . I had a counselor at Planned Parenthood who talked to me. She said my baby would never be adopted. Who was I to turn to?

My mother and father didn't want me to have the child. I was forbidden to see my boyfriend, and the people at Planned Parenthood said my baby would never be adopted. Now . . . would you mind telling me what *you* would have done? I didn't have a place to go, no money. Would *you* have taken me into your home? Paid my doctor bills and expenses?

My abortion is something I wish I had never done. I can remember looking at the doctor when it was done and saw him putting my baby in a plastic bag and then, throwing it away in a garbage bag. Do you know how that feels? . . . Have you ever lost something you loved dearly? I did, and I'm not proud of it. . . . If I had a place to go and people who cared about my baby and me, maybe my baby would be born and alive. It was supposed to be born this month. . . .

You're hurting girls that wanted their babies, but didn't have any alternative, but to have it aborted. But I want to say it hurts. . . .

You people are against abortion, but are you willing to help young girls and women who don't have the money or a place to live? . . . Some of us women and girls are not killers. We're human too. And I can tell you having an abortion is killing me slowly.

Carrie*

Before it was ever legal, abortion was promoted as a woman's right, a matter of freedom. The prohibition against abortion was denounced as another example of a male-dominated society's victimizing women, a terrible imposition. The argument was made with a vengeance: abortion should be legalized and accepted.

Today abortions are legal in the United States. For many thousands, perhaps millions, of women, abortion has become the terrible imposition; and they have become the second victim of a procedure that was supposed to make them free.

WHY I AM AN ACTIVIST

People come to oppose abortion for many different reasons. In 1978 I concluded I must actively oppose abortion because of a conviction that life created in God's image is destroyed every time an abortion is performed. That conclusion was reached only after three long years of study on every possible aspect of the issue—biological, ethical, psychological, medical, sociological, theological.

Of all the articles on abortion that I read, none suggested that abortion victimizes women. The issue was couched in exactly the opposite terms by abortion advocates. Opponents of abortion focused on the fetus as a tiny human being entitled to the right to life. The experience of abortion and pressures women are under to abort their offspring were never covered. Abortion opponents didn't question that women wanted abortions, and the advocates couldn't get beyond their angry slogans.

After resolving to fight abortion, I joined the Christian Action Council. Shortly thereafter, we committed ourselves to develop ministries providing alternatives to abortion. The goal of these "Crisis Pregnancy Centers" would be to compete with abortion clinics for the attention of women facing stressful or unwanted pregnancies. Efforts had previously been confined to education on abortion and active support for legislation drafted to stop the government from funding and promoting the practice.

As far as ministry was concerned, we had no idea what the

*The accounts and testimonies presented in this book are true, but individuals' names have been changed to protect their privacy.

reaction would be. We were somewhat fearful as to whether women faced with abortion would actually *want* our help. We were starting from scratch, because no program of ministry then existed anywhere.

We quickly learned that for many women, abortion is a horror. The letter quoted above portrays tragically the position of many teenagers at the time of their abortions. It was written by a young woman who was forced to abort. She wanted help, but no one was there to hear her cries. She wrote this letter to a Christian. It may as well have been you or I.

SURVEY OF PROTESTANT DENOMINATIONS

The vast majority of Protestant denominations have denounced abortion as evil. A study done in 1980 indicates that of ninety-nine denominations, fifty-nine have either adopted formal resolutions opposing abortion or have stated their opposition in other forms. Some make explicit exception for abortion to save the life of the mother; others do not. Another fifteen denominational groups have gone on record as generally opposed to abortion but would make exceptions in one or more of the hard cases (e.g., pregnancy resulting from rape or incest, pregnancy leading to the birth of a baby with deformities). Fourteen denominations either through formal resolution or other means have expressed support for abortion as the right of every woman. The remaining eleven denominations refused to take any position whatsoever on abortion.[1]

As expected, advocates of abortion applauded as denominations came out in support of abortion rights. A national organization was formed to represent their views in Washington. Those same advocates denounced denominations opposing abortion on the grounds that their views reflect narrow sectarian values that have no place in society at large.

Over the last eleven years, abortion advocates have solicited testimony from clergy who support abortion whenever hearings were held in Congress. At the same time, they have charged that similar attempts to influence legislators by ministers who oppose abortion violate the constitutional separation of church and state.

Are these charges true, and, if so, should they be limited to Protestants opposed to abortion? Or are those denominational statements that condemn abortion a basis for just law and a guide to keep people from tragedy?

1. Tj. Bosgra, *Abortion, the Bible, and the Church* (Honolulu, Hawaii: Hawaii Right to Life Educational Foundation, 1980), pp. 31-35.

The statements read as if the Christian leaders who wrote them believed they were stating the truth about abortion. But few attempts have subsequently been made to bring that witness to bear upon society. The failure to actually *do* something to curb abortion witnesses as well, of course. It serves to confirm the charge that opposition to abortion is a sectarian matter, for members only.

James's rebuke is apt: "Show me your faith without the works, and I will show you my faith by my works" (James 2:18). Formal statements count for nothing in the case of Carrie and other young women like her.

RESOLVE MUST STRENGTHEN

Perhaps Christians lack the resolve to stop abortion because of apathy toward evil. If so, this indicates a terrible indifference toward the holiness of God. Perhaps this grows out of a sort of inferiority complex, a poor self-image reinforced by a hostile press. On these points one can only speculate, but one point is quite clear. Christians identifying with Protestant denominations opposed to abortion represent a large segment of our society and the vast majority of Protestants in America. Their resolve must strengthen before the practice can be stopped.

Is it worth the sacrifice? Believers will decide for themselves. As long as women like Carrie cry out for help, however, the church will have a constant reminder of what happens when they do nothing.

1

Less Than Human, Entitled to Nothing

We hold these truths to be self-evident: That all men are created equal, that they are endowed by their Creator with certain inalienable rights, among these are life, liberty, and the pursuit of happiness, that to secure these rights governments are instituted among men.

Should the right to life be extended to the unborn? The question has sparked unparalleled controversy over the last twenty years in the United States. Initially the law was under attack by abortion proponents because existing statutes prohibited abortion. All this was changed, however, in 1973 when the Supreme Court handed them the victory they could not achieve through state legislatures. In a 7-2 decision known as *Roe v. Wade,* the High Court mandated a policy of elective abortion throughout the United States.

The High Court's sweeping opinion did nothing to resolve the controversy. On the contrary, it served only to shift and intensify it. Today it is abortion foes who fight to change the law.

A NATION DIVIDED

In recent years the Supreme Court has been under attack for a variety of decisions: school prayer, bussing, reapportionment. None of those has created the dissension and strife generated by the abortion decision. In fact no decision in recent history has so divided the nation.

One indication of the level of controversy surrounding abortion may be found in Congress. Since 1976 the House and Senate have cast more roll call votes on abortion than on any other issue. In spite of politicians' efforts to avoid it, abortion has consumed vast amounts of time, energy, and political capital. Another indication is the extent to which public protest has occurred. Every year since 1974, close to 100,000 citizens have converged upon the Capitol in the annual March for Life. This has become the largest annual march in US history. As the march in Washington, D.C., takes place every January 22, similar protests occur in dozens of state capitals and hundreds of cities across the country.

Longtime political analysts have observed that opposition to abortion has changed the face of American politics. An unheard-of coalition has developed between traditionally Democratic Roman Catholics in the Northeast, traditionally Democratic evangelicals in the South, and traditionally Republican evangelicals in the Midwest and Far West. The results have clearly been in evidence in elections where longstanding members of Congress have met with defeat because they supported abortion on demand, for example, Senators Dick Clark (Iowa, 1978), Birch Bayh (Indiana, 1980), Frank Church (Idaho, 1980), Thomas J. McIntyre (New Hampshire, 1978), and Robert Morgan (North Carolina, 1980). This same coalition was directly involved in electing Ronald Reagan to the presidency in 1980.

HISTORIC ANALOGY

Only once before in American history has so controversial an issue become crystalized around a decision by the US Supreme Court. Slavery provides us with an analogy that is worth investigation. In the midst of so many conflicting statements and so much rhetoric, a look at the lessons of history can do much to clarify our thinking about abortion.

The Declaration of Independence served as the charter of revolution for the colonists. It was premised upon a very liberating notion: a true and just God creates all men. He blesses them all with fundamental rights. When government selectively denies those rights to men, they have just occasion to revolt against it.

Subsequent to the Revolutionary War and the brief tenure of the Articles of Confederation, the Constitution was drafted as the new nation's charter of government. A free country rather than tyranny was the aim of the document, a nation safeguarding those rights for which Americans had fought. Unless the new government conformed to the ideals of the revolution that produced it, it too would be thrown off.

Tragically, the Constitution was not consistent in guaranteeing the rights of all who came under it, because all men were not considered equal. No revolution came, however; those denied justice were not in a position to protest or revolt. As Jefferson penned the lofty words of the Declaration, they were already in chains; their bondage was more than one hundred fifty years old. They were America's black slaves.

SLAVERY ACKNOWLEDGED

Slavery was acknowledged in the first article of the Constitution. In Article 1, Section 2, the issue of apportioning Congressional districts to the states was addressed. For purposes of reckoning the number of representatives, slaves were to be counted as three-fifths person each. The effect was to inflate the number of congressmen from states where slavery was widely practiced. With the three-fifths rule, the Constitution not only condoned slavery but supported it by giving to slave owners a political advantage in Congress.

The three-fifths rule was adopted as a concession to Southern states that feared the more populous North would dominate Congress.[1] Understanding the politics behind the rule did nothing to assuage the anguish of men like Jefferson, who could not reconcile slavery with the inalienable rights of life, liberty, and the pursuit of happiness. Equally troubling were the Constitution's provisions for taxing the importation of slaves (Article 1, Section 9, Par. 1) and for the extradition of escaped slaves across state lines (Article 4, Section 2, Par. 3). Jefferson sensed that even if the new nation condoned slavery, a just God would not. The compromise of truth that kept bondsmen in chains would not stand:

> God who gave us life gave us liberty. Can the liberties of a nation be secure when we have removed a conviction that these liberties are the gift of God? Indeed I tremble for my country when I reflect that God is just, that His justice cannot sleep forever. Commerce between master and slave is despotism. Nothing is more certainly

1. William C. Davis, *Brother Against Brother*, Civil War Series, vol. 1 (Alexandria, Va.: Time-Life, 1983), pp. 29-30.

written in the book of fate than that these people are to be free.
Establish the law for educating the common people. This it is the
business of the state to effect and on a general plan.

Jefferson's words are a warning to every generation of Americans that would deny to others the rights they cherish for themselves. Today they may be found engraved in stone on the walls
of the Jefferson Memorial in Washington, D.C.

SLAVE OR FREE?

As the new nation grew, so did the institution of slavery in the
South. In the North, opposition grew to this commerce in human
lives. It was economic survival versus conscience. Terrible conflict over slavery was certain. The issue that set it off was the
admission of new states forged from territories to the west:
Would they be slave or free?

On three occasions the issue was raised: regarding states
formed from the Louisana Purchase, specifically the admission
of Missouri, in 1820; regarding states formed from territory
taken in the Mexican-American War, specifically the admission
of California, in 1850; regarding the admission of states from the
Nebraska Territory, specifically the admission of Kansas, in
1854.

The Congress was divided, North against South. Opponents
argued that the institution of slavery is evil and should not be
permitted to infect the new territories. The advocates argued just
the opposite, that slavery is a positive good, providing security,
sustenance, and Christianity to poor souls who could not survive
if left to themselves. Congress made no attempt to resolve the
moral issue. Instead, the members resorted to political compromises to settle the immediate matters before them. With each
compromise, however, tension and hostility grew rather than
diminished. The people were not satisfied, justice was not satisfied, the conscience of the nation could find no peace.

Congress's attempts at compromise were certainly creative. In
the case of Missouri, Congress employed a theory of partition.
Missouri would be admitted as a slave state, and Maine would be
admitted as a free state; as a result the Senate would remain
evenly divided on slavery. As for the remainder of the Louisiana
Purchase, states formed from territory north of the 36°30' lati-
tude would be free, those from territory south of the line, slave.
The Missouri Compromise, as the decision came to be called,

contributed nothing to settling disputes that would arise later.[2]

In 1850 Congress determined that California would be admitted according to its own preference, as a free state. Several concessions were granted to slave states in return. The most significant of these was passage of the Fugitive Slave Act which created a Federal police force to round up escaped slaves and return them to their masters. "The affidavit of a reputed slave owner was all that was necessary to secure the arrest of a Negro. The alleged fugitive could not testify, nor summon witnesses, nor have a trial by jury."[3] Under the law, slaves were hunted down in Northern states where slavery was prohibited as well as in the South. As a result, resentment and outrage against slavery increased. Many citizens for the first time saw freedom crushed and the brutality of the practice exposed, as slaves were shackled and returned South.

POPULAR SOVEREIGNTY

Upon the application of Kansas for statehood, the debate over slavery raged once more. Under the Missouri Compromise there should have been no question about Kansas, since the entire state lay north of the 36°30′ demarcation. Nonetheless, opposition from Southern senators was fierce, and hostility between North and South increased. To resolve tension, Senator Stephen Douglas forged a compromise that became the Kansas-Nebraska Act. The Missouri Compromise was set aside. In its place he espoused the doctrine of "popular sovereignty," the notion that the people in each territory should be free to determine whether their state would be slave or free, without interference by Congress.[4] This was in essence a states' rights position on slavery that was applied to the territories.

"Popular sovereignty" may have sounded dignified and respectable, but it led directly to armed conflict and bloodshed. People began pouring into Kansas from North and South in order to gain control of the new government. Since Congress failed to provide any principled basis for resolving the conflict over slavery, the final arbiter would be force. It was for this reason that Northern firebrand Charles S. Sumner, senator from Maine,

2. Ibid., pp. 35-36.
3. Roy F. Nichols, *The Stakes of Power, 1845-1877* (New York: Hill and Wang, 1961), pp. 42-43.
4. Gerald M. Capers, *Stephen A. Douglas, Defender of the Union* (Boston: Little, Brown, 1959), pp. 44-48.

called the Kansas-Nebraska Act "the best bill on which Congress ever acted" because it "makes all future compromises impossible."[5] Senator David R. Atchison wrote to Senator Jefferson Davis of Mississippi, "We will be compelled to shoot, burn, and hang, but the thing will soon be over."[6]

The political compromises on slavery and their effects illustrate well that issues of justice must be decided around principles of justice. To do otherwise only increases the frustration and hostility people feel, adding layers of complexity to the issue at hand and making a peaceful resolution virtually impossible. None of the compromises were honorable.

At such a crucial juncture in American history, the Supreme Court chose to act on the matter of slavery. Rather than treating slavery as a violation of rights granted to men by God, the High Court instead rationalized slavery as a right guaranteed to men by the Constitution. If Congress's compromises lacked honor, the Supreme Court's Dred Scott decision carried with it boundless shame.

DRED SCOTT DECISION

Dred Scott was a black slave who served an Army surgeon, John Emerson of Missouri. As he was transferred to new installations, he would bring Scott with him. On two occasions, Emerson was stationed in regions where slavery was prohibited (Illinois and "Upper Louisiana," or the Wisconsin Territory). On this basis Scott sued for his freedom. How could he be legally bound as a slave when living in places where slavery was illegal? Had Scott been given his freedom in Illinois or Wisconsin, he never would have returned with Emerson to a slave state such as Missouri.

Two primary questions faced the Supreme Court. Did Dred Scott have standing as a citizen to sue in a Federal court? Was Scott in fact a free man?

The decision was written by Chief Justice Roger Taney, himself a slave owner. His response to the two questions was an emphatic "No." To reach his decision, Taney relied on an assumption about black slaves and their descendants: they were not "people" or "citizens" as the terms are used in the Constitution. Therefore, they are entitled to none of the rights or privileges guaranteed by the Constitution.

5. Davis, p. 72.
6. Ibid., p. 74.

We think they are not, and that they are not included and were not intended to be included under the word "citizen" in the Constitution, and can therefore claim none of the rights and privileges which that instrument provides for and secures to citizens of the United States.[7]

As a justification for keeping blacks in chains, Taney's premise was pure legalism. It assumed the Constitution rather than God Himself was the author of rights and freedoms. The question of enslaving blacks was reduced to a matter of definition.

To counter the moral argument against slavery, Taney argued that blacks were less than human anyway and thus entitled to nothing. It was proper for the Constitution to be exclusive.

They had for more than a century been regarded as beings of an inferior order, and altogether unfit to associate with the white race, either in social or political relations; and so far inferior, that they had no rights which the white man was bound to respect; and that the negro might justly and lawfully be reduced to slavery for his benefit. He was bought and sold, and treated as an ordinary article of merchandise and traffic, whenever a profit could be made by it.[8]

Taney relied almost exclusively on the precedent of slavery as a justification to its continuation. Slaves *had* been regarded as nothing more than a piece of property; therefore, slaves *were* nothing more than a piece of property. Taney never questioned the morality of slavery or the laws that made it legal: "It is not the province of the court to decide upon the justice or injustice, the policy or impolicy, of these laws."[9]

Taney concluded that prohibitions against the ownership of slaves in the territories were unconstitutional because these violate the right of the individual to own private property. Ironically, Taney invoked the Fifth Amendment in support of the right to own slaves: "No person shall be deprived of life, liberty, or property without due process of law." Thus the Missouri Compromise was unconstitutional; slavery must be permitted in territories throughout the Louisiana Purchase.

WAR OVER SLAVERY

And the war came. At the time, one-eighth of the population of

7. *Dred Scott v. Sandford*, 60 U.S. 393 at 404.
8. Ibid., at 407.
9. Ibid., at 405.

the United States was in chains. The Civil War would prove the costliest in American history. No one anticipated the extent of the bloodshed. To a stunned nation, Abraham Lincoln gave his second inaugural address. His words were comforting yet prophetic. The terrible judgment predicted by Jefferson had come to pass:

> The Almighty has His own purposes. "Woe unto the world because of offenses for it must needs be that offenses come but woe to that man by whom the offense cometh."
>
> If we shall suppose that American slavery is one of those offenses which in the Providence of God must needs come but which having continued through His appointed time He now wills to remove and that He gives to both North and South this terrible war as the woe due to those by whom the offense came shall we discern therein any departure from the divine attributes which the believers in a living God always ascribe to Him.
>
> Fondly do we hope—fervently do we pray—that this mighty scourge of war may speedily pass away. Yet if God wills that it continue until all the wealth piled by the bondsman's two hundred and fifty years of unrequited toil shall be sunk and until every drop of blood drawn with the lash shall be paid by another drawn with the sword as was said three thousand years ago so still it must be said, "The judgments of the Lord are true and righteous altogether."
>
> With malice toward none and charity for all, with firmness in the right as God gives us to see the right, let us strive on to finish the work we are in to bind up the nation's wounds, to care for him who shall have borne the battle and for his widow and his orphan—to do all which may achieve a just and lasting peace among ourselves and with all nations.[10]

After the Civil War, the Congress acted on the morality of slavery and the attitude that had produced it. It approved three constitutional amendments, the Thirteenth, Fourteenth, and Fifteenth, which then were ratified by the states. The Thirteenth Amendment specifically forbade slavery. The Fifteenth Amendment guaranteed to the former slaves their right to vote.

The Fourteenth Amendment was intended to assure that no class of human beings would ever again be denied freedom or rights by any state government. The key term used in the amendment to embrace the spectrum of humanity was "person." It was understood as an open-ended or inclusive term, extending to all people. Regardless of the value society might place on an individ-

---

10. The second innaugural address of President Abraham Lincoln is inscribed on the walls of the Lincoln Memorial in Washington, D.C.

ual or on a class of individuals, "no person . . . shall be deprived of life, liberty, or property without due process of law." The Fourteenth Amendment would serve as a constitutional barrier, defending them against injustice and prejudice.

Congressman John A. Bingham, who wrote the first section of the Fourteenth Amendment, expressed well the intent behind it:

> Before that great law, the only question to be asked of the creature claiming its protection is this: Is he a man? Every man is entitled to the protection of American law, because its divine spirit of equality declares that all men are created equal.[11]

CONCLUSION

Understanding the tragic consequences of slavery in American history, most of us have assumed that no one, let alone the Supreme Court, would dare to suggest that rights be stripped away from another class of human beings. The injustice of the deed would be apparent, and the memory is still too vivid. God's justice does not sleep forever. Besides, the Fourteenth Amendment precludes such injustices.

Unfortunately, human rights have again been stripped away from a class of people, and the US Supreme Court again was the crucial advocate of this position. The result has been a form of violence that, from the victims' perspective, is more brutal than the bloody lash of a master's whip against the back of his slave.

11. US, Congress, *Congressional Globe*, 40th Cong., 1st Sess., 1867, 542.

2

A Shameful Parallel

On January 22, 1973, the US Supreme Court handed down twin decisions on abortion, *Roe* v. *Wade* and the less significant *Doe* v. *Bolton*. At issue were statutes in the states of Texas and Georgia respectively, that restricted abortion. In particular the Texas statute prohibited abortion except as a life-saving procedure for the mother. This exception is extremely rare given advances in modern medicine, which allow successful treatment for most life-threatening conditions associated with pregnancy.

DELIBERATE DESTRUCTION

The Texas statutes, like those of every other state prior to 1967, originated with nineteenth-century abortion law reform spearheaded by the American Medical Association[1]. With the discovery of the human ovum in the 1820s and the realization that a distinct human life is created through the fertilization of the ovum with male sperm, the unavoidable conclusion was drawn: Throughout pregnancy the woman is "with child." In abortion the developing human is deliberately destroyed, regardless of the stage of pregnancy.

The older view that a new human life is present only from the point of "quickening," when the mother first feels the baby

1. *Roe* v. *Wade*, 410 U.S. 113 at 119.

move, could no longer be sustained. Under the leadership of Dr. Horatio Robinson Storer, physicians mounted a successful campaign to make abortion, except to save the life of the mother, a criminal offense at any point during pregnancy. Historian James Mohr has rightly dubbed these efforts "The Physicians' Crusade Against Abortion," because of their pivotal significance in changing the law.[2] Storer and his colleagues minced no words in condemning abortion as "the unwarrantable destruction of human life."[3]

AMA POSITIONS

Throughout the 1960s, the American Medical Association's strong opposition to abortion was transformed into equally strong support for the procedure. By 1971 the organization formally endorsed abortion when it serves "the best interests of the patient."[4]

The AMA was by no means the only organization to advocate permissive abortion laws. In addition to the AMA, the Supreme Court cited the American Public Health Workers Association and the American Bar Association as advocates of legal abortion.[5]

EUGENIC ABORTION

One event that had a powerful effect on attitudes toward abortion was the thalidomide tragedy in England. Assuming no danger was posed to their unborn children, a number of pregnant women had been given the tranquilizer thalidomide. As a result many of the children born to those women suffered severe limb deformities. Some babies were born with no arms, only hands projecting from shoulder sockets. Others were born with legs that did not extend below the knee. The deformities were severe enough to lead a number of English physicians to argue for "eugenic" abortion, that is, abortion in order to eliminate those with severe birth defects.

Literally "eugenic" means "good race"; eugenic abortions would eliminate the "defectives" who failed to make a social or

2. James C. Mohr, *Abortion in America, the Origins and Evolution of National Policy, 1800-1900* (New York: Oxford U., 1978), p. 147.
3. Ibid., p. 157.
4. *Roe v. Wade*, 410 U.S. 113 at 143.
5. Ibid., at 144-47.

racial contribution. The argument generally focused on the social cost of caring for these children and upon the notion that the affected individuals' lives were not worth living. The handicapped children themselves were never asked what they thought. Within a few years, this view had taken root in American soil through the American Law Institute.[6]

FEMINIST MOVEMENT

With the rise of feminism in the United States, a second source of agitation for abortion developed. NOW was organized in 1966 under the strong influence of Betty Friedan. More than any other feminist leader, Friedan is responsible for leading her movement to equate the liberation of women with "total reproductive freedom."[7] In essence the position holds that women should not be required to bear responsibilities that are not required of men. Men do not bear children; women are entitled to the same prerogative. The widespread availability and use of contraceptives does not guarantee pregnancy will not occur. Therefore, women must have access to abortion "as a backup to contraceptive failure."

With this reasoning in mind, one can understand how proponents of the Equal Rights Amendment argue it would guarantee to women not only abortion on demand, but abortion at taxpayer expense. Women are not equal to men unless they are rid of childbearing responsibilities. Given the sympathetic ear of federal and state courts for feminist concerns, this interpretation of the ERA cannot be lightly dismissed although the term *abortion* never appears in the text.

Although the ERA has yet to be added to the US Constitution, a number of state ERAs have been ratified. In Massachusetts, Hawaii, and Pennsylvania, attorneys for the American Civil Liberties Union have argued before state courts that the state ERAs mandate the use of state funds for abortion. On this interpretation, the ERA makes access to abortion more than a right—it's a tax-subsidized entitlement. In March 1984, Pennsylvania courts agreed.

6. Germain Grisez, *Abortion: the Myths, the Realities, and the Arguments* (New York: Corpus, 1972), pp. 236-44.
7. Bernard N. Nathanson, *Aborting America* (Garden City, N.Y.: Doubleday, 1979), pp. 32, 49-50, 57-58, 62, 121.

ACLU INVOLVEMENT

In 1968 the American Civil Liberties Union first threw its hat into the ring, joining the feminists in the bid to overturn existing laws on abortion. The eminent legal historian John T. Noonan has assessed the crucial role played by the ACLU: "The ACLU provided what was indispensible to the establishment of the [abortion] liberty—a cadre of specialists spread throughout the land, centrally directed from New York, expert in constitutional litigation."[8] In the name of individual freedom for the woman, the ACLU pressed the case for abortion on demand with a sympathetic federal judiciary. In the process they ignored the question of civil liberties for the unborn.

PLANNED PARENTHOOD

The fourth major source of agitation for abortion came from activists for population control, the most prominent of these being Planned Parenthood. In 1964 a Planned Parenthood pamphlet said, "Abortion kills the life of a baby, once it has begun." By the end of 1968, under the leadership of Dr. Alan Guttmacher, the organization had absolutely reversed its public position and began arguing that abortion is necessary to "prevent" unwanted children.[9]

ABORTION STATUTES

The first states to liberalize their abortion laws did so in 1967. By the end of 1970, eighteen states had passed abortion statutes. Most of the laws allowed abortion only in exceptional circumstances (e.g., when the pregnancy resulted from rape or incest, where the fetus has a genetic defect, or when the pregnancy threatens the mental health of the mother). Regardless of their purpose, the net effect of the laws was to sanction abortions for anyone and any reason.

Those opposed to abortion were caught off-guard. By the end of 1970, however, antiabortion forces had mobilized significant numbers of people. In 1971 and 1972, dozens of attempts were made to pass permissive laws in additional states. In every instance opponents of abortion defeated the proposals. In May

---

8. John T. Noonan, Jr., *A Private Choice, Abortion in America in the Seventies* (New York: Free Press, 1979), p. 36.
9. Ibid., p. 37.

1972, the New York State Legislature repealed the permissive abortion law it had passed two years earlier. To the chagrin of the majority, then Governor Nelson Rockefeller vetoed the repeal and so kept the New York abortion industry in operation.[10]

SUPREME COURT RULING

In November 1972, abortion referenda were held in North Dakota and in Michigan. By margins of 3:1 and 2:1 respectively, both drives for legalized abortion were defeated. Clearly the tide of battle had shifted. The public did not want permissive abortion. The stage was being set for a massive effort to repeal virtually all the permissive laws. Then, on January 22, 1973, the High Court handed down its abortion decision, stunning everyone and leaving opponents reeling.

In rendering its decision the Supreme Court made one crucial assumption that made the rest quite predictable: the unborn child—whether embryo, fetus, or premature infant—is a "potential life." The only justification offered was that this view is "less rigid" than "the belief that life begins at conception or at some other point prior to live birth."[11] No attempt was made to provide biological, legal, or ethical evidence in support of the notion. "Potential life" was unknown in legal terminology. Only in Aristotelian philosophy, constructed 2,000 years before modern science, did the phrase occur with any frequency.

In writing the decision, Justice Harry Blackmun offered no definition for the phrase. Definition would have given an identity to the unborn, but that was precisely what Blackmun wished to avoid. By being classified in this way, unborn humans were denied the status of human beings, entitled to rights. For purposes of the law, they were made less than human or, more accurately, not-yet human. The historic parallel to Chief Justice Taney's assignment of blacks to an "inferior order" is unmistakeable.

Having trivialized abortion by assigning the unborn baby to the netherworld status of "potential life," the Court proceeded to declare that women have a right to abortion that is derived from a broader constitutional right of privacy. This assertion, though frequently repeated, lacked boldness. Blackmun conceded, "The Constitution does not explicitly mention any right of privacy."[12]

10. Nathanson, p. 156.
11. *Roe* v. *Wade*, 410 U.S. 113 at 150.
12. Ibid., at 152.

He acknowledged the problem of deciding where to locate this in the document. Nevertheless, the Court was adamant that abortion is clearly guaranteed wherever it happens to be.

> This right of privacy, whether it be founded in the Fourteenth Amendment's concept of personal liberty and restriction upon state action, as we feel it is, or, as the District Court determined, in the Ninth Amendment's reservation of rights to the people, is broad enough to encompass a woman's decision whether or not to terminate her pregnancy.[13]

Remarkably, with as little direct constitutional support as this, the Court elevated the right to abortion alongside other "fundamental rights." As a result, laws prohibiting abortion would be impossible. Only limited regulation would be permitted.

> Where certain "fundamental rights" are involved, the Court has held that regulation limiting these rights may be justified only by a "compelling state interest," . . . and that legislative enactments must be narrowly drawn to express only the legitimate state interests at stake.[14]

At this point the decision was over half completed. Having denied the biological status of human life to the unborn and having fashioned a right to abortion, Blackmun turned his attention to the Fourteenth Amendment, with its broad guarantees that "no person . . . shall be deprived of life, liberty, or property without due process of law." Unless he excluded unborn children from its protection, any decision for abortion would be viewed as a violation of their constitutional rights. The Court acknowledged this: "If this suggestion of personhood is established . . . the fetus' right to life would then be guaranteed specifically by the [Fourteenth] Amendment."[15]

DRED SCOTT PARALLEL

The deed was accomplished with the stroke of a pen. Just as Taney decreed that "citizen" in the Constitution did not include blacks, Blackmun decided "person" is an exclusive term as well, applying to everyone except the unborn. The Fourteenth Amendment wall of legal protection, intended to guarantee the rights of

13. Ibid.
14. Ibid., at 155.
15. Ibid., at 156.

every human, had been breached, and the tragic lesson of *Dred Scott* was lost in the pages of an old history book.

Blackmun's arguments were feeble. He maintained that none of the instances where "person" was used in the Constitution "indicate with any assurance, that it has any prenatal application."[16] This is true. What he failed to consider was that in nearly every instance, the term was used of rights or prerogatives that are exercised only by adults. This argument was just as much a basis for denying protection to young children as to the unborn.

In addition he argued from the precedent of early nineteenth-century abortion laws; while condemning abortion, they did not regard the procedure as a criminal offense early in pregnancy.[17] In this he appealed to a standard of law that was based on ignorance concerning the development of life in the womb. He passed over a hundred years of law and knowledge in order to deny to unborn children legal status as persons.

Finally, in the decision the Court acknowledged the claim of abortion opponents that "life begins at conception and is present throughout pregnancy, and that, therefore, the State has a compelling interest in protecting that life from and after conception."[18] For a response, the Court resorted to the least damaging of three options.

THREE OPTIONS

The justices could *deny* that human "life begins at conception and is present throughout pregnancy," but that would have been such an obvious biological error that the credibility of the entire decision would have been suspect. As a second option, they could *agree* that "life begins at conception and is continuous throughout pregnancy." With that admission, however, the justices would expose their decision as a repudiation of the right to life and the standard of law on which it is based. Hardly did they want to face the torrent of criticism that would follow.

The only other option was to *dismiss* the question entirely without responding to it. That is what the Court did with a simple denial that any response was necessary. Apparently to avoid appearing arbitrary and dictatorial, Blackmun pled ignorance concerning the matter of life in the womb.

16. Ibid., at 157.
17. Ibid.
18. Ibid., at 159.

We need not resolve the difficult question of when life begins. When those trained in the respective disciplines of medicine, philosophy, and theology are unable to arrive at any consensus, the judiciary, at this point in the development of man's knowledge, is not in a position to speculate as to the answer.[19]

RIGHTS OF THE UNBORN

One last issue was considered by the Court before proceeding to its ruling, the fact that rights were already afforded unborn children in a variety of instances. They have inheritance rights. In their name lawsuits can be brought against individuals for harming them while in the womb. "Wrongful death" actions can be brought against individuals who accidentally injure unborn children to the point of their death. After giving those brief treatment, Justice Blackmun concluded, "In short, the unborn have never been recognized in the law as persons *in the whole sense*" (emphasis added).[20]

To this day, the law recognizes unborn children as persons entitled to all these rights. In fact, criminals who have assaulted pregnant women have been successfully prosecuted for murder when the unborn child has been killed. Nevertheless, the law regards the unborn as a non-person when a mother is willing to destroy him.

CONFLICT OF INTEREST

In all of its deliberations, the Supreme Court made unrealistic assumptions about the unborn. It also made an unhealthy assumption about the relationship between a mother and her child. In essence the Court assumed that a conflict of interest exists between a mother and her child, that the two exist as adversaries. By mandating permissive abortion, the Court elevated that view of the relationship between mother and child to the status of a social norm ruling in favor of the mother. Only when the child is not perceived as a threat to the mother does society provide him with protection and rights. The other view, that abortion is the enemy of both mother and child, was rejected.

EFFECT OF THE DECISION

The conclusion of the Court had the effect of overturning every law in the United States that attempted to prohibit abortion.

19. Ibid.
20. Ibid., at 161.

1. During the first third of pregnancy, abortion is legal for any reason as long as a licensed physician performs the procedure.
2. During the middle third of pregnancy, abortion also is legal for any reason, but states may pass laws intended to protect the health of the mother. This is a concession to the fact women face increased risk of medical complications from abortion as their pregnancies progress. Thus, states may require that these abortions be performed in facilities with medical equipment for emergencies.
3. During the last months of pregnancy, when the baby is clearly able to survive outside the womb—is viable—if given the best medical treatment available, the Court ruled that a state "may, if it chooses, regulate, and even proscribe, abortion except where it is necessary, in appropriate medical judgment, for the preservation of the life or health of the mother."[21]

Even in the last months of pregnancy, states are not required to protect unborn children. Rather, they are *allowed* to, excepting those cases where the doctor (e.g., the abortionist) is willing to testify that an abortion is necessary to preserve the mother's "life or health." These two exceptions may sound narrow, but in fact the health exception is defined so broadly as to permit abortion for any reason.

The Court used the United Nations definition of "health": "a state of complete physical, mental, and social well being, not simply the absence of illness and disease."[22] Virtually any reason for abortion is a health reason under this definition. Unfortunately the Supreme Court did not consider the United Nations' declaration of human rights, which includes: "The child, by reason of its physical and mental immaturity, needs special safeguards and care, including appropriate legal protection before as well as after birth."[23]

CONCLUSION

The Supreme Court's decision was so sweeping as to surprise even the strongest supporters of abortion. The eighteen state legislatures with revised laws that favored abortion had never entertained the notion that abortion should be legal in the last months of pregnancy. Even the most liberal laws enacted by leg-

21. Ibid., at 164-65.
22. C. Everett Koop, *The Right to Live; the Right to Die* (Wheaton: Tyndale, 1976), p. 41.
23. Ibid., p. 36.

islatures were now too restrictive. The statutes of thirty-two states that did prohibit abortion were suddenly overturned, with no recourse for appeal. The "land of the free" found itself with the most permissive abortion policy on earth. Only in recent years, after the Peoples Republic of China began a population control program including forced abortion, did the US lose that distinction. China's program is funded in part with US dollars through UNFPA* and applauded by officials in our own Agency for International Development.[24]

By any standard of comparison the Supreme Court's decision represented a revolution in law in the United States. Not only the old laws but the values and legal theory that undergirded them were discarded and replaced. The following chapter takes another look at the decision and reflects on what the Court was rejecting and installing in its place.

*United Nations Fund for Population Activities.

24. *The Richmond News Leader*, 28 June 1983.

3

Strategy of Deceit

THE BIBLICAL TRADITION

Inasmuch as American law is rooted in the tradition of common law with its foundation the Bible, Christian truth is a major part of our heritage. It weighed heavily against any sanction for abortion. Rather than addressing this directly, the Court countered with a single paragraph entitled "Ancient Attitudes." In twenty-eight lines the Court attempted to sum up the insights of past philosophies, religions, and legal theories regarding abortion. It failed to mention the biblical teaching against violence, the doctrine of the sanctity of human life, or the early church's opposition to abortion, infanticide, and suicide. The entire discussion focused upon pagan laws, pagan religions, and pagan philosophies that by and large supported abortion. It was as though the Bible, Judaism, and Christianity had never existed or didn't matter. On "ancient attitudes," the following declarations were made:

> These are not capable of precise determination. . . . Greek and Roman law afforded little protection to the unborn. If abortion was prosecuted in some places, it seems to have been based on a concept of a violation of the father's right to his offspring. *Ancient religion did not bar abortion* (emphasis added).[1]

1. *Roe v. Wade*, 410 U.S. 113 at 130.

21

The precedent of pagan religion was cited to show that legal abortion is an acceptable option for society. On this basis the Court might have argued for infanticide, suicide, and prostitution, because "ancient religion" supported those practices as well.

THE MEDICAL TRADITION

The Court had another task to perform besides replacing Christian truth with the standards of paganism. If permissive abortion was to be legal and commonly available in the United States, the longstanding rule of medical ethics, summarized in the Hippocratic Oath, must be discredited. The Hippocratic Oath, which medical students commonly recited upon graduation from medical school, is built around a pledge to "do no harm" to a patient. Accordingly, it contains a vow not to perform abortions and condemns suicide and euthanasia. The doctor is never to approach the patient as executioner, rather as healer and comforter.

The imaginative tribunal found little difficulty in dispensing with the ethic embodied in the oath. The argument begins as an *ad hominam* attack against the Pythagoreans who first espoused the oath. They were a dogmatic minority that believed the human life began with conception and that abortion kills an individual. The oath became popular, not because it was good or true or right, but because it conformed to the "emerging teachings of Christianity." This, the Court maintained, explains the oath's principle failing, "rigidity."

> What then of the famous Oath that has stood so long as the ethical guide of the medical profession and that bears the name of the great Greek, who has been described as the Father of Medicine, the "wisest and the greatest practitioner of his art," and the "most important and most complete medical personality of antiquity," who dominated the medical schools of his time, and who typified the sum of the medical knowledge of the past? . . . Most Greek thinkers . . . commended abortion, at least prior to viability. For the Pythagoreans, however, it was a matter of dogma. For them the embryo was animated from the moment of conception, and abortion meant destruction of a living being. . . . The Oath originated in a group representing only a small segment of Greek opinion . . . it certainly was not accepted by all ancient physicians. . . . But with the end of antiquity a decided change took place. Resistance against suicide and abortion became common. The Oath became popular.

The emerging teachings of Christianity were in agreement with the Pythagorean ethic. . . . This, it seems to us, is a satisfactory and acceptable explanation of the Hippocratic Oath's apparent rigidity.[2]

On the same grounds of "rigidity," the justices had earlier dismissed the view that human life begins with conception and adopted the fiction that only "potential life" exists within the womb. Because the facts of life and medical ethics militate against abortion, they were summarily rejected. There is no argument here, only presumption.

THE RIGHT TO LIFE

In all the Court's deliberations on abortion, the right to life was never seriously treated. Only one passing reference was made to it, as a protection under the Fourteenth Amendment.[3] No consideration was given to the conviction underlying that amendment or the rest of the Constitution, that fundamental rights are God-given and belong to everyone.

The Court could reject the sanctity of human life in the biblical witness with an appeal to pagan religion. It could reject the sanctity of human life in medical ethics by dismissing the Hippocratic Oath as too rigid. It could not, however, reject the sanctity of human life in law for this would involve an *outright* denial of the right to life. Had the Court done this, it would have exposed its disregard for that legal theory on which freedom and American constitutional law are based.

SANCTITY OF LIFE VERSUS QUALITY OF LIFE

Since the Court so handily dismissed the sanctity of human life, one wonders what other theory of man and social responsibility governed their decision. Ethicist John Fletcher may provide the answer:

> The nation's increasingly liberal outlook is a welcome trend away from the sanctity-of-life attitude toward a quality-of-life ethic.[4]

When the Supreme Court made the destruction of unborn humans a fundamental right in the Constitution, it was adopting a

2. Ibid., at 130-32.
3. Ibid., at 156.
4. Joseph Fletcher, *Time*, 29 January 1973, p. 47.

quality-of-life view of man. "Quality of life" is used to describe an ethic that at various times has been labelled utilitarianism or situation ethics. In the 1960s, when this approach to conduct resulted in the so-called "sexual revolution," it was popularly known as the "new morality."

In quality-of-life ethics, the only human obligation is to maximize pleasure and minimize pain. Pain and pleasure both are understood exclusively in materialistic terms. Spiritual values or moral absolutes are considered an impediment to the pleasure/pain principle because those limit the kinds of conduct an individual may wish to pursue. As an example, fornication or adultery may be pleasurable, but they are nonetheless condemned as immoral for a variety of reasons. In the light of biblical revelation, the end does not justify the means. The standard is what God requires.

The quality-of-life ethic is militantly atheistic and hostile to any conduct based on faith in a holy and just God. It is the ethic of humanism, which explains why *The Humanist* ran articles lauding the Supreme Court's decision. Wrote Ed Doerr and Paul Blanshard, "We feel like a champagne dinner in honor of the United States Supreme Court for its January [1973] decision on abortion."[5]

Quality-of-life ethics is focused upon the notion of duty to self rather than to God or to others. It is essentially self-serving, cloaked in the terminology of personal fulfillment, human potential, and self-realization. It cuts dramatically in two different but complementary directions on life-and-death questions like abortion.

The woman involved in a crisis pregnancy is obliged to maximize her own pleasure in life. If she determines that having a child would not be in her best interests, then abortion is, morally speaking, the right thing to do. Similarly, for society as a whole the cost of providing for the birth of children to the poor is high, absorbing funds that would otherwise go to advance social goals. Therefore, abortion should be promoted by the government and financed with taxpayers' dollars.

The other application of quality-of-life ethics is directly to the individuals destroyed by abortion. The quality of their lives is so minimal, it is argued, that society should not protect them. This argument is consistently applied to any fetus diagnosed as having a handicap or genetic defect, or to those seen as a social

5. Paul Blanshard and Ed Doerr, "A Glorious Victory," *The Humanist* 33, no. 3 (May-June 1973):5.

burden for financial reasons. Even if the unborn are perfectly healthy and conceived within the wealthiest of families, the argument still applies because they have not developed to the point of achieving "personhood" or "humanhood."

These terms refer to an undefined standard of physical, emotional, and relational abilities a human must maintain in order to have a life worth living—or protecting. This standard is never precisely defined but exists only as a concept in the minds of those desiring to justify the destruction of innocent life. Not only does it mean different things to different people, it can mean different things to the same ethicist.

As the chief proponent of quality-of-life ethics, Joseph Fletcher once maintained there are fifteen positive and five negative criteria for measuring the quality of one's life and whether humanhood has been achieved.[6] Several years after expressing this view, Fletcher economized, reducing the criteria to "four indicators of humanhood."[7]

As an ally in the struggle to implement the quality-of-life ethic into American law and social policy, Garrett Hardin maintains, "Whether the fetus is or is not a human being is a matter of definition, not fact; and we can define any way we wish."[8] With the stroke of a pen nonhumans may be made human or vice versa.

DECEITFUL ETHIC

How do we understand this ethic, which seems so twisted both in its use of language and in its treatment of individuals? As a starting point I recall a modern proverb among social activists: verbal engineering always precedes social engineering. If we are going to make the unacceptable acceptable, it must be made to sound acceptable. The deceitful use of language is necessary.

In 1970 a now famous editorial appeared in *California Medicine* advocating the "new ethic" based on the quality of life. This ethic, the author maintained, justifies both abortion and euthanasia. He granted this position represents a repudiation of the "old ethic," based upon the sanctity of human life, and honestly appraised the strategy of abortion proponents:

6. Joseph Fletcher, *Humanhood: Essays in Biomedical Ethics* (Buffalo, N.Y.: Prometheus, 1979), pp. 12-18.
7. Joseph Fletcher, "Four Indicators of Humanhood—The Enquiry Matures," *The Hastings Center Report* 4, no. 6 (December 1974):4-7.
8. Garrett Hardin, "Abortion—or Compulsory Pregnancy?" *Journal of Marriage and the Family* 30 (1968):250.

The process of eroding the old ethic and substituting the new has already begun. It may be seen most clearly in changing attitudes toward human abortion. . . . Since the old ethic has not yet been fully displaced it has been necessary to separate the idea of abortion from the idea of killing which continues to be socially abhorrent. The result has been a curious avoidance of the scientific fact, which everyone really knows, that human life begins at conception and is continuous whether intra- or extra-uterine until death . . . it is suggested this schizophrenic subterfuge is necessary because while a new ethic is being accepted the old one has not yet been rejected.[9]

The strategy of deceit has been deliberately used; if those who believe in the sanctity of human life and the right to life knew what was taking place in abortion, they would not stand for it. This may help explain the Supreme Court's decision. The Court claimed the onset of a human being's life is presently unknowable. It denied the humanity of the unborn and assigned to them instead the pseudoscientific status of "potential life." The justices defined abortion euphemistically as "termination of pregnancy." The fact that human life is destroyed was obscured. The notion that fundamental justice requires the protection of the innocent was never entertained.

The quality-of-life assumptions behind the Court's decision did surface at several points. The outright repudiation of the Hippocratic Oath is one example. In stating factors affecting their determination, Justice Blackmun included "population growth," "pollution," "poverty," and "the distress of all concerned associated with the unwanted child."[10] When the Court finally did acknowledge a possibility of state intervention to protect the unborn, they made the following points:

With respect to the States' important and legitimate interest in potential life, the "compelling" point [for protection] is at viability. This is so because the fetus then presumably has the capability of *meaningful life* outside the mother's womb (emphasis added).[11]

MEANINGFUL LIFE

What is "meaningful life"? And who is entitled to make that judgment? With this quality-of-life criterion for determining

9. *California Medicine* 113, no. 3 (September 1970):67-68.
10. *Roe* v. *Wade*, 410 U.S. 113 at 116 and 152.
11. Ibid., at 163.

whether an individual *may* be protected, the Court created a basis for approving the destruction of handicapped newborns, the elderly, and the infirm as well as the unborn.

CONGRESS RESPONDS

In 1981 the US Senate Subcommittee on Separation of Powers conducted extensive hearings on abortion in light of the Fourteenth Amendment's protection of human life. Twenty-two legal scholars, physicians, and scientists testified. They were evenly divided in their views on abortion. After hearing from these outstanding leaders in their respective fields, the Subcommittee made the following observation:

> Through these hearings we have also come to recognize that the fundamental question concerning the life and humanity of the unborn is twofold. Not only must government answer the biological, factual question of when the life of each human being begins; it must also address the question of whether to accord intrinsic worth and equal value to all human life, whether before or after birth.
>
> These two questions are distinct and separate. The question of when the life of a human being begins—when an individual member of the human species comes into existence—is answered by scientific, factual evidence. Science, however, is not relevant to the second question; science cannot tell us what value to give to each human life.[12]

The Senate subcommittee's observation confirmed what *California Medicine* confessed, that the question of when life begins is not really at issue. Rather, the value we place on human beings is under debate. Many of the witnesses who testified in behalf of abortion attempted to obscure this distinction, denying that the unborn are human beings. The Subcommittee was alert to this and made the following observation:

> Those witnesses who testified that science cannot say whether unborn children are human beings were speaking in every instance to the value question rather than the scientific question. No witness raised any evidence to refute the biological fact that from the moment of human conception there exists a distinct individual being who is alive and is of the human species. No witness challenged the scientific concensus that unborn children are "human beings" inso-

12. US, Congress, Senate, Subcommittee on Separation of Powers, *Report to the Committee on the Judiciary Regarding the Human Life Bill—S. 158*, 97th Cong., 1st Sess., p. 3.

far as the term is used to mean living beings of the human species. Instead, these witnesses invoked their value preferences to redefine the term "human being." . . .

A careful examination reveals the true nature of this line of argument. By redefining "human being" according to one's value preferences, one never has to admit believing that some human lives are unworthy of protection. Conveniently one can bury the value judgment that some human lives are not worth protecting beneath the statement that they are not human beings at all.[13]

THE COURT REBUKED

The conclusion of the Subcommittee represented a rebuke to the Supreme Court for its quality-of-life decision to deny the sanctity-of-life principle in the Fourteenth Amendment.

Because it affirms the Constitution, the Subcommittee cannot accept any legal rule that would allow judges, scientists, or medical professors to decide that some human lives are not worth living. We must instead affirm the intrinsic worth of *all* human life. We find that the fourteenth amendment embodies the sanctity of human life and that today the government must affirm this ethic by recognizing the "personhood" of all human beings. Earlier we found, based upon scientific examination, that the life of each human being begins at conception. Now, basing our decision not upon science but upon the values embodied in our Constitution, we affirm the sanctity of all human life.[14]

DISAGREEMENT WITHIN THE COURT

As with any decision that is extremely controversial, the Supreme Court's justices did not agree on the meaning of *Roe* v. *Wade.* Chief Justice Warren Burger concurred with the decision but flatly denied it would lead to abortion on demand.

I do not read the Court's holding today as having the sweeping consequences attributed to them by the dissenting Justices; the dissenting views discount the reality that the vast majority of physicians observe the standards of their profession, and act only on the basis of carefully deliberated medical judgments relating to life and health. Plainly the Court today rejects any claim that the Constitution requires abortion on demand.[15]

13. Ibid., pp. 11-12.
14. Ibid., p. 18.
15. *Doe* v. *Bolton,* 410 U.S. 179 at 208.

Justice Byron White was joined by William Rehnquist in voting against the decision. White was brutally frank and characterized its effect as permitting the extermination of human beings.

> The common claim before us is that for any one of such reasons or for no reason at all, and without asserting or claiming any threat to life or health, any woman is entitled to an abortion at her request if she is able to find a medical advisor willing to undertake the procedure. . . . I cannot accept the Court's exercise of its clear power of choice by interposing a constitutional barrier to state efforts to protect human life and by investing mothers and doctors with the constitutionally protected right to exterminate it.[16]

Over the last eleven years overwhelming evidence has accumulated to prove Justice White's analysis correct. The number of abortions in America climbed from 22,670 in 1969 to 586,760 in 1972. After the Court's decision in 1973, the number rose to 1,297,606 in 1980. According to the Centers for Disease Control, which publishes these statistics, the recent figures are probably low due to underreporting. According to Planned Parenthood's research arm, the Alan Guttmacher Institute, they may be off by as much as 20 percent.[17]

ABORTION STATISTICS

For every 1,000 babies born in the US, 359 are aborted. This is one of the highest overall abortion rates in the world. No nation has a higher teenage abortion rate (730 abortions for every 1,000 live births). Among unmarried women in the US, abortions now exceed live births by a ratio of 3:2.[18] Following is additional data on the percentage of abortions performed on various subgroups of American women:

White, 66.2	Black and Others, 28.5	Unknown, 5.4
Married, 21.7	Unmarried, 72.4	Unknown, 5.9
Under 25 Years, 63.8	25 Years or Older, 34.7	Unknown, 1.3
Previous Abortion, 30.9	No Previous Abortion, 64.4	Unknown, 4.7
Non-Mothers, 56.8	Mothers, 40.4	Unknown, 2.8[19]

16. Ibid., at 221-22.
17. Centers for Disease Control, Abortion Surveillance 1979-1980, (May 1983), pp. 7, 24. A copy may be obtained from: US Dept. of Health and Human Services, Public Health Service, Centers for Disease Control, Center for Health Promotion and Education, Division of Reproductive Health, Atlanta, GA 30333.
18. Ibid., pp. 15, 26, 31, 33.
19. Ibid., pp. 30, 32-34, 36-38.

The CDC reports that abortions are performed throughout the duration of pregnancy, from less than 8 weeks gestation to over 21 weeks of gestation.[20] This indicates that infants who have reached the point of survival outside the womb (viability) are being destroyed. A variety of procedures to accomplish abortion are now widely used: curettage, saline or prostaglandin instillation, dilatation and evacuation, and hysterotomy.[21] These are described in chapter 8.

The abortion industry operates in all fifty states, generating as much as $500 million a year. In no less than fourteen metropolitan areas, abortions outnumber live births. In 1976 Washington, D.C., was one of the first cities to join this list. It now includes Atlanta, Seattle-Everett, San Francisco-Oakland, Raleigh, Miami, and Reno.[22]

SUBSEQUENT RULINGS

Since its original decision, the Supreme Court has issued subsequent rulings that have reinforced and expanded the abortion right to the exclusion of other rights. As a result, your fifteen-year-old daughter can now get an abortion without your consent—even without your knowledge. The Supreme Court has ruled that parental consent laws or laws requiring only that parents be notified of their daughter's abortion are unconstitutional *unless* they provide a means for setting aside the very requirements they are designed to establish.[23]

In states where those laws have been passed, the process of circumventing parental consent or notification is simple. If a young woman entering an abortion clinic indicates she does not want her parents to know about her abortion, arrangements are made for her to appear before a judge. If the judge feels she is mature enough to make the abortion decision on her own, the clinic may provide her one, and her parents are not notified. If the judge determines she is too immature to make the abortion

20. Ibid., p. 36.
21. Ibid., p. 38.
22. This information is based upon a comparison of data in a 1981 Alan Guttmacher Institute report, *Abortion 1977-1979*, and data in an unpublished table listing live births for the Standard Metropolitan Statistical Areas of the US, from the Natality Division of the National Center for Health Statistics in Washington, D.C. Special thanks for making this information available: Mr. David Andrusko, National Right to Life Committee, 419 7th St. NW, Suite 402, Washington, D.C. 20004.
23. *H.L.* v. *Matheson*, 450 U.S. 398 (23 March 1981); *Planned Parenthood Association of Kansas City, Missouri, Inc.* v. *Ashcroft*, __U.S.__. (15 June 1983).

decision but nonetheless feels an abortion is in her best interests, then identical results follow. The abortion is performed, and her parents are kept ignorant of the entire incident.

In effect, the law regards parents as their daughter's enemies, without her best interests in mind, because they might prohibit her from seeking abortion. Accordingly, their authority and rights as parents have been stripped away and placed in the hands of judges. Nevertheless, it is the parents—not some judge or abortionist—who must deal with the aftermath of abortion in their daughter's life. It is the parents who will share their daughter's grief because they love her.

The Supreme Court has also ruled on laws requiring the consent of husbands before wives abort their offspring. In the opinion of the Court, these laws are unconstitutional. Known as *spousal consent statutes*, they were based upon the notion that both parents are responsible for the welfare of their children. If a husband objects to his wife's abortion, that objection should stand because it would save the life of his child.[24] The Supreme Court has denied fathers their authority in order to assure that women always have the opportunity to destroy their offspring before birth.

On several occasions legislatures have passed laws to prohibit abortions after viability. To date, all those have been struck down.[25] The Court *will* allow that two doctors be present when viable infants are aborted—one to kill the baby through abortion, and one to care for the infant should the first doctor fail.[26]

CONCLUSION

The Supreme Court's decision on abortion cannot be understood apart from its consequences. Viewing this ruling only in terms of a change in law trivializes the violence that is taking place and the violence that may occur in the future. *Roe* v. *Wade* gave respectability and legal sanction to a deceitful ethic that regards human life as expendable. Quality of life proponents are now on notice that they may proceed—with caution—to implement their entire social agenda. Whether in Congress, the Federal Courts, the federal bureaucracy, the medical profession, the legal

24. *Planned Parenthood of Central Missouri* v. *Danforth*, 428 U.S. 52 (1976).
25. In addition to *Planned Parenthood of Central Missouri* v. *Danforth*, 428 U.S. 52 (1976), *Colautti* v. *Franklin*, 47 U.S. *Law Week* 4094 (9 January 1979).
26. *Planned Parenthood Association of Kansas City, Missouri, Inc.* v. *Ashcroft*, ___U.S.___. (15 June 1983).

profession, or the halls of secular universities, they have been emboldened by the Supreme Court to continue efforts to gain social approval for the destruction of other groups of human beings deemed burdensome and useless.

4

The Sanctity
of Human Life

Many truths in the Word of God are summarized as doctrines. Some of those are easier to understand than others. Most Christians are familiar with the doctrines relating directly to God and to the redemption He provides in Jesus Christ. But there are other truths as well that God has revealed, obviously for our benefit, and we would do well to live by them. In fact only by them can we live.

The Reformer John Calvin observed in the opening of his *Institutes* that wisdom consists of two types of knowledge: the knowledge of God and the knowledge of man. These can only be understood in terms of each other. We cannot know who or what we are apart from the knowledge of God. Similarly, we cannot know who God is unless we understand by our sinfulness that all holiness belongs to Him.[1]

GENESIS

Beginning with the book of Genesis, we learn that whereas God can exist apart from man, man would not exist if it were not for God. Inescapably, we live in relation to Him. Our identity, and hence our value as individuals, is determined by this rela-

---

1. John Calvin, *Institutes of the Christian Religion*, 2 vols. (Grand Rapids: Eerdmans, 1975), 1:37-38.

tionship. The truth is summed up in the phrase *the sanctity of human life.*

In Genesis 1:31 we learn that after God created the universe and its inhabitants, He considered His handiwork and saw that it was very good. The entire creation was very good—not only the things about it but also the creatures within it.

Simply on the basis of the inherent goodness of God's creation, Christians have argued effectively for the conservation of natural resources, the preservation of places of natural beauty, and the prevention of cruelty to animals. Man, as powerful as he is, has no right to destroy the created order. This frightening prerogative rests only with One who has absolute dominion over it. And that One is God.

If that truth is sufficient to teach us respect for rocks and trees, tiny plants and little animals, then surely it is sufficient to teach us respect for human beings.

IN GOD'S IMAGE

Scripture of course teaches much more about man than the fact that we are part of a good creation. Specifically verses 26 and 27 of Genesis 1 state that when God created man, He made man different from any other creature.

> Then God said, "Let Us make man in Our image, according to Our likeness; and let them rule over the fish of the sea and over the birds of the sky and over the cattle and over all the earth, and over every creeping thing that creeps on the earth." And God created man in His own image, in the image of God He created him; male and female He created them.

No other ceature can claim the distinction of being created in the image of God. Because of that, human beings possess a special dignity and value. The core truth behind the phrase is fairly simple. We were created to be God's children.

In Hebrew, the phrases "created in the image of" or "made in the likeness of" connote a filial or son-to-father relationship. When God created man, He intended a creature who would relate to Him and *know* Him as "Father, which art in heaven." He also intended a creature who would *resemble* Him in holiness as a child resembles his parents.

The meaning of these phrases is well illustrated in Genesis 5:1-3, where they are used not only to describe Adam's relationship to God but also Seth's relationship to his father, Adam:

When God created man, He made him in the likeness of God. He created them male and female, and He blessed them and named them Man . . . when they were created. When Adam had lived one hundred and thirty years, he became the father of a son in his own likeness, according to his image, and named him Seth.

Luke's genealogy of Jesus (Luke 3) also clarifies what it means to be made in the image of God. Everyone is the son of someone until finally we reach Adam, who is described as the son of God. This decription is true because Adam was created in God's image.

OFFSPRING OF GOD

This truth is similarly reflected in Paul's sermon to the Greek philosophers, recorded in Acts 17. Paul was in Athens, a place where the people "used to spend their time in nothing other than telling or hearing something new" (Acts 17:21). As the philosophers heard Paul preaching Jesus and the resurrection, they wanted to know more about the new teaching as well as the teacher. They brought him to the Areopagus, a large pavilion that served as a forum for debate, and invited him to speak. His argument for Christ rested upon a fact recognized by even the Greek poets, that human beings were created to be the offspring of God:

> . . . He made from one, every nation of mankind to live on all the face of the earth, having determined their appointed times, and the boundaries of their habitation, that they should seek God, if perhaps they might grope for Him and find Him, though He is not far from each one of us; for in Him we live and move and exist, as even some of your own poets have said, "For we also are His offspring." Being then the offspring of God, we ought not to think that the Divine Nature is like gold or silver or stone, an image formed by the art and thought of man. Therefore having overlooked the times of ignorance, God is now declaring to men that all everywhere should repent, because He has fixed a day in which He will judge the world in righteousness through a Man whom He has appointed, having furnished proof to all men by raising Him from the dead. (Acts 17:26-31)

Paul does not hesitate to quote the authorities his audience relied on. To paraphrase his point, "Your poets have said, 'We also are his offspring.' Since you know we are His offspring, you ought to know better than to worship idols of gold and silver and stone." The truth that we are created in God's image to be His children served as a bridge for evangelizing Gentiles.

It also formed the church's basis for true ethics, or the knowledge of how we are to treat one another. Any time we bless another person or behave badly toward him, we have handled or mishandled one who bears the image of God. God's law was given to instruct us on the proper treatment of those so richly endowed and precious in His sight.

God places great value on us as individuals, and this is to be respected by men. Our worth is not based on what we do, how we look, or whom we know. Rather it is based on who we are, creatures made by God in His image. Regardless of our status in society, our health, or our deeds, there is a sanctity about our lives. We have been set apart from creation for the unique privilege of relating to God as our Father.

When we attack our neighbor, we war against God. When we deny protection to individuals and acquiesce in their destruction, we scorn their Creator and invite His judgment upon us. Proverbs 17:5 illustrates this point in speaking of the poor: "He who mocks the poor reproaches his Maker." Innocent, defenseless people have an advocate in God. He promises to vindicate them and to be a father to the fatherless (Psalm 82:3-4).

THE LEAST OF THESE

Under the New Covenant, Jesus reinforced this teaching. His advocacy of the weak and defenseless extends to the point of identifying with them: "To the extent that you did it to one of these brothers of mine, even the least of them, you did it to Me" (Matthew 25:40). No one is weaker or more defenseless than the unborn child.

RESULT OF ADAM'S SIN

If the created order today were unchanged since its creation, abortion would not exist. Because sin has entered into the world, the sanctity of human life has been denied.

When Adam chose to violate the command of God, he rejected the unique relationship he had with God. He denied the sanctity of his own life, refusing to relate to God as his Father, and refusing to walk in righteousness. Many expressions of man's rebellion against God have followed, but none is so dramatic as violence. In the shedding of innocent blood, men usurp the role of God over each other in order to kill one another.

Violence swiftly followed Adam's sin. The first son of Adam, Cain, killed the second son, Abel. Brother murdered brother. God sought out Cain as He had sought out Adam and Eve after their sin. He condemned the violence and pronounced judgment on Cain: "The voice of your brother's blood is crying to Me from the ground. And now you are cursed from the ground" (Genesis 4:10-11).

In spite of God's judgment against violence, violent practices spread as the human family expanded. As a result, by Noah's generation, God regretted that He made man and determined to destroy the whole earth in a flood. Violence in the earth is cited as the reason (Genesis 6:11). It was catastrophic. Everyone was destroyed except Noah and his family.

After the waters receded, God spoke to Noah as the second progenitor of the human race. He gave to him all the commands and all the promises He had given to Adam. He also gave an additional promise and an additional commandment, and those are related.

God promised never again to judge mankind with a flood, and He gave the rainbow as a sign of this promise (Genesis 9:8-17).

At the same time He commanded men to restrain the very condition that had provoked that judgment, violence. "Whoever sheds man's blood, by man his blood shall be shed, for in the image of God He made man (Genesis 9:6). This verse is widely recognized as the institution of capital punishment in the Bible, given to protect the innocent and punish the guilty.

CAPITAL PUNISHMENT

In contemporary theology, capital punishment is frequently presented as a contradiction of the sanctity of human life principle, although passages such as Genesis 9:6 teach precisely the opposite. It is worth considering why capital punishment is prescribed for the murder of the innocent. Clearly the Bible teaches that *every* sin is a capital offense against God. Every sin we commit calls forth the sentence of death upon us. Capital punishment, however, is not commanded by God except for very *few* sins.

The reason for the exclusive use of capital punishment for sins such as murder is provided in the verse we are considering: "For in the image of God He made man." Although every sin is deadly, some sins are more offensive to God than others because they represent the desecration of His image. Even a casual reading of the Old Testament reveals that violence and idolatry are more heinous to God than other sins. Both constitute direct assaults against His image.

GOD OPPOSES VIOLENCE

The clearest statement of God's opposition to violence occurs in the commandment given to Moses on Mt. Sinai "you shall not murder" (Exodus 20:13). The Hebrew term translated "murder" refers only to the killing of innocent people. It does not refer to self-defense or to the execution of criminals; different Hebrew terms denote those acts.

In the brevity of this commandment, we understand at once its breadth. No exceptions are offered. The prohibition against murder applies to every human being. No one is excluded from protection because everyone is created in God's image.

In the simplicity of the commandment, we understand its severity. "You shall not murder" is an absolute statement of God's will concerning human life. There is no ambiguity here, only clarity, which assures that any deviation invites judgment.

The judgment of God against violence is revealed again and again upon men and nations throughout both Testaments. It has been confirmed repeatedly through the course of human history. Nations that have exploited rather than protected the innocent no longer exist. Political instability and the destruction of nations reveals both the severity and the mercy of God. Oppressors do not last forever.

MISSION OF REDEMPTION

Because God has a father's heart toward us, He did not abandon mankind to violence and death. He dispatched His Son to deliver us from the power of sin and draw us back to Himself. At the cost of His life, Jesus accomplished this mission. He overcame every expression of sin and evil. He conquered every principality and power that enslaves men. He took upon Himself the curse of the law in order to deliver men who were under its curse. Justice was served, and the redemption of men was accomplished.

Christ's victory was demonstrated to men in the resurrection. Jesus was raised from the dead and ascended to heaven. As the triumphant Lord of lords He reigns today. "All power and authority" have been given to Him. In turn He gives to those who accept Him authority to walk as children of God in the earth (John 1:12).

Through Christ's mission of redemption, God's purpose in creating men is accomplished. The sanctity of human life is restored. Those who trust in Christ to deliver them from sin's power, consequences, and judgment come to know God as their Father; they even begin to resemble Him. They have become His children.

This transformation is accomplished only through the work of the Holy Spirit. In Romans 8, Paul writes to Christians, "For all who are being led by the Spirit of God, these are sons of God. For you have not received a spirit of slavery leading to fear again, but you have received a spirit of adoption as sons by which we cry out, 'Abba! Father!' The Spirit Himself bears witness with our spirit that we are children of God" (Romans 8:14-16). Paul similarly wrote to the Galatians (Galatians 4:6).

A number of powerful images are used to explain this work of grace that causes the hater of God to cry out in faith. The image of adoption is used in the passages quoted above. The best-known image is that provided by Jesus Himself, however, and it is birth: "Truly, truly I say to you, unless one is born again, he cannot see the kingdom of God" (John 3:3).

THE NEW SELF

This image and the extensive teaching of the New Testament on the means of salvation makes clear that believers in Christ come to resemble God not only in an outward fashion, through obedience to His righteous commands, but from the inside out, through the good work of God in them. Paul exhorted the Ephesians to "put on the new self, which in the likeness of God has been created in righteousness and holiness of the truth" (Ephesians 4:24). Similarly, Paul wrote to the Colossians: "Do not lie to one another, since you laid aside the old self with its evil practices, and have put on the new self who is being renewed to a true knowledge according to the image of the One who created him" (Colossians 3:9-10). The image of God is reflected in the believer as sin is overcome in his or her life. Solely as a result of God's grace, His longstanding command can now be obeyed: "You shall be holy for I am holy" (1 Peter 1:16).

CONCLUSION

Human life is sacred because God created us in His image, that we might be His children. This is true for every person whether he accepts this truth or not. On this basis every human being has great dignity and is entitled to protection and respect.

5

The Author of Life

Granted that human beings are created in the image of God, and violence is a terrible evil, how does the Bible regard the human embryo, fetus, or premature infant? As a human being made in God's image? Or as a subhuman living mass of tissue? Many passages of Scripture address this question. As we will see, they reveal not only that God regards the unborn as human beings but also that He is intimately involved with them—so much so that the unborn are considered God's handiwork, hardly to be discarded as an unwanted possession.

PSALM 139

> For Thou didst form my inward parts; Thou didst weave me in my mother's womb. I will give thanks to Thee, for I am fearfully and wonderfully made; wonderful are Thy works, and my soul knows it very well. My frame was not hidden from Thee, when I was made in secret, and skillfully wrought in the depths of the earth. Thine eyes have seen my unformed substance; and in Thy book they were all written, the days that were ordained for me, when as yet there was not one of them. (Psalm 139:13-16)

Psalm 139 is the inspired record of David's praising God as the sovereign Lord of his life. The king begins by acknowledging that God knows whatever he is doing at any given point in time

(vv. 1-3). The Lord is aware of David's thoughts before he expresses them (vv. 4). He cannot avoid the presence of God. If he journeys to heaven, God will be there (vv. 8). If he ventures to Sheol, he will find the Almighty (vv. 9). So too, in the remotest part of the sea (vv. 9). Even the darkness cannot conceal the king from God's sight (vv. 11-12). In verses 13-16, David considers the origin of his life and confesses that God not only was aware of him, but that He was forming him in the womb! This confession is true for every human being.

Psalm 139 teaches clearly that God is the Author of life, not in an abstract, philosophical sense but in a very dynamic way: "Thou didst weave me in my mother's womb." I recall a series of lectures in embryology presented when I was a pre-med student at the University of Illinois. The theme was simple. In studying prenatal development, we can describe what is taking place, but we cannot explain why.

Those who suggest the mystery of human development—perhaps of life itself—is solved by genetics and the knowledge of DNA face stiff opposition from experts in the field of embryology. Dr. E. Blechschmidt recently put the issue in these terms: "If we imagine, for instance, the genetic substance as a kind of cookbook, it would have value only if a cook were to use it, but it remains entirely unexplained who in the system of cells the cook is."[1] It is hoped all the mechanisms of human development will be uncovered, but the force of life that is necessary for any of these things to occur can never be understood scientifically. It is spiritual. The Author of life is at work.

David's response to this truth is an example for us all. It is gratitude: "I will give thanks to Thee, for I am fearfully and wonderfully made." Whenever we become aware that a human being has been conceived, whether planned by the parents or not, we may know God is the Author of that life, and humble gratitude is the proper response.

GOD MAKES NO MISTAKES

Couples certainly have unexpected pregnancies. We are confronted with this all the time in our Crisis Pregnancy Center ministry. Human failings, however, do not apply to God. He neither is surprised nor makes mistakes. He is the sovereign

---

1. E. Blechschmidt, "Human Being from the Very First," *New Perspectives on Human Abortion*, ed. Thomas W. Hilgers, et al. (Frederick, Md.: University Publications, 1981), p. 15.

Creator of every human being, regardless of the circumstances. No human being is conceived outside His will. Even through circumstances that are sinful—fornication, adultery, or violence—He can cause something as precious and redeemable as a new human being to come forth. When life comes, it comes as a gift, never as punishment (Psalm 127:3).

As we shall see, this truth became evident to Hagar, who conceived a child by Abraham (Genesis 16). This blessing is not limited to pregnant women in the Bible, however. We have witnessed this in the lives of thousands of women who obeyed God and chose life even though their pregnancies were difficult or embarrassing.

WORLD'S VIEW

The biblical view of pregnancy is dramatically different from the world's view. Planned Parenthood and their allies in the population control movement view the unexpected or unwanted pregnancy as a cause for despair. Daily, women in the United States are counseled to regard their pregnancies as a burden that means the end of joy and fulfillment. The world says, "Mistake!" Pregnancy is unhealthy, and women best rid themselves of this condition.

That viewpoint was well illustrated in a paper prepared for the Planned Parenthood Physicians' Association by Dr. Willard Cates. Its title was self-explanatory: "Abortion as a Treatment for Unwanted Pregnancy: The Number Two Sexually Transmitted Disease."[2] The theme of the paper was simple. The unwanted pregnancy is a type of venereal disease that has reached epidemic proportions, second only to gonorrhea. Abortion is simply a medical "treatment" for the condition.

A CAUSE FOR HOPE

When I see a pregnant woman, regardless of her circumstances, the first thing I recognize is hope, because God is at work within her. I want to help her see that. The baby is not a "mistake," even if her conduct was. The Lord of Life has gained her attention and now compels her to think of things she may have feared or ignored throughout her life—the existence of God, the meaning of life, the nature of love, accountability before God. He is giving her an opportunity to know Him, to love

2. Paper presented 11-12 November 1976, Miami Beach, Florida.

Him, and to carry out the lofty privilege of bringing a new human being into the world.

She may be isolated from virtually everyone and feel very much alone, but she is not alone. Even if she is alienated from God, He is not far from her. Through faith, she can know the One Who promises, "I will never desert you, nor will I ever forsake you" (Hebrews 13:5).

Apart from Christians who co-labor with God to make His presence and truth known, the pregnant woman may totally miss the opportunity she has. She is subject to so much false information concerning abortion and pressure to destroy her offspring that she may not respond to the truth God has placed within her, that it is good to nurture life.

Directors from two different Crisis Pregnancy Centers at opposite ends of the country recently expressed their amazement at the way the Lord brings people into their centers. It becomes clear, when they begin to work with clients, that He has already been working in their lives, preparing them for this meeting with Christians. On a number of occasions Christian women have come to a Crisis Pregnancy Center thinking they were entering an abortion clinic. When they realize the centers are ministries demonstrating Christ's love for them, they have seen that God does not reject them but calls them to repent and walk again with Him.

SPECIAL CREATION

Psalm 139 teaches us more than the fact that God is the Author of life in the womb. It teaches as well that the unborn child is a human being, a creature made in His image (verses 15 and 16).

David draws a parallel between his development in the womb and Adam's creation from the earth. Using figurative language in verse 15, he refers to his life before birth when "I was made in secret, and skillfully wrought in the depths of the earth." This is known as poetic allusion; it harks back to Genesis 2:7: God formed Adam from the dust of the earth. As surely as Adam was specially created by God, so too was David. That truth was a source of joy and gratitude.

David also confessed, "Thine eyes have seen my unformed substance" (v. 16). Even before David was known to others, he was known to God. The term translated "unformed substance" is a noun derivative of a verb meaning "to roll up." David was referring to the earliest points in his development before he even looked like a baby, probably before his mother knew she was pregnant. When David appeared to be no more than a shapeless mass, a "blob," God knew better, and His tender gaze was upon him, long before his birth.

The reference to God's "eyes" (v. 16) also is significant. Throughout the Old Testament the term is used to connote the sovereign oversight of God in the life of an individual or a group of people. It is never used to describe God's awareness of things. God's eyes were on David as a tiny developing human, growing toward a destiny known only to Him.

In these verses, the king rejoiced not in his "kingliness" but in his "creatureliness." David was "fearfully and wonderfully made." So is every other human being.

PSALM 51

"Behold, I was brought forth in iniquity, and in sin my mother conceived me" (Psalm 51:5).

Psalm 51 records David's repentance from his sin of adultery with Bathsheba. He acknowledges that his sin was not simply the result of an impulse to sin, momentary lust creasing the periphery of his heart. Rather, David confesses that his act of adultery reflected a principle of sin that had always been within him, what theologians call *original sin.*

Thus, David confessed, "I was brought forth in iniquity." The verb clearly connotes childbirth. David's reference is not to the circumstances of his birth, but rather to his spiritual condition at birth. In the next line David extends this reference back to his conception: "And in sin my mother conceived me." Again, not the circumstances surrounding David, but rather David himself is in view. (We may assume from other texts that David's conception was not the result of fornication or adultery.) From the time of his conception, David had been a sinner by nature. A similar reference to birth and conception is found in Job 3:3.

The Word of God does not claim to be a scientific textbook, but it is true on every matter to which it speaks. The Bible does not define the conception of a human being in terms of the union of sperm and ovum, but it does make clear that conception occurs at the outset of pregnancy. In Job 10:8–12, poetic imagery dramatically communicates that intimate relations resulting in pregnancy were the occasion of Job's beginning. (It is worthwhile to note that from the time fertilization was first understood, the term "conception" was made synonymous to it.)

CALLED BEFORE BIRTH

The Old Testament reveals that God deals with people as human beings, creatures made in His image, long before they are born. God set apart Jeremiah from his mother's womb (Jeremiah 1). He called Isaiah from his mother's womb (Isaiah 49), assuming the reference is to the prophet. In the New Testament, the apostle Paul indicates he, too, was set apart by God while in the womb (Galatians 1:15). The Bible gives no suggestion that God regards the unborn as less valuable in His sight than other human beings.

THE INCARNATION

The New Testament records the most powerful evidence for the sanctity of the unborn child's life when it recounts the incarnation of Jesus Christ, the event by which God became a man. Completely identifying with human beings, Jesus went through the full range of human development. Accordingly, the Bible teaches that Jesus' earthly, human existence began with His conception in Mary. Matthew 1:18-20 reveals that Christ was conceived in her by the Holy Spirit. Jesus Christ entered the world at the point of conception, because that is when human life begins.

MARY AND ELIZABETH

As a result of Christ's presence, relationships were immediately affected. When Mary, who had just become pregnant with Jesus, ventured to the hill country to see her cousin Elizabeth, who was six months pregnant with John the Baptist, the relationship between the two was forever transformed. Indeed the joy of the event could not be contained.

> And it came about that when Elizabeth heard Mary's greeting, the baby leaped in her womb; and Elizabeth was filled with the Holy Spirit. And she cried out with a loud voice, and said, "Blessed among women are you, and blessed is the fruit of your womb! And how has it happened to me, that the mother of my Lord should come to me? For behold, when the sound of your greeting reached my ears, the baby leaped in my womb for joy. And blessed is she

who believed that there would be a fulfillment of what had been spoken to her by the Lord." (Luke 1:41-45)

When Mary entered the house to see Elizabeth, she did not enter alone. The Son of God was growing within her. Mary was "blessed" because "blessed" was the fruit of her womb—not a blob of protoplasm, mere tissue and cells, but Jesus Christ. In fulfillment of the prophecy of Luke 1:15, John was filled with the Holy Spirit and leaped for joy. John was not a blob either, but a person, and God personally related to him.

A number of recent books and articles track the psychological development of unborn children.[3] These present many evidences for their emotional development months before they are born. That John would experience emotion in the womb in the sixth month of pregnancy was not a miracle. That God would graciously fill him with His Holy Spirit was.

Christ's mission of redemption began with His conception. That too often is overlooked. He identified fully with human embryos, fetuses, and infants. The truth of creation and the truth of redemption both lead to one conclusion, the sanctity of all human life.

A MODEL FOR CRISIS PREGNANCY MINISTRY

Many Christians use God's Word in arguing for the protection of unborn children from abortion. It provides a basis as well for ministry to women with crisis pregnancies.

Regularly I receive letters from men and women who have just heard about the Crisis Pregnancy Center ministry of the Christian Action Council. Very often we are told the work is innovative, but it isn't. We didn't discover this sort of outreach. We find in the Word of God a powerful illustration of God's directly ministering to a woman with a crisis pregnancy.

ABRAHAM AND HAGAR (GENESIS 16)

When God promised a son to Abraham, he and his wife, Sarah, were already advanced in years. As time went on, no baby was conceived, and Sarah grew impatient. Eventually she took matters into her own hands. She persuaded Abraham to take her handmaiden, Hagar, and conceive a child by her.

3. Thomas Verny, *The Secret Life of the Unborn Child* (New York: Summit, 1981).

When Hagar became pregnant, she began to resent her mistress. After all, Sarah had all the privilege and wealth that came from being Abraham's wife, but poor Hagar was performing the wifely duty. Jealousy raged within her, and she became outwardly hostile toward her mistress.

HAGAR FLEES

Sarah responded by blaming the domestic uproar on Abraham. The whole affair was his fault. Abraham determined to appease his hurt and angry wife, so he gave her permission to mistreat Hagar (Genesis 16:6). Soon afterward Hagar ran away into the wilderness.

This incident provides us with an excellent illustration of a crisis pregnancy. Clearly the child had been conceived in circumstances of sin. Sarah's unbelief led directly to Abraham's adultery with Hagar. As the father of the child, Abraham was not committed to the mother. He was married to another woman. Hagar suffered personally as a result and grew jealous of Sarah. Relationships began to unravel. Hostility grew to the point of harsh mistreatment.

Undoubtedly, Abraham wished the whole incident had never occurred. Sarah certainly came to resent her scheme. Hagar felt trapped and totally out of control. She felt she had no choice but to run away. The image provided by the text is dramatic—a pregnant woman, totally vulnerable, in a dangerous, cruel place. That is exactly where many women find themselves today as they pursue abortions.

GOD MINISTERS TO HAGAR

Hagar was angry, confused, and scared. She did not know what to do, where to go, or how to survive. The Lord did not abandon Hagar to despair and death. He sought her out and ministered to her in very practical terms: "Return to your mistress, and submit yourself to her authority" (Genesis 16:9). Hagar should return home. That would solve her immediate problem.

The Lord went on to minister to Hagar at the point of her greatest fear, a fear that will drive many women this day into abortion clinics. Most often we hear it expressed in this way: "I should never have become pregnant. What future can this child possibly have?"

> Moreover, the angel of the Lord said to her, "I will greatly multiply your descendants so that they shall be too many to count." The

angel of the Lord said to her further, "Behold, you are with child, and you shall bear a son; and you shall call his name Ishmael, because the Lord has given heed to your affliction. And He will be a wild donkey of a man, His hand will be against everyone, and everyone's hand will be against him; and he will live to the east of all his brothers. (Genesis 16:10-12)

The Lord comforted Hagar with the knowledge that her child would have a significant future in His sight. He pronounced upon them both the blessing of fertility. In a time when survival was a daily struggle, this was one of the greatest blessings. Those who received it became people of promise. They served a purpose in His plan for human history.

In addition, the Angel of the Lord made clear to her that this child came as no surprise to God. The offspring was a son, and God already had his name picked out! It would serve as a memorial to all generations, reminding them of God's mercy toward Hagar when she needed Him the most. Ishmael—"God hears." The Lord was merciful to Hagar in the midst of her affliction.

Through the Body of Christ today, our Lord continues to respond to the affliction of thousands of Hagars every year. Upon learning their children are unique creations of God, many women feel encouraged to carry their babies to term. They become aware not only of the dignity possessed by the child within them but of their own dignity and the privilege of nurturing the gift of life. When practical assistance from caring churches is added to this kind of counsel, most women choose life.

THE WITNESS OF CHURCH HISTORY

In light of so much clear teaching in the Bible on the value of human life before God, it should come as no surprise that the church has consistently opposed abortion since its inception. An outstanding book has been written on the subject by Michael J. Gorman, *Abortion and the Early Church*. In it he makes the following observation:

> Writers of the first three centuries laid the theological and literary foundation for all subsequent early Christian writings on abortion. We will see that three important themes emerged during these centuries: the fetus is the creation of God; abortion is murder; and the judgment of God falls on those guilty of abortion.[4]

4. Michael J. Gorman, *Abortion and the Early Church* (Downers Grove, Ill.: Inter-Varsity, 1982), p. 47.

Beginning with the *Didache*, the earliest known Christian teaching outside the New Testament, abortion was thoroughly condemned: "Thou shalt not murder a child by abortion/destruction."[5]

In the second century, Clement of Alexandria wrote, "For those who conceal sexual wantonness by taking stimulating drugs to bring on an abortion wholly lose their own humanity along with the fetus."[6] Clement's view was typical of Christian teaching on abortion. In fact Christian opposition was so widespread and well known in the second century that it was taken for granted. One reason for the notoriety of this opinion was that it differed remarkably from the prevailing notion that abortion was acceptable.

Athenagoras appealed to this common understanding of the Christian position before the Emperor Marcus Aurelius when he defended the church against the charge of cannibalism at the Lord's Supper. The believers' Communion language regarding "eating the body" and "drinking the blood" of the Lord led hostile unbelievers to assume that Christians were devouring one another! Athenagoras argued that couldn't possibly be true since Christians are opposed to all violence—even abortion.

> How could we kill a man—we who say that women who take drugs to procure abortion are guilty of homicide and that they will have to answer to God for this abortion? One cannot at the same time believe that the fetus in the womb is a living being—as such in God's care—and kill one already brought forth into the light.[7]

Over the centuries the church has been subject to two great divisions, the schism of 1054 between East and West and the Protestant Reformation of 1517. In spite of all the differences and disagreements they represent, the sanctity of human life was never at issue, nor was opposition to abortion. Thus did John Calvin, the Protestant Reformer, write the following commentary on Exodus 21:22-24:

> The fetus, though enclosed in the womb of its mother, is already a human being and it is almost a monstrous crime to rob it of the life which it has not yet begun to enjoy. If it seems more horrible to kill a man in his own house than in a field, because a man's house is his

5. Ibid., p. 49.
6. Germain Grisez, *Abortion: the Myths, the Realities, and the Arguments* (New York: Corpus, 1972), p. 139.
7. Ibid., p. 140.

place of most secure refuge, it ought surely to be deemed more atrocious to destroy a fetus in the womb before it has come to light.[8]

The beliefs of Christian leaders who have preceded us do not alone determine the content of our faith. Only the Bible is the final authority. Nevertheless, it is a comfort to know we do not engage in innovative interpretations of Scripture that are so tenuous as to have totally missed the attention of our forefathers in the faith. In defending the sanctity of human life and opposing abortion, we stand in a noble tradition, well within the mainstream of Christian orthodoxy.

8. John Calvin, *Commentaries on the Four Last Books of Moses*, trans. Charles William Bingham, 4 vols. (Grand Rapids: Eerdmans, 1950), 3:41-42.

6

The Experience of Abortion

Abortion has been subject to a good deal of misplaced sympathy. Many people who oppose abortion in principle nonetheless believe it is a social necessity for women with crisis pregnancies. On this view, the argument goes, denying access to abortion is unloving and unkind.

With all due respect, I must maintain this sympathy is misplaced. It assumes that abortion can somehow solve the problems facing the woman with a crisis pregnancy. Since I first joined the ranks of those working to stop abortion, many of my perspectives and attitudes have changed. They have had to because they could not withstand the test of experience. There is one conviction about abortion, however, that has been reinforced time and again through ministry experience: abortion accomplishes none of the good things that are claimed for it. Abortion is evil; it is destructive to everyone involved.

ABORTION AND THE POOR

Abortion is not a solution to poverty. For the impoverished woman, abortion only increases the pain she knows already in her life. It represents a tragic verdict that the life she knows is not worth living. Abortion imparts no dignity or hope; rather it is a yielding to that force of despair that wars against the will to live.

It is significant that among the poor especially, value is placed in people rather than on things. In the ghettos of America where mothers rather than fathers represent stability and authority in the home, it is the children who are valued most. It is the children who provide dignity, purpose, and love to their mothers. The little ones embody all their hopes and dreams. Abortion is especially tragic in this situation; it destroys the living and the reason for living.

In fact, the principle argument advanced for aborting the children of the poor is hardly motivated by a desire to benefit them. Repeatedly the argument has been advanced by Planned Parenthood and other abortion supporters that it is cheaper to abort the children of the poor than it is to subsidize through welfare their delivery, birth, and growth.[1] Abortion then is not presented as an attempt to break the cycle of poverty, but to reduce its cost to the taxpaying public.

Even worse is the argument frequently made that the children of the poor represent a terrible *social* cost. This view is fatalistic, assuming that children born into low income homes will inevitably become social statistics—thieves, murderers, rapists. More accurately, in modern jargon, the view is deterministic.

ABORTION AND RELATIONSHIPS

Very often we hear from women who had abortions because they feared they would lose their husbands or boyfriends if they carried their babies to term. This fear could be the result of a direct or implied threat from the father. Or it may be an assumption made by the mother in light of many factors including finances, career goals, and living conditions.

The peculiar tragedy in this case is that abortion does not strengthen weak relationships. It brings no peace to couples who are upset or angry with each other. In fact, abortion is a wedge that drives couples apart. It introduces guilt and resentment into relationships, which speed the very outcome women so desperately want to avoid, total brokenness whether in divorce or "splitting." One husband recently described the effect of abortion on his marriage in this way:

> I firmly believe the living Hell Diahnn and I went through was due to overwhelming guilt [over the abortion]. I started abusing Diahnn,

---

1. "Abortion: Private Morality, Public Responsibility." A copy may be obtained from: Planned Parenthood Federation of America, 810 7th Ave. New York, NY 10019.

physically and verbally, blaming her for the abortion. I resented her, she resented me for agreeing to the abortion, and we resented ourselves. I got into drugs and alcohol, she sank deeper into depression; our marriage was over.[2]

It may surprise you to know that this couple's marriage did not collapse. They were reconciled to each other after first being reconciled to God. In His mercy Christ opened their hearts to receive His forgiveness; in turn, they were able to forgive each other. Very often, however, these stories do not have such a happy ending. A young man from the West Coast recently shared his experience:

> While this [abortion] was not the only reason for our subsequent divorce, it was a major one. I blamed her for being so insistent on having the abortion. I felt that she had coerced me into making a decision that was really against my inner feelings. I never forgave her while we were together, because I didn't want to face the fact that I was a co-conspirator with her. I only knew that the child was gone, and could never be replaced.
> We separated one year after the abortion and divorced a few months after that. I don't know what side effects she might have as a result of that abortion because I haven't seen her since the divorce. But I do know how it affected my life.[3]

Women's magazines regularly feature articles that deal with the strain abortion puts on relationships. In *Glamour*, one piece was provocatively titled "How Abortion Tests a Relationship: Could Yours Survive This Emotional Crisis?"[4] In another, author James Lincoln Collier made the following observation:

> Male feelings also do not end with the procedure itself. A man is usually very concerned about how a woman will feel toward him afterward, and how he will feel toward her. Understandably, a considerable number of couples break up after the abortion. Recalls one young man, "I don't know what went wrong, I just didn't feel the same way about her anymore. I guess I felt guilty about it, and I didn't want to be reminded of that."[5]

2. Testimony gathered by the Christian Action Council. Correspondence on file.
3. Testimony gathered by the Crisis Pregnancy Center of San Francisco. Correspondence on file.
4. P. Span, "How Abortion Tests a Relationship: Could Yours Survive This Emotional Crisis?" *Glamour*, December 1980, pp. 200-201.
5. James Lincoln Collier, "Abortion: How Men Feel About One of the Biggest Issues in a Woman's Life," *Glamour*, February 1980, p. 245.

Bruce Rappaport, program director of the Men's Support Center, an abortion counseling organization for men, maintains breakups after abortion are common:

> There's a lot of feeling between a man and a woman at this time. . . . We've done no official study, but places where we work estimate half the people they see have had their relationship broken up over abortion.[6]

In her book *The Ambivalence of Abortion* Linda Bird Franke drew an even stronger conclusion regarding the effects of abortion on relationships between single adults.

> In my research, almost every relationship between single people broke up either before or after the abortion. What had been pleasure became pain. What had been frivolous became heavy. Sex, which had brought intimacy and relief, brought memories of pain and guilt.[7]

IRREVERSIBLE SCARS

Inasmuch as abortion is promoted around an ethic that is essentially self-serving, it is significant to note that for so many women who have had them, abortions have not led to a better "quality of life." They have not led to fulfillment as the way was cleared to pursue personal goals or career ambitions. Happiness and joy were not the outcome.

In fact we find abortion injures the heart. The result is irreversible sorrow and regret, and the scar is deep. It affects the capacity to enjoy life and colors both experiences and relationships. Inescapably after an abortion, as with any great tragedy, the woman lives in its reflection. One young woman, an urban teen, shared spontaneously about her experience.

> Looking back, I honestly feel that no woman should ever go through an abortion. The feelings of guilt will always be there. If the person does choose to have children later on, you always think of the child as your second baby, not as your first. Even when you go to the hospital the doctors ask you, "Is this your first pregnancy?" It hurts to have to say, "No," but yet you have no other children to show for it. It hurts to say that.

6. Bruce Rappaport, "Abortion: Are Men There When Women Need Them Most?" *Mademoiselle*, April 1981, p. 253.
7. Linda Bird Franke, *The Ambivalence of Abortion* (New York: Random House, 1978), p. 47.

With the abortion, after it was over and done with, I tried not to think about it but you always think about it. When I look at my daughter, I always think of her as my second child, never as my first. My first child is gone.

I felt I had to replace my first child. I got pregnant in little over a year right after my abortion. I felt I had to replace the child that I lost.

Every time you look at a child you think and then you find yourself counting the years—"Well, my child would have been one today," or "My child would have been four." . . . You never see another child without thinking about yours and wondering what your child would have been like. And you wonder the classic question: "I wonder if it would have been a girl or a boy?"[8]

After enduring the procedure, women discover they have only initiated their experience with abortion. The agony reflected in the interview above is not limited to teens. In fact, studies now indicate abortion regret is greater in older women than in younger women. A thirty-seven-year-old woman gave us her reflections:

After seventeen years I still have not really fully faced the fact that I did not have an abortion, but I aborted my baby. It's a very painful thing and there's no turning back from it. It's something that a part of me still feels like hiding. I'm a very open person, and I rarely talk to anyone about me having an abortion, because it's such a dead end.

The scars it leaves you with can never be totally healed. I think the scar that it's left me with is that there's a kind of numbness, maybe protectiveness or a blocking out, that to admit or call myself a murderer . . . and sometimes to think that here my other daughter that I gave up for adoption is a grown women, has met the Lord, we've had a reunion, and this other baby would have been grown up too. I think that when we're young we don't realize twenty years passes so quickly. It's something I really regret.[9]

EMOTIONAL EFFECTS

It is disappointing to discover so few studies have been done on the emotional effects of abortion. Most tend to be biased or

8. *Understanding Pregnancy Alternatives*, an educational videotape produced by the Christian Action Council in May 1983, includes interviews with women who have faced abortions. The testimony cited comes from the interviews.
9. Ibid.

invalid because of the sampling technique, the interview process employed, or the period of observation and follow-up. The latter factor is especially important. The period of follow-up on women who have had abortions tends to be too short. There is no occasion to observe anniversary reactions to the abortion or to the projected date of the baby's delivery, although these are common. *Long-term* studies on the psychological impact of abortion on individuals or on family relationships do not exist. In part • that is because elective abortion is so recent to our society. In addition the evidence of interviews suggests that the results would not be pleasing to a secular establishment that insists abortion is simple, easy, and quickly over.

DETACHMENT

The most frequent emotion of women who have just had an abortion is relief. The pregnancy, the crisis, the abortion—these are over and done with. They can now proceed with life as usual. That is what they have been told, and they desperately cling to that promise. Often the reality of the procedure itself, the loss of life it guarantees, the mother's responsibility in this, and the assault it makes against a woman's psyche with its natural desire to nurture life, have not been faced. Before the procedure is performed, women typically expend a great deal of energy avoiding those issues, or trying to. In the language of counseling, they seek to detach themselves from what is taking place. That was well illustrated in the tragic report of a woman who aborted her unborn male after learning he was afflicted with Down's syndrome. The author recounts her experience of waiting, just prior to her prostaglandin abortion:

> The baby kicks another time and I stitch more frantically. I start saying the word fetus over and over to myself . . . no baby, no baby . . . just a Down's syndrome fetus . . .[10]

The abortion industry fosters this condition of emotional detachment in clients. This is not difficult because they are so vulnerable. Most women are largely ignorant about abortion as they enter a clinic or hospital. They are so threatened by their pregnancy they prefer to avoid any direct consideration of it. One young woman described her reaction to pregnancy this way:

10. Katherine G. Levine, "What I Thought During My Abortion," *Mademoiselle*, May 1979, p. 110.

"I was shocked. I really didn't believe it because I didn't think it could happen to me. I felt like it was something happening to all the other girls but not to me."[11]

As with people facing any crisis, these women are looking for help and will accept direction they might otherwise reject. They tend to respond favorably to authority figures, like doctors in white coats. They are reluctant to question advice when it points to a way out of their immediate crisis.

Abortion clinics exploit vulnerable women in two ways. They keep them as ignorant as possible of what they are paying for. Frequently the term "abortion" is not used at all, rather "termination." When asked about abortion, many clinic counselors respond that what is being removed is merely "fetal tissue," "a ball of cells," "the conceptus," "products of conception," "like the yolk of an egg." The notion that abortionists provide women with personal attention and thorough counsel on pregnancy and abortion before proceeding is a myth.

In conducting interviews for this book, I was introduced to one young woman from the Southwest whose experience underscored the disinformation that comes from abortion clinics. As a single college student, Annie was shocked to learn that she was pregnant. After telling her boyfriend the news, he urged her to get an abortion.

Annie made the appointment. The clinic personnel told her to call "anytime you want to talk." Feeling lonely and confused, she confided in her sister. Annie was in for a jolt. Having written a paper on pregnancy, her sister knew something about the development of the unborn and the experience of pain in the fetus. She pointed these things out to Annie, who didn't know what to believe.

> I had to call the abortion clinic to find out for sure. When I reached them, I told the counselor who I was and asked, "Will the baby feel it, and what will it look like?" The counselor said, "It won't look like anything more than a little ball of cotton, and it won't be able to feel anything."[12]

Annie wasn't convinced. She called a nearby Crisis Pregnancy Center and set up an appointment for the next morning. When she saw pictures of unborn infants in the first trimester of pregnancy and learned more about fetal pain, she made up her mind to carry the baby to term.

11. *Understanding Pregnancy Alternatives.*
12. Testimony gathered by the Christian Action Council, interview on file.

Annie recently gave birth to a beautiful, healthy daughter, and everyone is doing fine. Understandably, she resents the abortion clinic personnel for misleading her. Through the grace of God, this did not result in an abortion as it has for so many others. I asked Annie about the Christian counselor who worked with her at the Crisis Pregnancy Center. She responded instantly, "I love her so much for helping me!"

In a provocative book entitled *Techniques of Abortion*, Dr. Selig Neubardt reports that the numbers of saline abortions his doctors perform (e.g., ten per morning) tire them out so that their interaction with clients is likely to become broken and uneven. To remedy this a taped message is played for each woman as the abortion proceeds so the same things are said to everyone. In alerting the client to the expulsion of the fetus, which will occur, she is told, "You will easily recognize the fetus." But that is all.[13]

The truth about abortion becomes clear only after the procedure. One young woman shared the following testimony with me recently. It illustrates the truth about "abortion counseling."

> The doctor took me into his office after the examination to give me the results of my pregnancy test. Actually I think I knew the results were positive and I was real shaky.
>
> He explained the results were positive. Then he told me that from the examination I was ten to twelve weeks pregnant and asked what I wanted to do. I told him that I was afraid and didn't want anyone to know about it. "You can come in and have an abortion tomorrow morning then," he said.
>
> The next morning, my boyfriend drove me down. The doctor was late because he was out delivering a baby. Up to this point I thought he was being helpful and really nice. When he came in the office, he started going on and on about the delivery, how wonderful it was, how big the baby was and everything. All the blood drained from my head.
>
> I had to sign a release form that if anything happened to me he was not responsible. When I signed it, he said to me, "I have to tell you what your options are. To have the baby and keep it or give it up for adoption. Or to have an abortion." That was the extent of the counseling.
>
> Then he went into the examining room and a nurse prepared me for my abortion. The whole thing felt like a dream. He performed the abortion and then when it was over, he lifted the sack in front of

13. Selig Neubardt, *Techniques of Abortion* (Boston: Little, Brown, 1977), pp. 70-71.

my face and asked if I wanted to see it. He said it was kind of hard to tell, but he thought it might have been a boy. I started throwing up.[14]

CHEMICAL CALM

In addition to carefully cultivated ignorance before the procedure, some clinics also resort to the use of drugs. Over the last five years providing women with sedatives soon after their arrival has become routine procedure in most clinics. Any anxiety or hesitancy these patients feel soon fades as they are chemically removed to another world where a feeling of calm reigns.

The ignorance and detachment fostered by abortion proponents now has the sanction of the US Supreme Court. This was provided in June 1983, when the High Court struck down as unconstitutional a city ordinance passed in Akron, Ohio.[15] It was called the "Informed Consent" ordinance because its principle aim was to require that abortion clinics in Akron inform their patients of the facts of pregnancy, fetal development, and abortion—both the procedure and the risks. Then, if the patient elected to proceed with abortion, she would truly be giving her "informed consent." It is instructive to consider the six provisions that the Supreme Court found offensive.

1. The law required that abortions after the first trimester of pregnancy be performed in a hospital rather than an abortion clinic. This reflected the Supreme Court's acknowledgment in 1973 that abortions performed after the first trimester of pregnancy pose greater health risks to the mothers.
2. It prohibited a physician from performing an abortion on an unmarried girl who is under fifteen years of age, unless that physician had the consent of one of her parents or a court order for the procedure.
3. Under the ordinance, attending physicians would have been legally responsible to inform their patients of the status of their pregnancy, to explain the method of abortion to be used, to describe the particular state of development reached by the unborn child, and to detail the possible physical or emotional complications that could result.

14. Testimony gathered by the Christian Action Council, interview on file.
15. *Akron* v. *Akron Center for Reproductive Health, Inc., et al.*,___U.S.___. (15 June 1983).

4. The ordinance required abortionists to alert their patients to the availability of help to pursue alternatives to abortion.

5. It further required that twenty-four hours must elapse between the patient's signing a consent form for abortion and the actual onset of the procedure. This would give patients an opportunity to reflect on the information they had been given before going ahead with abortion.

6. Lastly, the Akron Ordinance stipulated that the remains of the dead fetus be disposed of in a "humane and sanitary manner."

The rationale provided by the Supreme Court for striking down those provisions varied from lofty constitutional assertions to minor technical charges. The High Court, whose 1973 decision gave rise to the abortion clinic industry, determined to be its guardian. Not only do unborn children go unprotected to the clinics, but so do the mothers who carry them.

PSYCHOLOGICAL TRAUMA

The abortion scenario, which is acted out thousands of times daily in the US, is an invitation to an emotional hell at some time in the mother's future. It may not occur for years, but eventually the fact of what took place reaches her. Human beings erect strong emotional barriers to defend themselves from things they regret or feel guilty over. That can only be done at the expense of tremendous amounts of emotional energy. As a result personality distortion and mental illness may occur.

Psychiatric journals occasionally print case studies on this problem. One article was entitled "Obsessive-Compulsive Neurosis After Viewing the Fetus During Therapeutic Abortion."[16] It recounted the story of a nineteen-year-old woman whose abortion was recommended by a psychiatrist as a mental health safeguard. At the time of her abortion no medical personnel were present with her, so she had the opportunity to study the dead infant. She was especially affected at seeing the tiny but well-formed toes and fingers.

In a strange sort of self-retaliation, she concluded that her own hands and feet were dirty and hurt other people. She began wash-

16. Steven Lipper and W. Morton Feigenbaum, "Obsessive-Compulsive Neurosis After Viewing the Fetus During Therapeutic Abortion," *American Journal of Psychotherapy* 30(1976):666-74.

ing her hands thirty to forty times each day and refused to wear shoes or socks. Soon she was continually washing all of her possessions. She could no longer function normally. Fifteen months after her abortion, this young woman was admitted to a psychiatric unit.[17]

In some cases the reality of abortion breaks in on a woman very suddenly and unexpectedly. This may be triggered by any number of events such as the birth of a child, the death of a loved one, or seeing the picture of an unborn child. A young woman describes what happened to her one evening several years after her abortion.

> All of a sudden, I was thinking about the abortion, and I couldn't understand why I was thinking about it. I started to become very anxious and just totally depressed. I cried a lot and had a lot of guilt feelings. And it shocked me that this is what happened, that I had actually interrupted a pregnancy. I think that what was so hard was my denial through the whole thing. I had a lot of physical symptoms related to this like dizziness. My pulse was very rapid, and I was short of breath when I'd get so upset. I can remember crying a lot, and just a deep sense of hurting.[18]

To the glory of God, this woman has been delivered from her guilt and depression. She credits this deliverance to Christ's forgiveness and His unconditional love, which she realized through Christian counseling and the support of her family and friends. Many women, however, have no contact with anyone who knows the gospel.

The difficulty women have dealing with the emotional and spiritual aftermath of abortion finds expression in a variety of ways, public as well as private. WEBA, Women Exploited by Abortion, is a nationwide self-help organization that ministers to women who have had abortions. In addition, members speak out publicly so other women might know the truth and be warned.

DEALING WITH GRIEF

Over the last five years dozens of articles have been written by women who have gone through abortion. They serve as a form of public confession by women who are struggling to justify what they have done or at least to deal with their grief. These articles

17. Ibid., p. 668.
18. *Understanding Pregnancy Alternatives.*

are painful to read, even more painful to write. Among the pieces that have been published in women's magazines and newspapers, the following titles are especially indicative: "Why I Ended My Baby's Life";[19] "My Doctor Said I Should Have an Abortion";[20] "Diary of My Decision: Why I Had an Abortion";[21] "What I Thought During My Abortion."[22] Other articles analyze the grief that affects women who have destroyed their offspring: "On Paying the Price of Abortion";[23] "Are You Sorry You Had an Abortion?";[24] "We've Won the Right to Legal Abortion, but We're Still Learning the Physical and Emotional Results."[25] All these articles appeared in magazines that for years have endorsed abortion as a simple matter of reproductive rights. Those who have adopted this attitude are shocked to find themselves relating to the "fetal tissue" they destroyed as to a dead son or daughter. Often that shift occurs even before the abortion itself.

In "An Apology to a Little Boy I Won't Ever See" the anonymous author recounts her feelings before her abortion:

> I give serious thought to having this child and raising it alone, and I face the fact that I am not the person to meet that challenge, that burden. Call it selfishness. Call it quality of life. Call it caring about what you can offer the children you have. *Oh baby, I think to myself, I love you so much that I want everything to be perfect for you. I want to be able to give you everything. I want you to have all the things, all the opportunities. I can't give you those now. This isn't the right time for you baby.*
>
> And I am angry. I am angry at Billie Jean King and Gloria Steinem and every woman who ever had an abortion and didn't tell me about this kind of pain. There is a conspiracy among the sisterhood not to tell each other about guilt and self-hatred and terror. Having an abortion is not like having a wart removed or your nails done or your hair cut, and anyone who tells you it is is a liar or worse. To decide to have an abortion is to make a life-and-death decision, and most people I know don't make those casually. Yes, it is convenient and legal and a subject for polite conversation these days. And yes, a part of me is dying too.[26]

19. *Glamour*, May 1982, p. 134.
20. *Good Housekeeping*, March 1982, p. 32.
21. *Redbook*, September 1979, p. 62.
22. *Mademoiselle*, May 1979, p. 110.
23. *Mademoiselle*, March 1978, p. 100.
24. *Good Housekeeping*, July 1977, p. 120.
25. *Glamour*, January 1978, p. 110.
26. These excerpts come from an article first published in the Providence, Rhode Island, *Evening Bulletin*, 23 April 1980. It was subsequently reprinted in *Human Life Review*.

This sort of public grieving has become ritualized in Japan, where over fifty million abortions have been performed since the practice was legalized in 1952. Buddhist temples have been erected to memorialize "water babies," those who perish by abortion, in order to secure peace for their departed souls. For the price of $340 to $640 each, grieving mothers can purchase small stone Buddhas erected as memorials at one temple. With over 10,000 of these statues now in place, the temple grounds have become a commercial attraction. For a small price visitors are admitted to browse and take pictures.[27]

Priests at many temples offer prayers regularly for the souls of the departed babies. The fee at one temple is $120 for the first "water baby" and $40 for each additional one. In exchange for the money, the priest promises, "We will give the best possible care to the soul of your unborn child." In the first seven years of the temple's operation, women contracted for prayers for over 120,000 aborted infants.[28]

This exploitation of women's grief is yet another destructive effect of abortion. Although the phenomenon occurs only in Japan at present, the suggestion has been seriously advanced to develop similar rituals in the US.[29] Aborted women are too vulnerable in their grief for American profiteers to ignore them.

MEN AND ABORTION

The grief of abortion does not end with the mother. One reason that so many couples break up after abortion is that the man as well as the woman has been affected. Arthur Shostak, professor of sociology at Drexel University, in Philadelphia, has conducted studies regarding abortion's impact on the fathers. He reports that close to one-third of young men involved with abortion experience strong emotional reactions that persist long after the abortion has been performed. Those feelings include guilt, remorse, sadness, and nightmares. When asked if "males generally have an easy time of it and have few, if any, lingering disturbing thoughts," 72 percent of the men interviewed disagreed.[30]

27-28. Information included under these footnotes was presented in a television documentary produced and aired in Japan during March 1983. A transcript of the news program was made available through: The Christian A/V Center c/o The Student Christian Center, 1, 2 Chome Surugadi Chiyoda-ku, Tokyo 101, Japan.

29. Carol Lynn Mithers, "The Intelligent Woman's Guide to Sex," *Mademoiselle*, September 1983, p. 66.

30. *San Francisco Examiner and Chronicle*, 18 May 1980, p. 29.

Shostak explains that men experience abortion "as a loss of fatherhood." "I have had men break down and cry when I was interviewing them. They've never spoken about it before. There's been no catharsis for them. They speculate; they say, 'What would have happened if I had told her that I wanted this child?' "[31]

When the word *fetus* was used in one interview with a young man, his response summed up well the experience of so many: "The man's eyes filled up with tears," Shostak said. "He said to me, 'It's not a fetus we're talking about. It's my son. He would be 3 years old now.' "[32]

Shostak has requested funding from the National Institutes of Health in order to carry on his critical research. Funding has been denied. He explained their refusal in an interview with the *San Francisco Examiner and Chronicle*.

> They told me off the record that this work could be construed as anti abortion. It could indicate that the absence of counseling is leaving behind a destructive residual in many men, it would be seized upon by antiabortionists. So they didn't want to fund any investigations of what happens to these men.[33]

CHILDREN AND ABORTION

Statistics gathered by the Centers for Disease Control indicate that just over 40 percent of women who abort have carried at least one child to term.[34] This means that many aborted infants had brothers or sisters. Abortion dramatically affects them as well. Even for those children born to women after a previous abortion, the deed can be a cause of great misery and suffering. The widespread acceptance of abortion conveys to all children the frightening message that the love they receive is conditional.

Those are the conclusions drawn by psychiatrist Philip Ney as a result of his studies on how abortion effects unaborted siblings. He refers to them as "abortion surivors" because they respond as do children who have faced a major disaster in their lives. In an article in *Child Psychiatry and Human Development*, Dr. Ney cites a number of studies confirming young children's awareness

31. Quoted by Steve Chapman, *Chicago Tribune*, 8 June 1983.
32. Ibid.
33. *San Francisco Examiner and Chronicle*, 18 May 1980, p. 29.
34. Centers for Disease Control, *Abortion Surveillance 1979-1980* (May 1983), p. 34. A copy may be obtained from Centers for Disease Control, Atlanta, GA 30333.

of their mothers' pregnancies, miscarriages, or abortions. These incidents can effect them deeply, much to the parents' surprise:

> A seven-year-old patient reported a dream in which three siblings went with him to play in a sand bank. While playing, the undermined bank collapsed and buried his siblings. Who they were he could not tell me but he knew they were brothers and/or sisters. His mother admitted to three early miscarriages but insisted her child could not have known.[35]

Three possible syndromes may develop in the brother or sister of an aborted infant. These represent the psychological effect of abortion as a disaster in the child's life.

> The "haunted child" survives to live in distrust of what may be in store for him while parents conspire not to burden him with the facts. The child is haunted by a mystery, knowing and yet not knowing. He is afraid to ask for clarification in case he discovers something more awful than he already expects.
>
> The "bound child" reflects a parental need to control those forces that destroyed his sibling. If an abortion was done for convenience, social pressure or economic necessity, the parents struggle to make sure it cannot happen again. Preconsciously aware of their destructiveness, the parents overprotect the child against projected hostilities. As the child is kept free from exploring the world, so his intelligence, adaptability and curiosity are crimped.
>
> The "substitute child," maybe an abortion survivor, is especially wanted to replace the child that is no more. This child carries a heavy burden of expectation that he may not be able to fulfill. When he is disappointing, the parents may react with enraged frustration. They may have "terminated" the life of one child that could have been all they hoped for. Now this child continually lets them down.[36]

Perhaps the most alarming impact of abortion on surviving siblings surfaces in the maternal relationship. Child abuse rates are higher among women who have aborted than among those who have not:

> Lenoski's evidence indicates that 90 percent of battered children are wanted pregnancies. Barker found higher rates of abortion among women who have abused their children and also among siblings of abused children. Our study indicates that child abuse is more fre-

35. Philip G. Ney, "A Consideration of Abortion Survivors," *Child Psychiatry and Human Development* 13, no. 3 (Spring 1983):170. Used by permission.
36. Ibid., p. 171.

quent among mothers who have previously had an abortion. The mother's guilt or high expectations may be reasons why there is this high correlation. A more plausible cause is that because of guilt, there is antepartum depression that interferes with the mother's ability to bond. Children not well bonded appear to be at higher risk to a parent's occasional rage or neglect.[37]

One of the early arguments for abortion was that it would reduce child abuse because unwanted children would be aborted before their parents had opportunity to batter them. Just the opposite effect has occurred. The violence of abortion begets further violence.

Even if child abuse does not occur (and it does not in most cases), Dr. Ney relates that the failed ability to bond in an aborted mother can have other adverse effects on her next child.

> Some mothers who have had an abortion develop an aversion to touching babies. An intelligent young woman told me "I desperately wanted a baby after my abortion, but when they handed it to me I handed it right back, something was wrong." Abortion may be a major factor in reducing parent-infant skin contact and therefore the development of the child's intelligence, independence and maturity.[38]

In the concluding section of his paper, Dr. Ney raises a poignant issue:

> The knowledge they have been chosen to live creates peculiar psychological problems which may retard their development, subject them to an increased risk of abuse, neglect, existential guilt, as well as the possibility of becoming parents who have difficulty relating to their children. Having been told they must appreciate being alive, they do not complain now. We might wonder what happens in the future when abortion survivors hold in their hands the fate of those aged or enfeebled parents and professionals who regarded them so callously when as unborn children they were so vulnerable.[39]

The issue Dr. Ney raises has nothing to do with vengeance. Rather, what are children today being taught about regard for human life when their brothers or sisters are being aborted and when they themselves live only because they are wanted? Does this not teach that the unwanted are expendable? Has not this lesson been taught to them by their own parents?

37. Ibid., p. 172.
38. Ibid., p. 173.
39. Ibid., p. 177.

CONCLUSION

In studying the effects of abortion on mothers, fathers, and siblings, it is clear that abortion is a major hazard to the mental health of our citizenry. Rather than accept the responsibility they instinctively feel to love a newly conceived infant, parents suppress that instinct and misplace their guilt on the child, calling him or her "unwanted." Within themselves this argument is unpersuasive, however, and they come to experience abortion as violence against their own flesh and blood. Because it is.

7

The Target of Abortion

"Our generation is the first ever to have a reasonably complete picture of the development of the human from conception."[1]

Unborn humans are amazingly beautiful. Growing rapidly and forcefully, these tiny individuals exert tremendous determination to enter the world of the living. If we are going to understand what abortion truly is, we must consider the victim in some detail.

Prior to the 1960s knowledge of the unborn was acquired principally through pathological examinations. Embryos, fetuses, and premature infants that had been subject to miscarriage or criminal abortion provided one of the few sources of data for doctors and scientists. Small corpses rather than living individuals were under study. The only way to observe an unborn child in the womb was through the use of X-rays. Those proved dangerous to infants and useless before their bone structures began to form. The only other means of monitoring fetal activity was indirect, involving the use of electrocardiographic recordings of the fetal heart.[2]

1. Robert L. Sassone, ed., *The Tiniest Humans* (Santa Ana, Calif.: Robert L. Sassone, 1977), p. 12.
2. Sir A. William Liley, "A Day in the Life of the Fetus," in *New Perspectives on Human Abortion*, ed. Thomas W. Hilgers, et al. (Frederick, Md.: University Publications, 1981), p. 30.

Nonetheless, a great deal was being learned. Enough in fact that in the early sixties the unborn child was first treated directly as a patient. Dr. William Albert Liley of New Zealand successfully completed an intrauterine blood transfusion to an unborn child who was subject to the rh factor. As a result, the baby was born without suffering from the effects of rh incompatibility with his mother, and the medical community worldwide was presented with a new frontier, providing direct care for the preborn baby. The fact that obstetricians are confronted with the responsibility for two human beings in pregnancy was highlighted as never before.[3]

LIFE MAGAZINE PHOTOGRAPHS

On the popular level, the humanity of the unborn was brought to world attention in 1965 when photographs of unborn infants were published as the lead feature in the April issue of *Life* magazine.[4] The photos, taken by Swedish photographer Leonnart Nillsen, educated millions of people to the wonder of life in the womb. The rapid, complex development of the tiny embryo or fetus was vividly portrayed in a series of photos covering infants throughout the duration of pregnancy. What few people knew was that the pictures were taken of human beings who had been aborted.[5]

OBSERVING THE UNBORN

Over the last two decades two techniques have been refined for observing the unborn in their mothers' wombs. The first is fetoscopy, which involves the insertion of a long, narrow fiberoptic tube into the uterus of the mother. With this the unborn child can be directly observed and photographed. Movies are now commercially available showing the fetus in his native environment, swimming, turning, sleeping, sucking his thumb, as well as engaging in other activities.[6]

The second technique is known has ultrasonography. This has become immensely popular because it makes observation of the

3. Sassone, p. 12.
4. *Life*, 30 April 1965. "Life Before Birth" is available as "Educational Reprint 27" from Media International Distribution Center, P.O. Box 67, Pine Bluff, NC, 28373.
5. *Life*, April 1983, p. 39.
6. A good example of this is the film *First Days of Life*, available through For Life, Inc., P.O. Drawer 1279, Depot Station, Tryon, NC, 28782.

unborn possible with no invasion of the uterus whatsoever. Ultrasound is an imaging technique based on the use of low frequency sound waves. These are projected through the abdomen of the mother and reflected off the baby as well as the mother's organs and tissues. The returning sound waves are computer enhanced to produce an image on a television screen. Because the equipment is relatively inexpensive, it may be found in the offices of many obstetricians. Routinely, expectant mothers can view their babies long before birth—in fact, before they have even felt the babies move within them.

One effect of this technology is to foster in the mother a strong emotional attachment to her baby, long before birth. Known as maternal bonding, this psychological mechanism has traditionally occurred at birth when the mother first sees her baby. Now, it is not necessary to wait that long.

For women considering abortion, ultrasound can cause an amazing change of mind. Two examples were recently provided in the *New England Journal of Medicine*. Researchers interviewed a thirty-year-old woman at a large inner-city hospital as she viewed her fetus on a television monitor.

"How do you feel about seeing what is inside you?" She answered crisply, "It certainly makes you think twice about abortion!" When asked to say more, she told of the surprise she felt on viewing the fetal form, especially on seeing it move: "I feel that it is human. It belongs to me. I couldn't have an abortion now."[7]

A second interview was conducted with a thirty-two-year-old woman at a genetics clinic at the National Institutes of Health. Her response was similar.

The mother was asked about her experiences with ultrasound. She said, "It really made a difference to see that it was alive." Asked about her position on the moral choice she had to make, she said, "I'm going all the way with the baby. I believe it is human."[8]

Authors John Fletcher and Mark Evans acknowledge that ultrasound may "result in fewer abortions and more desired pregnancies." They express concern that it could "become a weapon

7. John C. Fletcher and Mark J. Evans, "Maternal Bonding in Early Fetal Ultrasound Examinations," *New England Journal of Medicine* 308, no. 7 (7 February 1983):392.
8. Ibid., p. 392.

in the moral struggle" over abortion and the use of fetal therapy. Those advocating treatment for the unborn and opposing abortion might use ultrasound as "a potent (and unfair?) maneuver."[9] With techniques such as ultrasound, mothers can observe the son or daughter within them. Rather than reacting with unqualified enthusiasm to this new ability to educate the patient, the response of professionals such as Fletcher and Evans is tempered by the commitment to keep the killing option not just available but acceptable. For them ultrasound conveys a knowledge of "uterine contents" that is dangerous. In that case, let us take a few moments and think dangerously.

THE DEVELOPMENT OF THE UNBORN BABY IN THE WOMB

"Life has a very very long history, but each human being has a very neat beginning: the moment of conception."[10] At conception a sperm cell from the father plunges into the much larger ovum of the mother. This fusion is accomplished in part through enzymes secreted by the sperm, which dissolve away the protective outer layer of the ovum. This usually occurs in one of the mother's two fallopian tubes (the narrow tubes leading from the womb to the ovaries). Genetic material from the father that had been carried by the sperm now recombines with an equal complement of material from the mother's ovum. Each parent thus contributes equally twenty-three chromosomes to the genetic heritage of their offspring. The result of this event, also known as fertilization, is a unique human individual composed of a single cell.

THE FIRST WEEK

Immediately the fertilized ovum demonstrates its distinctive nature. Whereas an ovum or sperm cell soon dies once freed from the body of which it is a part, the fertilized ovum begins to divide and multiply. Over the next seven days the tiny individual will grow to several hundred cells while swept along on the most perilous journey of human existence.

Lacking any form of self-propulsion or steering, the new human is at the mercy of forces within the fallopian tube and

9. Ibid., p. 393.
10. Opening remarks of Dr. Jerome Lejeune before the Separation of Powers subcommittee of the US Senate Judiciary Committee, during hearings on the humanity of the unborn in May 1981. Dr. Lejeune is the renowned geneticist who discovered the genetic basis for Down's syndrome.

uterus, especially the hairlike cilia that line the tube. Eventually, however, he or she (the sex was determined at fertilization) enters the womb, prepared to nest in its soft, blood-rich lining. Because of cellular multiplication the embryo looks much like a very tiny mulberry. Already the growth pattern has become differentiated so that cell types can be distinguished, and multiplication rates vary.[11]

Once contact has been made with the lining of the uterus, the embryo "sticks" to it. Since the nutrition present in the original ovum is all but depleted, a new source of nourishment, direct from the mother, is about to be found:

> Soon it vigorously erodes through the uterine lining as though it were an invading parasite intent on nesting down for the next nine months. The uterus at first reacts to this invasion of the blastocyst as it would to the presence of an enemy. The lining tissues actively swell outward to engulf the embryo, and at the same time marshal thousands of white blood cells to clean up any debris. Then resistance turns to welcome. The blood vessels of the uterus become greatly engorged with blood, the lining glands secrete their fluids more actively, and the uterine tissues seem to make a place for the embryo—some tissues even form a protective cordon around the embryo.[12]

THE SECOND WEEK

Before the second week is complete the embryo produces cells that form the amnion, a protective capsule that will house him or her in a fluid environment. This will serve as a source of protection cushioning the individual from sudden jolts and assuring a well-regulated temperature. In addition a yolk sac is formed that will produce the reproductive cells and the first blood cells needed by the embryo as he or she continues to develop. Lacking functioning organs and glands, a placenta also develops to accomodate the needs that will later be met by those structures. The placenta allows for the exchange of nutrients, waste products, oxygen, and hormones between mother and child. With every beat of the mother's heart, her offspring will be nourished and cleansed. The embryo is connected to this life support system by an umbilical cord, eventually composed of three tubes—two arteries, and one vein.[13]

11. Robert Rugh and Landrum B. Shettles, *From Conception to Birth* (New York: Harper and Row, 1971), p. 23.
12. Ibid., pp. 25-26.
13. Ibid., pp. 28-29.

THE THIRD WEEK

The embryo has been growing rapidly, doubling in size almost daily. With the establishment of a home base, remarkable development of body systems now begins. The first to advance is the most important and the most complex. It is the central nervous system including the brain. Man is, after all, a "cerebral being."

Because of this early start for the brain and its subsequent development, the head of the unborn will be disproportionately large throughout pregnancy when compared with that of a child or adult. "Throughout its growth, the brain influences that of all other organs."[14] By twenty days after conception, the foundation has been created for the new human's brain, spinal cord, and entire nervous system.[15]

The nervous system is not the only dramatic advance for the embryo during the third week of life. A brain requires the support of a heart, and by eighteen days after conception a tiny heart has formed as a single tube that will soon differentiate into two and then four chambers. Within the following week it will begin to beat, irregularly at first, but soon very steadily up to 100,000 times every day. Even before reaching one month of age, the embryo's heart, prominent and bulging from his chest, is circulating blood.[16] Technicians skilled in the use of sonography have been able to observe its palpitations.

THE FOURTH WEEK

By the end of the first month, the embryo is 10,000 times larger than when first proceeding down the mother's fallopian tube.[17] Still one-fourth inch in length, he or she is able to fit on a penny. An internal skeleton has begun to form, composed of living tissues. So have a mouth and body cavity. The sense organs (nose, eyes, and ears) have begun to form. Small "limb buds" are present and will soon become arms and legs. The embryo also has a small "tail," but this will disappear within a week as the buttocks grows.[18]

14. E. Blechschmidt, "Human Being from the Very First," in New Perspectives on Human Abortion, ed. Thomas W. Hilgers, et al. (Frederick, Md.: University Publications, 1981), p. 19.
15. Rugh and Shettles, p. 33.
16. Leslie Brainerd Arey, Developmental Anatomy (Philadelphia: W. B. Saunders, 1965), pp. 97-98.
17. Linda Ferrill Annis, The Child Before Birth (Ithaca, N.Y.: Cornell U., 1978), p. 27.
18. Arey, pp. 92, 98.

THE FIFTH WEEK

By the end of the fifth week of life (or the seventh week of pregnancy, since the duration of pregnancy is reckoned from the first day of the mother's last menstrual period), the unborn is "recognizably human," with a body that has "plumped out into a baby shape."[19] The development of human facial features is dramatic and continues throughout the second month. The eyes, nostrils, ears, mouth, lips, and tongue are clearly visible. Even the teeth have begun to develop. The differentiation of the brain has occurred to the point at which the cerebral cortex may be observed, and the pituitary gland is now forming.[20] Rudimentary lungs, liver, kidneys, gall bladder, and spleen are developing as the heart beats 160 times a minute.[21] Because all muscle blocks in the human body are now present, movement may begin.[22]

THE SIXTH WEEK

During the following week all the major internal organs that are present in the adult appear in the embryo. Those that are not operational need only time to mature. Even the toes and fingers, the last extremities to develop, are asserting themselves. The little son or daughter may begin to test out those brand new knees and kick, but Mom will not feel anything for another eight weeks or so. The brain "glimmers through skin as thin as waxed paper, revealing every tiny branching blood vessel beneath."[23] The eyes have become pigmented, and the olfactory nerve network (creating the sensation of smell) is connected.[24] Brain activity can now be measured as can the heartbeat. Because so much growth and development have occurred, the embryo reaches a new level of maturity and receives a new name, *fetus*. Contrary to the claim that "fetus" implies an insignificant nonhuman mass of tissue, the term signifies a new stage of human dvelopment for an individual who has made remarkable progress already.

19. Sheila Kitzinger, *The Complete Book of Pregnancy and Childbirth* (New York: Knopf, 1982), p. 63.
20. Rugh and Shettles, pp. 44-45.
21. John T. Queenan, ed., *A New Life, Pregnancy, Birth, and Your Child's First Year* (New York: Van Nostrand Reinhold, 1982), pp. 50-51.
22. Physician members of the Value of Life Committee in Brighton, Massachusetts, prepared a very helpful publication from which this data is taken, "When Did Your Life Begin?" A copy may be obtained from: Value of Life Committee, 637 Cambridge St., Brighton, MA 02135.
23. Kitzinger, p. 63.
24. Rugh and Shettles, p. 47.

THE SEVENTH WEEK

Bone begins replacing cartilage during week number seven. Brain growth is accompanied by muscle development, so that coordination is increasing. As a result, "the movement of the arms and legs of the fetus are both frequent and purposeful."[25] In particular the little fetus will begin touching his mouth with his hands.[26] Over the next three weeks, he will become quite an acrobat. His or her sporting behavior is helped along by the buoyancy of the amniotic fluid. When not occupied with exercise, comfort determines his position.

THE EIGHTH WEEK

With the conclusion of the following week, the tiny child is two months old. His height is 1¼ inches, and he weighs about ¹/₃₀ of an ounce. If his mouth is lightly stroked, his entire body will shudder.[27] Local reactions will not develop until after birth. He is just now beginning to swallow.[28]

> If one can imagine a one-inch miniature doll with a very large head but gracefully formed arms and legs, Oriental slitlike eyes and small ear lobes over slight depressions on the sides of the head, and a rather bulbous abdomen, he would have a fair mental picture of a two-month-old-fetus.[29]

THE THIRD MONTH

By the end of the third month the tiny human will attain a height of 3 inches. His individuality will begin to assert itself, especially with facial expressions. If Mom and Dad could behold their child, they might see a family resemblance. The baby has begun to inhale and exhale amniotic fluid, strengthening his lungs. If aborted alive, he will struggle to breathe, and if his mouth is stimulated he will respond with the sucking reflex.[30] His eyelids have fused for protection; they will not open before the sixth month of pregnancy. Fingernails, toenails, and hair follicles have begun to form. His skin is very sensitive to touch.[31]

25. Queenan, p. 51.
26. Blechschmidt, p. 24.
27. Annis, p. 27.
28. Liley, p. 33.
29. Rugh and Shettles, p. 54.
30. Annis, p. 30.
31. Rugh and Shettles, pp. 58-61.

There is no question that this individual can suffer and experience acute pain.

One might think that with so much growth and development, no energy is available for exercise, but that is not the case.

> You cannot feel these movements, but it is kicking, curling its toes up and down, rotating its feet and wrists, clenching and unclenching its fists, pressing its lips together, frowning and making other facial expressions. . . . There is still plenty of room in the uterus, so the fetus can swoop and undulate in its own enclosed sea.[32]

Dr. William Albert Liley has observed that until infants have grown so large as to be restricted by the walls of the womb, their method of changing ends is very practical: "They propel themselves around with their legs and feet—usually walking backward—with their heads leading the movement, but occasionally walk around forward with their heads trailing."[33]

THE FOURTH MONTH

During the fourth month of life, the fetus grows to 6 inches in length and, just like a baby outside the womb, begins to suck his thumb. (Actually the thumb-sucking of a nine week aborted infant has been photographed.)[34] Only now does Mom feel him moving.[35]

THE FIFTH AND SIXTH MONTHS

Over the following two months the growing child reaches 12 inches in height. As the mother walks, she in effect rocks him so that when she is busiest, the baby often is asleep. If for some reason amniotic fluid is removed from his mouth and vocal cords, the baby may be heard crying within the womb.[36] And if he drinks too much of the fluid, he may get a case of the hiccups that lasts for half an hour. If born prematurely during the sixth month, he has a good chance of surviving. He is no longer a "fetus" but a premature infant.

During this period sensitivity increases in several ways. The eyes have opened so there is a much greater awareness of light. Sensitivity to taste is probably greater than at any other time in

32. Kitzinger, p. 65.
33. Liley, p. 31.
34. Ibid., p. 34.
35. Annis, p. 32.
36. Ibid., p. 32.

the course of life since both the inside of the mouth and tongue are covered with taste buds (these first began appearing during the third month). In addition, loud noises outside the womb can trigger a strong reaction.[37]

THE LAST THREE MONTHS

During the last three months of pregnancy, the infant grows to about 20 inches and weighs 7½ pounds. An outer layer of "baby fat" has been steadily accumulating so his body completely fills the womb. Around thirty-six to thirty-eight weeks, he will descend headfirst into the pelvis. Believe it or not, that is the most comfortable position for him. In the very last weeks of pregnancy, the life support system that has served so well, the placenta, begins to deteriorate. Three hundred quarts of blood have been daily passing from baby to placenta. The infant has no choice. For the sake of his survival, he must soon be born.[38]

The nine months of growth in the womb is a wonderful adventure. Quite properly did the poet Coleridge write, "Yes—this history of a man for the nine months preceding his birth would probably be far more interesting and contain events of greater moment, than all the three score and ten years that follow it."[39] Truly we are fearfully and wonderfully made.

THE UNBORN AS PATIENT

With the onset of observation and diagnostic techniques for treating unborn children, and with knowledge accumulated from research on monkeys and lab animals, dramatic advances are now being made in providing actual prenatal medical care.

Unborn children may now be treated surgically within the womb. At least eight medical centers in the US are equipped to perform the delicate operations.[40] In 1981, guided by ultrasound imaging, doctors inserted a catheter into the bladder of a sick baby boy suffering from a condition known as hydronephrosis. (Incidentally, his healthy twin sister was not affected by the procedure.) After the birth of the child and with subsequent surgery, his doctor reported, "His renal and pulmonary functions are normal, and he's doing fine."[41]

37. Kitzinger, p. 66.
38. Rugh and Shettles, pp. 30, 83.
39. Annis, p. 15.
40. *New York Times Magazine*, 28 February 1982, p. 20.
41. *Contemporary Ob/Gyn*, April 1983, pp. 218-19.

Surgery to relieve the build-up of fluid in the ventricles of the brain (hydrocephaly) has also been successful. In dozens of cases, a shunt has been placed in the skull of the unborn patient, venting fluid that is pressing on the brain. The result is a reduced incidence of brain damage and retardation.

In at least one instance, prenatal surgery has been undertaken to inflate the collapsed lung of a tiny infant. Six months after her birth, the patient, Emily Pinion, graced the cover of the *New York Times Magazine*. The subsequent article, devoted to her case and others, was appropriately titled "Saving Babies Before Birth," because that is exactly what is taking place.[42]

In the near future, surgery may also be employed to correct diaphragmatic hernias, to seal spina bifida lesions, to repair gastroschisis, and to conduct allogenic bone transplants.[43] In addition, operations on the unborn may not be confined within the womb. Several attempts have been made to remove the fetus for surgery and then to replace him. Results to date have been mixed.

CONCLUSION

Advances in fetal medicine are forcing physicians to reconsider the ethics of abortion. More to the point, it is giving them a bad conscience. Made legally killable on the premise they are less-than-human beings, unborn children are subject to life-saving care and treatment as human beings. The same profession that kills them also treats them as patients.

John Fletcher of N.I.H. has written several significant articles on what he calls "the apparent inconsistency of encouraging fetal therapy on the one hand and respecting parental choice about abortion on the other." He asks, "Should the moral status of the wanted fetus with a treatable defect outweigh that of an unwanted fetus with the same treatable defect?"[44]

Other authors in the medical literature are raising related questions: "Whether we call the fetus a person, a patient, or a fetus, what rights will we accord it? When will we leave all decisions regarding its health to its mother, and when, if ever, will we as a society decide to restrict the autonomy of pregnant women for the sake of their fetuses? The more things we can do for the fetus

42. *New York Times Magazine*, 28 February 1982, p. 48.
43. Sherman Elias and George J. Annas, "Perspectives on Fetal Surgery," *American Journal of Obstetrics and Gynecology* 145, no. 7 (1 April 1983):809.
44. *New York Times Magazine*, 28 February 1982: p. 48.

in utero, the more relevant and real this question becomes."[45]

Pulitzer prize winning columnist George Will put the issue sharply in focus in a 1981 commentary in *Newsweek:*

> Prenatal medicine should raise troubling thoughts in a nation in which abortion is the most frequently performed operation, a nation in which last year 1.5 million abortions ended about one-third of all pregnancies. Science and society are out of sync. The most humane of sciences, medicine, can now treat as patients those who the law says lack an essential human attribute: rights. Mothers can kill any fetus medicine can treat.[46]

45. Elias, p. 811.
46. *Newsweek*, 22 June 1981, p. 92.

8

The Techniques of Abortion

The techniques of abortion are violent. They must be since their purpose is death. Multiple techniques exist due to the rapid growth and development of unborn children. A suction abortion, for example, is very effective in destroying a six-week embryo. He or she can easily be torn apart and drawn through a suction tube. At fourteen weeks, however, the tiny being is 3½ inches long and cannot be successfully dismantled by suction alone. This is due to both size and the presence of bone, which is rapidly replacing cartilage in the skeleton. The plurality of abortion methods testifies to the fact that a growing, developing human is present within the mother, not a stagnant bit of undefined life.

ABORTION TECHNIQUES IN THE FIRST TRIMESTER

In the first months of pregnancy, two similar abortion techniques are employed. These are suction curettage and D & C, or dilatation and curettage. Both rely on a suction tube inserted into the uterus through the birth canal. They also involve scraping the uterus clean with a curet, a long instrument with a cutting loop shaped like a spoon. This is used to pry the placenta away from the mother's womb and to chop and mash the developing human into pieces that can be sucked through the vacuum tube.

PREPARATION

In preparation for her abortion, the client receives several shots of local anesthetic to the mouth of the womb, or cervix. These serve to block pain stimuli in the uterus from reaching the brain so that discomfort is reduced. Because of the high tension and anxiety felt by many women, some react very sharply to the shots themselves and must be forcefully restrained lest they injure themselves.[1]

In addition the abortionist must determine the size of the fetus to be destroyed. This information dictates what size suction tube is necessary to accommodate the dismembered body parts and placenta. It also alerts him to the extent to which he must stretch open the cervix, or mouth of the womb.

PRE-ABORTION EXAMINATIONS

To determine fetal size, standard pelvic examinations are generally done, but the size and position of the uterus can be misleading. To achieve more precise information, abortionists may resort to the use of a Doppler apparatus. Essentially a stethoscope with a hearing aid, this instrument is used to detect and locate the heartbeat of the young fetus. In a different setting, women are overjoyed as their doctors let them hear this dramatic sign of the new life within. For the abortionist, however, this sign of life signals the best way to destroy life.[2]

Abortionists also use ultrasound to directly visualize the unborn child. As the small one tumbles and romps within his liquid world, he is quite literally being sized up for a deadly assault.

In the early days of legal abortion, before 1973, the procedure was justified on psychiatric grounds. The argument was made that abortion is necessary to preserve mental health. In retrospect abortion advocates acknowledge "the searching, stretching, and even manufacturing of 'indications' for therapeutic abortion that psychiatrists had done under the old law."[3] We have already seen it is abortion that poses the grave threat to mental health. Some women emotionally cannot cope with the procedure. For this reason part of the preparation for abortion may include a mental health assessment.

1. Selig Neubardt, *Techniques of Abortion* (Boston: Little, Brown, 1977), p. 20.
2. Ibid., p. 24.
3. John F. McDermott and Walter F. Char, "Abortion Repeal in Hawaii, An Unexpected Crisis in Patient Care," *American Journal of Orthopsychiatry* 41, no. 4 (July 1971):620.

Psychiatric problems are extremely important to uncover before the patient undergoes clinic abortion. . . . There are enough problems inherent in interrupting a pregnancy in a clinic not equipped for full-scale surgery without adding the risk of hysterical reactions that can mimic serious medical conditions.[4]

DILATION AND SUCTION

Having determined to proceed with a suction abortion, the abortionist grasps the mouth of the womb, or cervix, with an instrument called a tenaculum. Then he begins stretching open the cervix by inserting a series of sausage-shaped devices known as dilators. Once it has been sufficiently opened to accept the suction tube, this is inserted to the far end of the uterus. The suction machine to which it is attached is turned on, and strong suction, more than two dozen times the force of a household vacuum cleaner, develops. As the suction tube is rotated within the womb, the membrane and fluid surrounding the fetus are quickly sucked away and the little being himself is soon torn apart. Finally the placenta, which is well-connected to the lining of the uterus, is pulled away. One manual of instruction describes this phase of the abortion:

> At any point that material is felt to be flowing into the tube, motion is stopped until the flow stops. Then the slow up-and-down gradual rotation pattern is continued. Blood-tinged fluid and bits of pink tissue will be seen flowing through the plastic tubing during the entire suction curettage.[5]

Once no more "tissue" is observed, a curet is inserted to scrape the wall of the uterus. This assures that the products of conception have been completely removed. Suction may be applied one last time.

Although most abortions in the first trimester of pregnancy are performed by this method, a number of complications do arise, especially among women who have never been pregnant before. Frequently they involve damage to the cervix.

DAMAGED CERVIX

In the early weeks of pregnancy, the mouth of the uterus is nearly as long as the pregnant body of the uterus. The cervix then

4. Neubardt, pp. 25-26.
5. Ibid., p. 38.

is a long ring of muscle that is tightly closed so the pregnancy can be protected and maintained. It is designed to open, or dilate, very gradually over the course of days from the inside of the womb outward. It is stimulated to do this at the time of miscarriage or birth by a series of mild contractions beginning at the top of the uterus. In clinic abortion, the cervix is forced open in a matter of minutes from the outside in. As a result it may tear if it refuses to give way.[6] For example, as the abortionist bears down on the cervix with a dilator, the instrument holding the cervix in place can rip out. In the practice of an abortionist, this is bound to happen "sooner or later."[7]

If this injury permanently damages the muscle, the cervix may become "incompetent," or unable to contain future pregnancies. That means miscarriages, premature births, or low birth weight babies beset with many health problems.[8]

The risk of damage is especially high to a woman in her first pregnancy because the cervix has never been stretched open before. In this condition it is known as a "green" cervix, one that has yet to mature through childbirth. Although many risks associated with abortion are due simply to the fact that it is surgical in nature (e.g., anesthetic reaction), cervical damage is an unavoidable risk due to the violence of the procedure. Even when a woman has determined with her mind to destroy her offspring, her body does not concur so readily.

PERFORATION OF THE UTERUS

Another complication is perforation of the uterus. One specialist in abortion has observed that perforation is inevitable if one does enough abortions or dilatation and curettage procedures.[9] Under local anesthetic, perforation is immediately evident because the client begins writhing in pain.

Perforation may occur as a result of a dilator piercing through

6. *Understanding Pregnancy Alternatives.* This educational videotape produced by the Christian Action Council includes a lecture from Dr. William F. Colliton on medical risks in abortion. These are cited in the text. Dr. Colliton is chairman of the Department of Obstetrics and Gynecology at Holy Cross Hospital in Silver Spring, Maryland.
7. Neubardt, p. 37.
8. Richard Calvert, "Premature Births and Low Birth Weight Babies in Pregnancies Following Induced Abortion" (June 1980). This monograph is a survey of medical articles concerning the impact of abortion on the subsequent reproductive health of women. A copy may be obtained from the Christian Action Council, 422 C. St. NE, Washington, D.C. 20002.
9. Neubardt, p. 45.

a uterus that is sharply bent above the cervix. Although surgery is not always required, scarring does result, and that can lead to permanent sterility.

Perforation of the uterus can also occur with the suction tube itself, and that is much more serious. Surgery is always required, and it often involves a complete hysterectomy as well as surgery on other abdominal organs.[10] The problem is that the suction that is so effective in tearing apart the "products of conception" is equally effective in tearing apart the mother's bowel or major arteries. These are easily recognized as they pass down the suction hose. Women have bled to death as a result.

Once a suction abortion or any abortion is completed, medical personnel must examine the remains of the fetus as well as the placenta. To make matters easier, the body parts—head, arms, legs, gut, and so on—are often crudely reassembled. Unless everything that is in the uterus has been removed, infection will result. Even with the administration of antibiotics and a clean uterus, pelvic infection is a major risk. This can contribute to sterility. In fact, P.I.D., or pelvic inflammatory disease, has become one of the leading causes of infertility in the world, however it is contracted. In addition it is the primary factor in the threefold increase in ectopic, or tubal, pregnancies in the US. This condition always results in the death of the child and threatens the life of the mother.[11]

The suction curettage procedure is a more recent technique than the dilatation and curettage, and it is more widely used in this country. There are two principal reasons for this. The first is economics. Suction abortions are relatively easy to perform, and the skilled abortionist can perform them more rapidly than the D & C. In addition the suction machine rather than the abortionist is immediately responsible for what is occurring in the uterus. Psychologically then, the suction abortion is easier on medical personnel. Nonetheless, the D & C is still in common use. It is directly resorted to when the suction technique by itself fails to dislodge the fetus and placenta.

D & C

With the D & C, the cervix is dilated as described above. Instead of proceeding with suction, however, a sharp curet is

10. Ibid., pp. 46-47.
11. Martin Quan, et al., "Pelvic Inflammatory Disease," *Journal of Family Practice* 16, no. 1:131-40.

inserted into the womb. Repeatedly it is drawn through the inside of the womb and rotated. Where resistance is encountered the scraping is concentrated. The body parts and placenta are then withdrawn; suction is commonly used. As with the suction abortion, perforation of the uterus, damage to the cervix, infection, and heavy bleeding may occur, with similar results. In addition the curet may nick the wall of the uterus without perforation. The resulting formation of scar tissue increases the possibility of sterility in the future.

SECOND TRIMESTER ABORTIONS

After the first three months of pregnancy, different abortion techniques are used to accommodate the increased size of the baby as well the uterus. They take advantage of the fact that the fluid-filled space around the infant has greatly expanded and now can be transformed from a safe haven into a deadly, hostile environment. These techniques are commonly called *instillation techniques* because they call for instilling, or injecting, lethal chemicals into the amniotic sac. Their effect is to kill the offspring and induce a premature labor pattern. The mother in turn delivers a tiny, dead baby. As we will discover, however, that does not always occur. Too often for the abortionist, these techniques result in the birth of a severely damaged but live baby. Very suddenly the legal nonperson is transformed into a human being entitled to protection and care under the law.

SALINE ABORTION

Throughout the 1970s, the most common second trimester abortion technique was the saline abortion.[12] In this procedure a 3½-to-4 inch needle is inserted through the abdominal wall of the mother and into the amniotic sac. Approximately 200 milliliters of amniotic fluid are withdrawn. An equal quantity of saline solution is infused in its place. The chemical used is sodium chloride, simple table salt. This may not sound particularly dangerous, but the salt solution is hyperconcentrated. We have circulating in our blood-stream the equivalent of .9 percent saline solution. The saline used in an abortion is a 20 percent solution.[13] It creates an osmotic effect, which means that the less concentrated fluids in the infant rush into the surrounding envi-

12. *Centers For Disease Control, Abortion Surveillance 1979-1980* (May 1983), p. 6.
13. *Understanding Pregnancy Alternatives.*

ronment in an attempt to even out the concentration of salt both within and outside the child. Through this process the tissues and organs of the child begin to hemorrhage and are destroyed. Huge bruises appear all over the body surface as arteries and veins rupture. When abortionists describe the effect of saline as the "dehydration of the fetus," they have not begun to tell the story.

Saline has another effect as well. Because the salt is so concentrated, it chemically burns human tissue. The child assaulted with saline looks as though he has succumbed to an attack with napalm. Much of the outer skin has simply been burned away.

No one can imagine how excruciating the pain is. We do know that physicians recognize immediately the effect of instilling saline into the woman's gut rather than the amniotic sac. The pain is so unbearable the client may throw herself off the table. This is exactly what the unborn child does in his mother's womb. In fact the mother can feel this:

> I went in and I asked, "What are you going to do to me?" All he did was look at my stomach and say, "I'm going to take a little fluid out, put a little fluid in, you'll have severe cramps and expel the fetus." I said, "Is that all?" He said, "That's all."
>
> It did not sound too bad. But what the doctor described to me was not the truth.
>
> Once they put in the saline there is no way to reverse it. And for the next hour and a half I felt my daughter thrash around violently while she was being choked, poisoned, burned, and suffocated to death. I didn't know any of that was going to happen. And I remember talking to her and I remember telling her I didn't want to do this, I wished she could live. And yet she was dying and I remember her very last kick on her left side. She had no strength left. . . .
>
> I delivered my daughter whose name is now Charmaine Marie. She was 14 inches long. She weighed over a pound and a half. She had a head of hair and her eyes were opening.[14]

Abortion is violence. It is a brutal way to kill. In a 1972 conference on abortion, sponsored in part by the Planned Parenthood Federation of America, abortionist Thomas Kerenyi reported on "techniques of late abortion." Speaking of saline, he reported on a study done to show the killing potential of the procedure. After injecting women with the poison, ultrasound was used to monitor fetal heart rates and so to determine the rate at which the unborn died. Ultrasound confirmed a rapid rise in the heart

14. *Action Line* 7, no. 9 (15 October 1983):2-3.

rate of the infants once the saline was instilled. In all probability this is caused by pain, frantic activity to avoid the poison, and the emotion of fear itself. Very gradually then over the course of an hour or more, the heart rate plummeted to zero.[15]

The period between the instillation of saline and the onset of labor can vary greatly. Usually labor begins twenty-four to thirty-six hours after the injection, depending on the use of a chemical stimulant for labor. Frequently clients are encouraged to walk around as they go into labor. Then, as the dead infant begins to descend through the birth canal they may be encouraged to pass the tiny corpse into a toilet.[16]

COMPLICATIONS

Any number of complications can occur as a result of saline abortion. Infection rates are much higher than for first trimester procedures, especially when the amniotic sac ruptures and delay occurs before the onset of labor. "Mortality figures from New York State suggest that fatal sepsis is one of the inevitable rare occurrences in saline amnioinfusion."[17] Not infrequently infections from this procedure require a complete hysterectomy in order to save the client's life. Because saline is so poisonous, there is always the risk of death to the mother if it spreads outside her womb and circulates in her bloodstream.

Delays between the administration of saline and the onset of labor are very stressful on patients. To induce labor earlier, oxytocin may be administered, but this drug is very risky. It may result in a lethal complication known as water intoxication, whose classic symptoms are: headache followed by convulsions and coma; death may soon occur.[18] The treatment consists of heavy doses of salt.

Another inevitable complication from the combination of saline and oxytocin is the forced delivery of the infant through a tear in the uterus rather than through the cervix. This is caused by the combination of strong uterine contractions and a narrowly dilated cervix.

15. Thomas Kerenyi, "Techniques of Late Abortion," *Abortion Techniques and Services* (Amsterdam: Excerpta Medica, 1972), pp. 20-21.
16. Neubardt, p. 71.
17. Ibid., p. 88.
18. Neubardt, p. 87.

PROSTAGLANDIN ABORTION

In fact, the death rate from saline is high enough that the government of Japan has outlawed the procedure there. A similar attempt to do so in the US was struck down by the Supreme Court as unconstitutional.[19] Nevertheless, abortionists are resorting to other techniques, if for no other reason than to reduce the risk of malpractice suits. Hormones called prostaglandins are now synthetically produced in this country for use in late abortions. While posing a lower risk of death to women, their use has resulted in a much higher incidence of unintended live births.

Prostaglandins are synthetically produced by the Upjohn company. These compounds cause smooth muscle to contract. As abortion inducers, the drugs cause the uterus to contract so vigorously that the developing fetus is expelled. The mother is very much a part of the process as with the saline procedure.

SIDE EFFECTS

The side reactions to the use of prostaglandins are severe. The violent contractions of the uterus are very painful. These also explain why the incidence of infants exploding through the uterine wall is higher than in the case of saline. Diarrhea and vomiting are common since the gut as well as the uterus is composed of smooth muscle.

In an effort to minimize those effects on the mother, a variety of approaches have been used to administer the chemicals, with limited success. In the US, prostaglandin usually is injected directly into the amniotic sac as in the case of saline. In order to induce labor within twenty-four hours of injection, the required doses of prostaglandin are so high that a large percentage of women will experience the side effects. To quote one abortion practitioner, "As to side effects, the degree of discomfort experienced from uterine activity induced by prostaglandins is not inconsiderable."[20] That is the epitome of understatement.

Once the contractions have ceased and the fetus has been pushed out of the uterus, the mother's physical pain subsides and she experiences considerable relief. In fact, if she is lying down,

19. *Planned Parenthood of Central Missouri v. Danforth*, 428 U.S. 52 (1976).
20. I.L. Craft, "Intra-amniotic Prostaglandin E_2 and $F_{2\alpha}$ for Induction of Midtrimester Abortion," *The Use of Prostaglandin E_2 and $F_{2\alpha}$ in Obstetrics and Gynecology* (Miami: Symposia Specialists, 1973), p. 90. This book was the result of a symposium sponsored by Upjohn concerning the use of prostaglandins.

she may be totally unaware that the tiny infant remains lodged in her birth canal:

> [I]n a considerable number of patients the products of conception were found on vaginal examination when the patients were subjectively free from discomfort, indicating a need for intermittent vaginal examinations to assess the progress of abortion.[21]

Prostaglandin abortions are risky even though the chemicals themselves are not as deadly to women as saline. By the second trimester of pregnancy the placenta is well rooted in the lining of the uterus so that incomplete abortion and heavy blood loss are common. A study conducted in California assessed complications from 276 prostaglandin abortions. Eleven percent of the women undergoing the procedure hemorrhaged, and thirty-four percent suffered incomplete abortions. In three cases the pregnancies had to be ended surgically by entering the womb through the abdominal wall.[22] This procedure is known as a hysterotomy abortion. Today many physicians are questioning the claim of five years ago that prostaglandins are less risky than saline.

GUILT

Instillation abortions are very hard on women. They experience labor, and an actual birth process occurs, but the result is a dead infant rather than live baby. This terrible contradiction is experienced as such by many women. Even though the intent is a dead fetus, the maternal desire to nurture life remains: "It is clear that the amnio abortion process is similar to birth in many ways, and is so perceived by the patient. Many ask us—'Can I see my baby?' "[23]

EFFECT ON MEDICAL PERSONNEL

Medical personnel, especially nurses, can be equally as affected. When these second trimester abortions are performed, the physicians' involvement with their clients is minimal. It is limited to injecting the poison, managing any complications, and re-

21. Ibid., p. 89.
22. Sadja Goldsmith, et al., "Second Trimester Abortion by Dilation and Extraction [Evacuation] (D and E): Surgical Techniques and Psychological Reactions." Paper presented at the annual meeting of the Association of Planned Parenthood Physicians in Atlanta, Georgia, 13-14 October 1977, p. 8.
23. Ibid., p. 5.

ceiving payment for service rendered. This perfunctory involvement angers many nursing personnel and easily becomes a source of staff tension.[24] When clients enter labor and the tiny corpse finally comes forth, it is the nurses who are expected to comfort the mother and handle the body.

Resentment and anger over this allocation of "dirty work" to nurses has led to revolts in hospitals in cities including Cleveland, Grand Rapids, and Fort Lauderdale. As a result the institutions no longer permit late abortions.[25] In Grand Rapids the revolt against physician authority began as nurses left a tiny corpse "lying in its mother's bed for an hour and a half, despite angry calls from the attending physician, who finally went in and removed it himself."[26]

When tensions over abortion involvement do not reach the point of revolt, they are expressed in other ways. Nursing personnel have reported nightmares, bouts of depression, and excessive drinking. Patient care suffers as resentment is directed toward the mothers.[27] Various obsessive behaviors have developed. In one case a nurse's aide involved in first trimester procedures "spent much of her time obsessively planning or performing the baptism of fetal parts to the point that it was interfering with her performance."[28]

Especially at hospitals where nursing staff assist in births as well as in abortions, nurses suffer from their abortion involvement.

> One young nurse . . . showed how she rocked a fetus in her arms, an aborted fetus which she said had been warm and breathing, one which she would formerly ordinarily put in an incubator, but now was supposed to go into formaldehyde.[29]

THE DREADED COMPLICATION

The emotional trauma of successful abortion is severe, but it is nothing when compared to unsuccessful abortions where babies are born alive. Abortion expert Thomas Kerenyi has labeled these incidents the "dreaded complication" of late abortion. On

24. Francis J. Kane, et al., "Emotional Reactions in Abortion Services Personnel," *Archives of General Psychiatry* 28 (March 1973):411.
25. Liz Jeffries and Rick Edmonds, "Abortion: The Dreaded Complication," *Today*, 2 August 1981, p. 14.
26. Ibid., p. 17.
27. Kane, p. 411.
28. McDermott, p. 623.
29. Ibid., p. 622.

August 2, 1981, the *Philadelphia Inquirer* featured a seven-page exposé using Kerenyi's phrase for a title. Many examples of live births, personnel reactions, and cover-ups were reported.

Because of the numbers of abortions performed after twenty weeks of gestation, live births are a daily occurrence in the US. One official with the Centers for Disease Control estimates at least 400-500 cases occur each year. Precise figures are not available since abortionists are unwilling to report on babies delivered alive. "It's like turning yourself in to the IRS for an audit," says the official. "What is there to gain?"[30]

Prostaglandin abortions result in far more live births than salines because prostaglandin is not directly lethal to the fetus. The aim is to push him from the womb before he is able to survive. One study indicates live births are forty times more frequent than with saline.[31] This is particularly a problem when prostaglandin is administered in the form of a suppository or tampon tipped with the drug.

> This warning was carried in the September 12, 1977, issue of *Weekly Pharmacy Reports*, pointing out the approved Prostin labelling notes that suppository form, unlike saline injection form, "does not appear to directly effect the integrity of the feto-placental unit and therefore, there exists a possibility that a live-born fetus may occur, particularly as gestational age approaches the end of the second trimester." So likely is a live birth after a prostaglandin abortion that a medical representative of Upjohn advises using Prostin E "only in hospitals with certain intensive care facilities."[32]

A report on 150,000 abortions performed in upstate New York revealed thirty-eight cases of live births.[33] This does not begin to tell the story, however. In June 1983, news broke in Madison, Wisconsin, of six live births from abortion in two hospitals there.[34] During the same month, Dr. Francis Schaeffer led a memorial service in Atlanta, Georgia, for fourteen babies who were born alive through abortions at Midtown Hospital, "Georgia's only licensed hospital specializing in abortion." The infants subsequently had died.[35] Two babies who survived abortions at Wil-

30. Jeffries, p. 14.
31. Ibid., p. 17.
32. Francis A. Schaeffer and C. Everett Koop, *Whatever Happened to the Human Race?* (Old Tappan, N.J.: Revell, 1979), p. 43.
33. Jeffries, p. 18.
34. *The New York Times*, 24 March 1983.
35. Information available from Georgia Department of Human Resources, Department of Vital Records, 47 Trinity Ave. SW, Atlanta, GA 30334.

mington Medical Center in Delaware were later adopted. These incidents occurred five weeks apart in the spring of 1979.[36]

Many physicians refuse to face the issue of live births because they cannot bring themselves to acknowledge the humanity of their victims. Dr. Warren Pearse, executive director of the American College of Obstetrics and Gynecology, gave the following answer when asked what doctors typically do to determine whether an aborted fetus is alive.

> "What you would do next [after expulsion] is nothing," Pearse said. "You assume the infant is dead unless it shows signs of life. You're dealing with a dead fetus unless there is sustained cardiac action or sustained respiration—it's not enough if there's a single heartbeat or an occasional gasp."[37]

Gasping for air, twitching and moving about, babies born struggling to survive abortion are unforgettable to their mothers. After watching these infants die, the scene is replayed mentally over and over again, and a cycle of self-punishment may begin.

D & E

In order to eliminate the pain and trauma of birth for the mother and the possibility of live births, another abortion technique has been developed for use from the eleventh or twelfth week of pregnancy onward. It is known as the D and E, or dilatation and evacuation. In the US, it has become the most common late abortion technique.[38]

In order for a D and E to be performed, women are frequently given a general anethsetic so they are oblivious to the entire procedure. Even with a local pain killer, they are not positioned to see what is taking place.

In using the D and E, the discovery was soon made that the emotional trauma of abortion had not been eliminated but merely transferred from the client to the medical personnel performing it. The reason for that is clear from the procedure itself.

After dilating the cervix considerably further than in the case of first trimester abortions, the doctor inserts a narrow forceps that resembles pliers. The baby is then methodically cut to pieces, the technical term being *morcellation*. In a paper present-

36. Jeffries, p. 16.
37. Ibid., p. 16.
38. CDC, *Abortion Surveillance* p. 6.

ed to the Association of Planned Parenthood Physicians in 1978, the technique was described:

> The fetus was extracted in small pieces to minimize cervical trauma. The fetal head was often the most difficult object to crush and remove because of its size and contour. The operator kept track of each portion of the fetal skeleton. . . .[39]

"A VERY DANGEROUS TECHNIQUE"

The D and E is a very difficult procedure to perform, medically and emotionally. Perforation of the uterus and damage to the cervix are much more likely to occur because grasping and cutting tools are directly inserted into the uterus and worked by hand. According to Dr. Bernard Nathanson, one of the early abortion practitioners in New York, the D and E "is a very dangerous technique in the hands of anyone less than highly skilled."[40]

MEDICAL REACTION

In 1978 Dr. Warren Hern and Billie Corrigan presented a paper on the emotional effects of the D and E on medical personnel. They operate one of the busiest abortion practices in the Rocky Mountain states, the Boulder Abortion Clinic.

Of the fifteen medical staff interviewed, "four expressed feelings of resentment, irritation or anger toward patients who had waited so long before seeking abortion." "Nine were quite preoccupied with the medical risks. . . ." In addition, two believed that performing D and E abortions must eventually cause pyschological damage to the doctors.[41]

Two members of the abortion clinic staff reported similar dreams "of vomiting fetuses along with a sense of horror." Several indicated that "the emotional strain affected interpersonal relationships significantly or resulted in other behavior such as an obsessive need to talk about the experience."[42]

Dr. Julius Butler, a professor of obstetrics and gynecology at

39. Goldsmith, p. 3.
40. Jeffries, p. 16.
41. Warren M. Hern and Billie Corrigan, "What About Us? Staff Reactions to the D and E Procedure." Paper presented at the annual meeting of the Association of Planned Parenthood Physicians, San Diego, Calif., 26 October 1978, pp. 4-5.
42. Ibid., p. 6.

the University of Minnesota Medical School, concurs that the emotional impact of the D and E, not its safety, is the main point at issue.

> "Remember," he said, "there is a human being at the other end of the table taking that kid apart."
> "We've had guys drinking too much, taking drugs, even a suicide or two. There have been no studies I know of of the problem, but the unwritten kind of statistics we see is alarming."[43]

Hern and Corrigan summarize well the horror of the D and E for physicians. Quite simply, it is the unavoidable reality that these abortions are killing unborn humans. Knowing full well what they are doing, and suffering the effects of it, these abortionists as well as others are nonetheless bent on practicing their art.

> We have reached a point in this particular technology where there is no possibility of denial of an act of destruction by the operator. . . . The sensations of dismemberment flow through the forceps like an electric current. It is the crucible of a raging controversy, the confrontation of a modern existential dilemma. The more we seem to solve the problem, the more intractable it becomes.[44]

THIRD TRIMESTER ABORTIONS

There is no question that abortions are being performed in the last three months of pregnancy, after the child is able to survive outside the womb. The abortion of infants at thirty or more weeks of gestation is a matter of record.[45] *The New England Journal of Medicine* recently featured an article that discussed a number of third trimester abortions, including one at thirty-six weeks. The piece was entitled "When Is Termination of Pregnancy During the Third Trimester Morally Justifiable?"[46] How often these late abortions are performed, we do not know. Abortionists do not volunteer such statistics. Facilities licensed to perform second trimester abortions would not declare a miscalculation in fetal age that resulted in the destruction of an older infant, say of twenty-eight weeks. The Centers for Disease Control reports on

43. Jeffries, p. 18.
44. Hern, p. 9.
45. Jeffries, p. 18.
46. Frank A. Chervanak, M.D., et al., "When Is Termination of Pregnancy During the Third Trimester Morally Justifiable?" *The New England Journal of Medicine* 310, no. 8 (23 February 1984):501-504.

the number of reported abortions performed after twenty-one weeks but provides no further information on gestational age.

HYSTEROTOMY

The procedures used to destroy viable infants include saline and prostaglandin abortions, the D and E, and a technique mentioned above, the *hysterotomy.*

The hysterotomy abortion is major surgery. It is identical to a caesarian section except that the intent is to destroy the child rather than to deliver a live baby. This procedure nearly always results in a live birth. To kill the infant the umbilical cord may be clamped. The effect is to suffocate the baby because no attempts are made to clear his nose and throat of the mucus so he can breathe. An equally effective procedure is simply to deliver the infant intact and then leave him unattended to die of exposure. The *Philadelphia Inquirer* exposé contained a physician's brief description of what takes place.

> As the infant is lifted from the womb, said one obstetrician, "He is only sleeping, like his mother. She is under anesthesia, and so is he. You want to know how they kill him? They put a towel over his face so he can't breathe. And by the time they get him to the lab, he is dead."[47]

In studying the reports on abortion from the Centers for Disease Control, it becomes clear that the standard abortion techniques described above do not encompass all the means used to destroy the unborn. Invariably in listing means of abortion, there is a column marked "other." I have often wondered what the term encompasses. We do have some indication.

The *New England Journal of Medicine* featured an article that describes how to abort one twin without destroying the other.[48] Using ultrasound, Dr. Thomas Kerenyi guided a needle through the mother's abdomen and then punctured the heart of a twin who had been diagnosed as having Down's syndrome. He withdrew approximately 40-50 percent of the infant's blood, and the baby died. Several months later, the mother gave birth to the survivor and discharged the remains of the dead infant. At a news conference shortly thereafter, Dr. Kerenyi described the

47. Ibid., p. 17.
48. Thomas D. Kerenyi and Usha Chitkara, "Selective Birth in Twin Pregnancy with Discordancy for Down's Syndrome," *New England Journal of Medicine* 304, no. 25 (18 June 1981):1525-27.

corpse as "flat, fragile and paperlike . . . like a rose that had been pressed in the Bible for five years."[49] But that was not a rose pressed lovingly in a Bible. It was the remains of an infant.

CONCLUSION

Life and death. In light of this information on abortion procedures and their destructive consequences, the challenge facing Christians is clear. But whose motivation will be greater? Christ's love in Christians that compels them to stop the violence, or the profit motive in the abortionists that compels them to practice violence? Are Christians more loyal to their God than the abortionists are to theirs? That question will be answered by what Christians do or refuse to do.

49. J. Robert Nelson, "Stepping Out of Down's Syndrome," *Christian Century* 98, no. 25 (12-19 August 1981):789.

9

The Legacy of
Abortion, Part 1:
Fetal Experimentation

Once legal protection was removed from unborn children in order to sanction abortion, they immediately became vulnerable to other forms of exploitation. Profiteers in the US and Europe have found a variety of uses for fetal corpses. Cruel experiments on live aborted infants and on fetuses scheduled for abortion are also occurring.

THE USE OF FETAL CORPSES

A 1981 article in the *Journal of Clinical Pathology* details the contribution to medical research made by the Fetal Tissue Bank at London's Marsden Hospital. Written by the director, the efficient operation of the Fetal Tissue Bank is described:

> Fetuses are collected within the London area and brought back to the hospital as rapidly as possible for immediate dissection by surgical theatre techniques in a "sterile" room. . . . Each fetus is given a number, and the tissues are distributed, the names of the recipients being recorded.[1]

Organs and tissues dissected from the corpses are distributed primarily to medical researchers for "non-clinical" uses. The au-

1. Sylvia D. Lawlor, "Conception and Development of the Fetal Tissue Bank," *Journal of Clinical Pathology* (1981):34, 240.

thor recounts a special problem the bank encountered in the early seventies as obstetricians began performing most abortions by techniques that yield "disrupted fetuses" rather than whole fetuses. Relatively few viable cells could be harvested. As a result, "if the bank were to continue to meet its commitment" as a major supplier of fetal tissue, a new retrieval technique would have to be found. A method was devised whereby organs could be identified and extracted from the gruesome remains of fetuses destroyed in suction abortions. Thus, virologists continue to have their "source of fetal tissues."[2]

Virtually every organ or tissue from the destroyed fetus can be used—from the liver, lung, and nasal mucosa for virology studies to the gonads for studies in developmental biology; from the pancreas, breast, and thymus for immunology studies to the muscle and brain for studies in cellular biology.[3]

These uses of fetal tissues are not limited to England but are broadly representative of uses now made of fetal tissues in the US. In 1980, for example, the Food and Drug Administration approved a new vaccine against human rabies. The cells used in its manufacture were derived from aborted fetal lung tissue.[4]

A recent article in *Medical World News* reports experiments successfully completed at the University of Colorado Medical Center in Denver. The research was used to refine "a new test using human fetal organs grafted in mice" which "may tell for sure whether pregnant women can safely take a new drug."

> Dr. Robboy, a Harvard associate professor of pathology, said his team took human genital structures from five-to 17-week-old female fetuses and grafted them into athyumic "nude" mice, which are unable to reject foreign tissue. The grafts were tucked under membranes covering the recipient mice's kidneys, where abundant blood vessels vascularized them.[5]

From that point the effects of DES (diethylstilbestrol) were studied on the developing female reproductive tracts. Evidently an additional aim of the research was to determine just how long and large the "human specimen" may be grown. Some of the mice

2. Ibid., pp. 240-41.
3. Ibid., p. 242.
4. Nick Thimmesch, "Our Grisley Human Fetal Industry," *Victoria Advocate*, 18 December 1981.
5. A formal account of this entire experiment may be found in Stanley J. Robboy, Osamu Taguchi, and Gerald R. Cunha, "Normal Development of the Human Female Reproductive Tract and Alterations Resulting from Exposure to Diethylstilbestrol," *Human Pathology* 13, no. 3 [March 1982]:190-98.

were kept alive with "human implants that are eight months post-conception." One of the researchers involved pointed out that "athymic rats under development could incubate even bigger human specimens."[6]

"FRESHNESS" ESSENTIAL

In harvesting fetal tissues for research, "freshness" is essential. Tissue samples for research generally must contain living cells. As a result, the process of retrieving organs and tissues may be initiated on aborted babies who are not yet dead.

In 1973 the State of Connecticut submitted a written interview to the Supreme Court as evidence in an abortion-related case. Dr. Baker (a pseudonym) was asked about medical events at the Yale-New Haven Medical Center:

Q. Are you a medical doctor?
A. Yes.
Q. Was there a case where some type of surgical procedure was performed on a baby after induced abortion?
A. I did not actually observe the operation itself.
Q. Can you tell us anything about it, to the extent that you know?
A. A baby was aborted by hysterotomy. Then it was taken to another room with a medical student.
Q. Did you first observe the baby being taken out of the mother?
A. Yes.
Q. What, if anything, happened then that you observed?
A. It was taken out of the room. Then this medical student followed it.
Q. Do you know why it was taken out of the room?
A. Well, they wanted to get something out of it.
Q. How did you know they were trying to get something out of it?
A. That's what they said, I just overheard it. They were going to get some kind of an abdominal organ, I think it was the liver. I was not very sure.
Q. You overheard this from whom, a nurse?
A. From a doctor.
Q. Was this the doctor that was presumably going to take this liver or whatever it was?
A. Yes, and the obstetrician that was performing the operation.
Q. When it was taken out of the room, did it have any movements?
A. It had some movements.
Q. Doctor, prior to the infant leaving the room, did it do anything noteworthy? Any noteworthy bodily functions?
A. Some form of movements of the arm.
Q. Were there any excretions at all?

6. Ibid.

A. Excretions, urine, yes.

Q. Tell us about that. Can you give us the details?

A. Well I would say when they picked this fetus up by the feet I could see that he urinated, he was a male infant.

Q. It was urinating?

A. Yes.

Q. You're sure of that?

A. Yes.

Q. What, if anything, did they do with the baby afterwards that you observed? They took it out of the room?

A. They just took it out of the room immediately.

Q. Then what, if anything, happened that you observed?

A. Nothing else. It was taken out of the room and I didn't see it.

Q. Did a medical student accompany it out of the room?

A. The medical student went out.

Q. With the doctor?

A. Yes, this lady doctor. I don't know what her name is and I can't even recognize her if I see her.

Q. Do you have any idea where she was from?

A. Either Boston or Hartford.

Q. Then what, if anything, occurred?

A. The lady doctor proceeded to open the abdomen of the fetus.

Q. You did not see this yourself?

A. No.

Q. This is based on what type of information, if any?

A. On what the medical student told me.

Q. Can you describe how the medical student appeared when he returned?

A. He was sort of pale, he said he felt sort of sick in his stomach. That's why he left the room and went back to the operating room where I was.

Q. Do you recall what, if anything, the medical student said?

A. He just said he couldn't stand it.

Q. Did he show any fear at the sight of blood prior to this incident?

A. No.[7]

Federal funds are allocated to sponsor much of the current research using aborted fetuses. In a letter dated November 19, 1982, to Congressman William E. Dannemeyer, Dr. Mortimer B. Lipsett, Director of the National Institute of Child Health and

---

7. On February 26, 1973, the appeals in two abortion cases from Connecticut (*Markle* v. *Abele*, 72-56 original law and 72-730 May 1972 law) were dismissed by the US Supreme Court. On March 14, 1973, the Attorney General of Connecticut petitioned the Court for a rehearing in these two cases. The State presented to the Court relevant materials developed in the record of their cases on the lower level. Among these was an affidavit of an anonymous "Dr. Baker" regarding medical events at the Yale-New Haven Medical Center (pp. 37-41 of the brief).

Human Development, acknowledged, "The fetal research that is currently being supported by the National Institutes of Health in the five specific areas to which you refer is being conducted on continuing pregnancies, *non-living fetuses or infants,* or living infants who are receiving routine medical care" (emphasis added).

Lipsett's reference to federally sponsored research on "continuing pregnancies" and on "living infants" presumably is to non-harmful research. Nonetheless many instances of cruel experimentation on living fetuses have occurred and are well documented.

EXPERIMENTS ON THE UNBORN PRIOR TO THEIR ABORTION

Fetoscopy, as mentioned above, is a technique used to examine the unborn child. It involves the insertion of a hollow tube into the uterus. Not only may unborn infants be viewed, but small samples of blood or tissue may be gathered from them as well. In developing fetoscopy, unborn children scheduled for abortion were used in experiments. The goal of this research was to refine the technique in order to reduce fetal mortality, or the extent to which fetoscopy itself damaged the unborn or triggered spontaneous miscarriage.[8] In these experiments infants scheduled for abortion were admittedly used because the research was potentially harmful or fatal.

The US government became a direct sponsor of this activity in June 1979, when Secretary of Health Joseph Califano approved the use of federal funds "to assess the safety of fetoscopy" at the Charles R. Drew Postgraduate Medical School in Los Angeles.[9] The decision provoked considerable furor since it involved waiving existing standards governing federally funded research on human subjects. Specifically the research failed to hold forth any benefit to the mothers or fetuses involved. In addition, it posed not minimal but considerable risk to the subjects.[10]

EXPERIMENTS ON LIVE ABORTED INFANTS

Of all the types of experimentation on the human fetus now documented, none are so disconcerting as the experiments per-

8. Charles H. Rodeck, "Value of Fetoscopy in Prenatal Diagnosis," *Journal of the Royal Society of Medicine* 73 (January 1980):29.
9. Statement by Secretary of H. E. W. Joseph A. Califano, Jr., released 19 June 1979.
10. Ibid.

formed on live infants after abortions. One of these involved hooking aborted infants to an artificial placenta. Eight fetuses obtained by hysterotomy were placed in tanks of saline solution. Small "tubes were inserted in the umbilical arteries and veins— for pumping in and removing oxygenated blood."[11]

The largest fetus lived five hours. "Irregular gasping movements . . . occurred in the middle of the experiment but there was no proper respiration." When the pumping in of oxygenated blood was terminated, the gasping increased. The "heart slowed . . . and eventually stopped." As controversial as this research was, it nonetheless won the Foundation Prize Award from the American Association of Obstetricians and Gynecologists.[12]

In another piece of research performed in Helsinki, Finland, by American and Finnish scientists, twelve fetuses were obtained by hysterotomy. Their heads were then severed and their brains perfused with chemicals so various metabolic processes could be studied. This experiment along with others provoked a storm of criticism in Congress because it was conducted in part with NIH funds. When research team leader Dr. Peter A. J. Adam presented a report to the combined meeting of the American Pediatric Society and the Society for Pediatric Research, "no one even raised an eyebrow," according to *Medical World News*.[13]

Various commercial as well as research uses have been found for live aborted infants, particularly in the cosmetics industry. Although the documentation of incidents has yet to surface in the American press, the practice has been exposed in Europe. In 1983 the Research Committee of the European Parliament commissioned a study by Italian member Alberto Ghergo:

> In his report—as yet to be adopted by the research Committee—the Italian MEP says that in [unnamed] European embryological laboratories experiments are being carried out on foetuses of between 12 and 21 weeks old. These are removed whole and alive by means of hysterectomy (Caesarean Section). He does not name the EEC countries involved.
>
> The embryos are dissected in order to remove certain organs (pancreas, thymus, brain, etc.) which are frozen by liquid nitrogen vapours. Other embryos are frozen on extraction from the mother's womb to be set aside for various uses.

11. Maggie Scarf, "The Fetus as Guinea Pig," *New York Times Magazine*, 19 October 1975, p. 92. Used by permission.
12. Ibid.
13. *Medical World News*, 8 June 1973, p. 21.

According to his report, the use of foetuses has given rise to a dense network of economic interests "ranging from traffic in them, with financial incentives to encourage mothers to become donors, to laboratory manipulation."

Mr. Ghergo said the laboratories experimenting on live embryos served the cosmetic industries in the preparation of beauty products such as powders and creams. They also serve allegedly scientific products for rejuvenation and anti-diabetic purposes. Other laboratories claimed to be concerned only with research.[14]

The *Gazette du Palais*, a respected French legal journal, reported in 1981 the import of frozen fetal corpses by the French cosmetics industry.

Frontier customs men intercepted a lorry coming from central Europe loaded with frozen human fetuses destined for the laboratories of French cosmetics firms. In some of France's neighboring countries there are fetus "banks," and a real trade in fetuses has begun. . . . Trade in particular is developing between France and Great Britain where there is an important fetal tissue bank."[15]

According to the journal, "many beauty establishments are prospering in France thanks to the use of living cells taken from the fetus."[16] Dead infants are being used to make women appear beautiful. Blending fetal cells into their own skin helps rejuvenate it and provide a more youthful appearance. One cannot help recalling the use of corpses by the Nazis to make everything from fertilizer to household articles.

A number of contemporary bioethicists, including Joseph Fletcher, argue that experiments on live unborn or aborted humans are acceptable because these contribute to medical knowledge and our ability to care for others.[17] In this way the valueless fetus takes on value in suffering and death.

CONCLUSION

This justification for killing or inflicting harm on human beings begs the question. Does the end justify the means? I suspect the victims would say no. They are never asked and couldn't

14. Val Dorgan, "Foetuses Experiments," *Cork Examiner,* 25 August 1983.
15. *Cornerstone* 2, no. 64 (April 1983):22.
16. Ibid.
17. Joseph Fletcher, *Humanhood: Essays in Biomedical Ethics* (Buffalo, N.Y.: Prometheus, 1979), pp. 93-105.

answer if they were. Stripping all human dignity and value from the unborn, we approve of killing tiny humans for a "good" purpose, when it has already been determined they are going to die for no purpose.

Dr. Peter A. J. Adam, who led the research on the metabolism of the fetal brain, put the matters as cooly and as pragmatically as is possible: "Whose right are we going to protect when we've already decided the fetus won't live?"[18]

18. *Medical World News*, 8 June 1973, p. 21.

10

The Legacy of Abortion, Part 2: Infanticide

INFANTICIDE

The Supreme Court's decision on abortion was in reality a decision for infanticide as well. Prior to 1973, the term *abortion* was defined in *Webster's New World Dictionary* as the "expulsion of a fetus from the womb before it is viable." The notion of aborting viable infants, or those able to survive outside the womb, did not exist. If someone did undertake the destruction of a child late in pregnancy or shortly after birth, then that individual was guilty of infanticide, "the murder of a baby."

EXTENDED DEFINITION

In reaching its abortion decision, the Supreme Court extended the definition of abortion to include the destruction of viable infants prior to their birth, and hence, a measure of infanticide. Although the Court did not approve the killing of newborns (this question was not before them), it did sanction the killing of infants in the womb who, in many instances, are older than premature babies receiving intensive care.

This cruel contradiction in medical practice drove Dr. C. Everett Koop, then Surgeon-in-Chief of Philadelphia's Children's Hospital and later US Surgeon General, to speak out:

It was the schizophrenia of our society that convinced me that I could not just continue to work with children individually and not speak out against what is happening in our society. When I realized perhaps for the first time that while we struggled with the postoperative care of a premature infant upon whom we had operated, and realized the hours of skilled physician and nursing care as well as the extraordinary technological advances that combined to offer this youngster a chance for survival, in the intensive care unit for infants in our institution, while a hundred yards down the street in an equally fine hospital, perfectly normal babies were being destroyed before birth. . . . The day I realized that, I sat down and wrote *The Right to Live, the Right to Die.*[1]

Birth, after all, is a profane event. It happens to everyone without altering the identity or increasing the value of anyone. This explains in large measure why people who accept the sanctity of human life oppose abortion. It also helps to explain why abortion advocates and those using a "quality-of-life" calculus to determine human value support infanticide.

HANDICAPPED NEWBORNS

Within months after the Supreme Court's decision, pediatricians began arguing for public acceptance of infanticide for newborns with birth defects or handicaps. Appearing in leading medical journals, their articles carried the imprimatur of the medical establishment. The published pieces were not theoretical in nature. They revealed the willingness of physicians to bring on the deaths of handicapped newborns and their actual participation as well.

BASIC CARE DENIED

In an article in the *New England Journal of Medicine,* Doctor Raymond Duff and Professor A.G.M. Campbell of Yale University acknowledged that during the course of two years, 14 percent of the babies who died in the intensive care nursery at Yale-New Haven Hospital expired through physician choice.[2] Frequently

---

1. C. Everett Koop, "The Silent Domino, Infanticide," printed in the *Congressional Record* 125, at E3686—E3688 and at E3915—E3917 (17-18 July 1979).
2. Raymond S. Duff and A. G. M. Campbell, "Moral and Ethical Dilemmas in the Special Care Nursery," *New England Journal of Medicine* 289, no. 17 (October 1973):891.

that choice included a decision to deny food and water to handicapped infants. In other instances the choice included failure to provide antibiotics or corrective surgery. Duff and Campbell argued that death should be a "management option" in the newborn intensive care nursery.[3]

The issue in infanticide is not whether a terminally ill child will be permitted to die, but whether a less-than-perfect child will be permitted to live. Infanticide is advocated precisely for those handicapped babies who can live if nourishment and medical care are provided. It was murder fifteen years ago, and it is murder today.

Since that 1973 article on infanticide at Yale-New Haven Hospital, a number of reports and investigations have followed. On June 14, 1981, the *Hartford Courant* ran an exposé entitled "Defective Newborns Are Dying by Design."[4] The article revealed that the repertoire of means used to end life at the hospital has grown. It includes not only passive measures such as starvation but the more active measure of administering lethal drug overdoses. Regarding the latter, the author reported her interview with Dr. Duff:

> In some of the cases, he said, parents approached doctors about the possibility of overdose. Other times, he and other doctors suggested the option, assuring parents they would sign the death certificate, no questions asked.
>
> The parents, he said, ended their infants' lives with morphine or phenobarbital prescribed by the doctors and usually dissolved in a baby bottle.
>
> The doctor said that although all such deaths he knows about occurred at home, he "wouldn't discount it happening in the hospital. But it becomes more difficult in a public institution where we have to account for all our medications."
>
> This daring practice and its acknowledgment by a doctor signals how routine the concept of non-treatment of defective newborns has become in medical practice and how far some professionals have taken it.[5]

As a result of the *Hartford Courant* series, hearings were called by the Connecticut State Senate Public Health Subcommittee. Considerable testimony was taken on the matter of infanticide.

3. Ibid., p. 894.
4. Diane Brozek, "Defective Newborns Are Dying by Design," *Hartford Courant*, 14 June 1981.
5. Ibid.

The focus of attention was on Yale-New Haven Hospital, but records from eleven hospitals across the state were considered. As a result, two cases of infant death were forwarded to the State's Attorney for review. One of those involved a Down's syndrome baby who had starved to death over the course of twenty-three days.

JAMES

As a result of news coverage given to the hearings, Connecticut Senator Regina Smith received a letter from a gentleman who described what had taken place at Yale-New Haven Hospital after his baby was born with birth defects. His letter is now a matter of public record. Much of the text follows.

> On April 8, 1975 a son was born to my wife Irene and I at Yale New Haven Hospital. He was our second child and we named him James. James was six weeks premature and spent the first eighteen days of his life in Newborn Intensive Care. It was during this time that we were informed that James was suffering from different medical problems that were not yet fully diagnosed. . . . It was then that we were called into conference with a Doctor Duff, who we were told was the head of Pediatrics for the hospital. Doctor Duff told us that James was going to be a great burden to us throughout our lives. He also told us that James would be a vegetable and a helpless human being. He told us to consider very seriously abandoning the child. My wife and I were totally shocked, we wonder how Doctor Duff could say these things when a full diagnoses hadn't even been arrived at. After discussing the matter with our own personal pediatrician we decided that no one was going to take James away from us no matter what his condition turned out to be. The final diagnoses was that James had Cerebral Palsy. His mental aptitude was perfectly normal. He had a physical handicap. James is now attending the First grade at Savin Rock Community School. He has reieved all A grades on his first report card. He walks under his own power. He is mainstreamed with all the rest of the children and gets along with all of them.
>
> I wish that you could see James and talk to him, he is a very warm, wonderful, and amiable person, hardly a vegetable, which I always thought was something that you ate. (Spelling errors as in original letter)[6]

6. Statement of findings by State Senator Regina R. Smith, press release 30 April 1982.

Proponents of infanticide argue that this should be an option for parents. As with abortion, it should be a matter of choice. In 1973, Nobel laureate James D. Watson espoused this position in an article in *Prism* magazine. He argued as well that it may be necessary to pretend the newborn is not alive in order to rationalize his death.

> If a child were not declared alive until three days after birth, then all parents could be allowed the choice only a few are given under the present system. The doctor could allow the child to die if the parents so choose and save a lot of misery and suffering. I believe this view is the only rational, compassionate attitude to have.[7]

KIMBERLY

In theory infanticide may be presented as a neutral option to parents. In practice, that is not the case. Those physicians prepared to starve a newborn infant obviously approve of infanticide. The agitation to do so comes from them. That they are hardly passive instruments in the hands of distraught parents was well illustrated in another letter that came to Senator Smith during the infanticide hearings in Connecticut.

> Our daughter Kimberly, was born March 26, 1975. She was diagnosed as having a birth defect. Later in recovery, the Neurological Team at Yale New Haven Hospital . . . came in to tell my husband and I that our daughter was born with Spina Bifida . . . we had to make an immediate decision as to whether or not to allow her [the doctor] to perform surgery on our daughter to close the opening on her back. She explained that without the surgery, infection would set in and further complications would arise, including the chance of death.
>
> Kimberly was placed in the Newborn Special Care Unit at Yale New Haven Hospital. My husband and I were approached by Dr. Duff. He wanted to know if we fully understood the future life we would be faced with. Our daughter would be a burden to us and would need constant care and may never amount to anything other than to be a vegetable, is what he had told us. There was the possibility that she would cause us much pain. We asked him is he was advises us against the surgery, asking us to take the chance of our daughter dying. He told us it was something that we should consider. . . .
>
> We strongly feel that Dr. Duff had no right to approach us and

7. James D. Watson, "Children from the Laboratory," *Prism*, May 1973, p. 13.

advise us at all. The Neurological Team had already done this. This time is a very trying time for the parents and being persuaded in the direction of ending the newborn child's life is something that might be regretted later if parents were to decide this way without feeling that there are other alternatives. If parents truly feel that they could not cope with such a child, they could decide to place the child up for adoption. No doctor should be allowed to persuade parents in the direction ending one's life. This is GOD'S right only! (Spelling errors as in original)[8]

The practice of infanticide is by no means limited to Yale-New Haven Hospital. The situation there has been extensively considered because it has been the subject of articles by practicing physicians as well as investigative reporters.

On March 9, 1980, the headlines of the *Birmingham News* (Alabama) read: "Doctors Let Some Retarded Babies Die by Withholding Care." In this exposé of Children's Hospital in Birmingham, the issue was the neglect of newborns with birth defects. One case reported was a newborn child with Down's syndrome who was unable to swallow. The routine surgery needed to correct the defect was not given; neither food nor water was administered. After thirty-one days, the baby died.

It is routine for newborns to languish longer than adults when denied food and water. That is because babies proportionately have greater quantities of fats and water stored in their bodies. Nonetheless, thirty-one days was an unusually long period of starvation, and some other factor was obviously at work. In fact, nurses were sneaking intravenous fluids into the infant at night. After these clandestine attempts to care for the baby were discovered, the feedings stopped.

The willingness of staff at Children's Hospital to withhold care is known well beyond its boundaries. Reporter Carl Carter included in his exposé an incident involving the transfer of a Downs syndrome child from Los Angeles to Birmingham because the California hospital would not permit the baby to go untreated. The staff surgeon at Children's Hospital was critical of the doctor who transferred the baby. "That [the transfer] was just a cowardly way out of it," he said. "This was dirty pool. He should have fought it out right there."[9]

Although clearly illegal, infanticide is nonetheless widely prac-

8. Findings of Senator Smith.
9. In Carl Carter, "Doctors Let Some Retarded Babies Die by Withholding Care," *Birmingham* (Alabama) *News*, 9 March 1980.

ticed. The American Medical Association, the American Academy of Pediatrics, and other medical societies have failed to condemn it. No physician has been subject to professional discipline by the medical community, and no physician has been successfully prosecuted under the law. Infanticide occurs behind closed doors, and few are willing to talk about it. For this reason, Dr. Koop has called infanticide the "second domino," which "fell silently" following the first, abortion on demand.[10]

INFANT DOE

In April 1982, this silent domino caused a great clamor. On April 9, a little boy was born in Bloomington, Indiana. He was, in the words of parents who love their retarded children, a "special child." Known to the world only as "Infant Doe," the boy had Down's syndrome. He also suffered from a correctible defect, a detached esophagus, which prevented him from taking foods orally. The surgery to correct this would have been routine. The parents, in consultation with their physician, determined the baby was to receive no surgery and no intravenous nourishment.

County prosecutors and concerned citizens frantically pursued legal avenues to save the baby. Two county courts refused to order that the baby be fed. The matter was then appealed to the State Supreme Court. "The child is at this very moment starving to death," the prosecutor told the four judges. "If this court does not act today, this child will be starved to death."[11] Three of the four judges turned a deaf ear to this plea for mercy. On April 16, while attorneys were enroute to Washington to make a last ditch appeal to the US Supreme Court, the baby died. He was seven days old.

No less than ten families had come forward during those days, offering to adopt the baby. The parents would not have it. And the courts sustained them by denying to the child his right to life. This was the first time law had been used to enforce the starvation death of an infant. This was also the first time that the press throughout the nation had brought the issue to the attention of the American public.

Editorials appeared around the country. The reaction was intense. Columnist Stephen Chapman wrote in the *Chicago Tribune*, "It is a measure of abortion's effect on our thinking that in

10. Koop, "The Silent Domino."
11. *Action Line* 6, no. 4 (14 May 1982).

at least one state it is now permissible to do to a deformed, retarded infant what would be illegal if done to a dog or a cat."[12] Columnist George Will, himself the father of a much loved Down's syndrome son, wrote perhaps the most eloquent condemnation of the violence.

> Such homicides can no longer be considered aberrations, or culturally incongruous. They are part of a social program to serve the convenience of adults by authorizing adults to destroy inconvenient young life. The parents' legal arguments, conducted in private, reportedly emphasized—what else?—"freedom of choice." The freedom to choose to kill inconvenient life is being extended, precisely as predicted, beyond fetal life to categories of inconvenient infants, such as Down's syndrome babies. . . .
>
> The trick is to argue that the lives of certain kinds of newborns, like the lives of fetuses, are not sufficiently "meaningful"—a word that figured in the 1973 ruling [on abortion]—to permit any protection that inconveniences an adult's freedom of choice.[13]

Rachel Ginder of Anderson, Indiana, wrote a letter to the editor in response to the death of Infant Doe. She and her husband have cared for many handicapped and retarded children. One in particular was a Down's syndrome baby with multiple physical defects. His life lasted twenty-three months.

> I don't feel I have a right to judge Family Doe for their inability to cope with their newborn . . . but I CAN, from having "been there," say that they had NO right to take their child's right to live away from him.
>
> It's no disgrace to admit to not being able to cope, but it is unforgivable to literally murder by starvation their child! There are many alternatives available that could be considered "courageous" as they put it.
>
> You, see, we know about that too . . . for we adopted our little one from a situation like this . . . starving to death at birth. We felt he deserved a chance at life . . . a chance to be loved by a family who wanted him . . . that could really love him and provide the medical help necessary for however long he might live. He had a full life with many friends who cared and shared. He was a much loved baby with whom we shared much happiness and will never forget. Those who knew him best will never be the same.

12. Stephen Chapman,
13. George F. Will, "The Killing Will Not Stop," *Washington Post,* 22 April 1983. Used by permission.

These innocent children, victims of neglect and abuse, cannot
speak for themselves. We must do it for them![14]

HOTLINE NOTICES POSTED

Like many citizens, President Reagan was deeply affected by
the death of Infant Doe. As a result, the Department of Health
and Human Services issued regulations requiring all federally
funded hospitals to post notices in their delivery, maternity, and
pediatric wards, which read in part: "Any person having knowledge that a handicapped infant is being discriminatorily denied
food or customary medical care should immediately contact the
Handicapped Infant Hotline." A toll-free number was posted so
that nurses or other personnel could call anonymously without
fear of losing their jobs.

The American Academy of Pediatrics and the National Association of Children's Hospitals and Related Organizations vigorously opposed the regulations. In an amazing example of double-
speak, AAP President James Strain complained, "The regulations
would inject federal investigators into the pediatric wards of this
country in a way that is dangerous to the health and lives of
seriously ill infants."[15] In a joint effort on March 21, 1983, the
two organizations took their case before a sympathetic federal
judge.

The judge, Gerhard Gesell, labeled the regulations "arbitrary
and capricious" and proceeded to strike them down. The decision
itself rested on technicalities, but Gesell went on to express dis-
satisfaction with the substance of the regulations. In a chilling
though nonbinding part of his decision, the judge suggested that
legal theory behind Roe v. Wade could be used to strip newborn
infants of all legal rights: "To the extent the regulation is read to
eliminate the role of the infant's parents in choosing an appropriate course of medical treatment, its application may in some
cases infringe upon the interest outlined in such cases as . . .
Roe v. Wade.[16]

Although the posted notices were taken down, the hotline
phone service was not disconnected. Calls continued to come in.
On July 5, 1983, the Surgeon General credited the hotline with

14. Letter on file with the Christian Action Council.
15. Action Line 7, no. 3 (31 March 1983).
16. American Academy of Pediatrics, National Association of Children's Hospi-
    tals and Related Institutions, Children's Hospital National Medical Center v.
    Margaret M. Heckler, Civil Action No. 83-0774, p. 19.

saving three babies within the previous two week period. "All three of those children are doing well," Dr. Koop said. "They all got treatment and the only reason they got treatment, as far as we can tell, is because somebody called. As soon as we investigated, the hospital decided they'd better treat and they did."

As this book is completed, the battle over regulations and statutes continues to rage. Infanticide is now subject to open debate in Washington, D.C. The American Medical Association has joined the ranks of other medical groups opposing attempts to safeguard the rights of handicapped newborns. They argue that the medical community is fully capable of policing itself. If that is true, why has it failed to do so?

SURVEY RESULTS

A 1977 survey of pediatricians and pediatric surgeons revealed that 76.8 percent of pediatric surgeons and 59.5 percent of pediatricians would "acquiesce in a parent's decision" to deny a Down's syndrome baby life-saving surgery to correct an intestinal obstruction. Nearly one quarter, 23.6 percent, of pediatric surgeons surveyed said they would encourage parents to make such a decision. When asked, "If you were the parent of a newborn infant with Down's syndrome and intestinal obstruction, would you consent to intestinal surgery?" only 27 percent of the surgeons answered yes.[17] Nearly three in four would allow their own children to die of starvation. The force of law must be used to constrain doctors to give handicapped infants the care they need.

DEBATE RESUMED

On August 1, 1983, Congressman Chris Smith underscored the need for strong laws to protect life when he brought to the House's attention the lead commentary of the July 1983 issue of *Pediatrics*. Written by bioethicist Peter Singer and entitled "Sanctity of Life or Quality of Life," the article begins by recounting how abortion and infanticide have served to erode the sanctity of life ethic. It then decrees that viewpoint obsolete: "We can no longer base our ethics on the idea that human beings are a special

17. Anthony Shaw, Judson G. Randolph, and Barbara Manard, "Ethical Issues in Pediatric Surgery," *Pediatrics* 60:588-95.

form of creation, singled out from all other animals, and alone possessing an immortal soul."[18]

In his statement to his colleagues, Congressman Smith emphasized the theme of the article, which is the prevailing view among many pediatricians.

> If we compare a severely defective human infant with a nonhuman animal, a dog or a pig, for example, we will often find the nonhuman to have superior capacities, both actual and potential, for rationality, selfconsciousness, communication, and anything else that can plausibly be considered morally significant. . . .[19]

Singer embraces the conclusion that must inevitably come to one who rejects the intrinsic value of human life. A healthy dog or pig has more value than a handicapped baby.

The quality-of-life ethic is cruel and ruthless because it makes no room for mercy or love. On this view, caring for people with severe handicaps is unethical. These are worthless animals who should not be given time or energy. Better to train the family dog—or pig.

RESOURCES AVAILABLE

The United States is the wealthiest nation in the world as well as the most technologically advanced. With these resources at its disposal, the medical profession has developed capabilities to care for and rehabilitate handicapped newborns that weren't even imagined fifty years ago. As a result most of these children can live largely "normal" lives even though physically or mentally they are not "normal." Many children facing profound physical handicaps are gifted intellectually or artistically. Among those who are mentally retarded, one can find the most loving people. Retardation and handicaps are not synonymous with suffering and unhappiness. Dr. Koop is most eloquent on this point.

> I am frequently told by people who have never had the privilege of working with handicapped children who are being rehabilitated into our society after the correction of a congenital defect that such infants should be allowed to die or even encouraged to die because their lives could obviously be nothing but unhappy and miserable. Yet it has been my constant experience that disability and unhappi-

18. *The Congressional Record* 125, at E3904 (1 August 1983).
19. Ibid., at E3903.

ness to do not go hand in hand. Some of the most unhappy children I have known have been completely normal. On the other hand there is a remarkable joy and happiness in the lives of most handicapped children. Some have borne burdens which I would have found difficult to face indeed.[20]

Regardless of the effectiveness of their therapy, each of these children is a human being created in the image of God. Each has his or her own ability to love and respond to love, to know happiness and contentment. This is true even among the severely retarded, those who are cruelly called "vegetables."

MELISSA

In the summer of 1983 I met a "vegetable." Her name is Melissa, and she is just two years old. Born with very little brain tissue, Melissa is severely retarded. When a light is shone on her head, the back of her skull transluminates because there is nothing inside.

At birth, Melissa was abandoned by her parents and could easily have become another victim of infanticide. The attending physician explained to all concerned that she could not possibly live more than a few weeks, let alone see, walk, speak, or respond with human emotion.

I met Melissa in a rural Indiana home where she now lives as the adopted daughter of Ronald and Rachel Ginder. As a result of their Christlike love and encouragement, Melissa is now called "a miracle child" by just about everyone. She is a beautiful child with hazel eyes and brown hair. She was humming along with music as I entered the room where she lay.

Her mother explained, "Melissa enjoys music, especially classical."

"How can you tell?" I asked.

"Oh, a mother can tell what her children like," she replied with a smile. "She also makes special sounds to let me know when she is hungry or just wants some lovin'."

"Loving?"

"There's no doubt about it. Melissa loves to be held and loved. She also knows when I need some affection." And with that, Melissa was swept into her mother's arms and gently roughed up. Melissa smiled and suddenly seemed to gaze into her mother's face.

20. Koop, "The Silent Domino."

"She looks like she can see," I said.

"Well, the doctor doesn't understand it, but it seems that way to him, too. Melissa definitely responds to bright light. He says her brain hasn't changed. She's just using everything she's got."

Spending the afternoon with Melissa and her mother, Rachel, was quite an experience. Rachel wanted me to meet Melissa in order to encourage me. "You can tell this child has a soul, and it's healthy," she said. "That makes this baby valuable."

One thing was perfectly clear to me. That beautiful little girl was hungry to receive and give love. Those who justify starving an infant like Melissa in the name of ending her pain deceive themselves and commit an unspeakable crime.

CONCLUSION

Arthur Dyck, professor of population ethics at Harvard School of Public Health, puts the issue of infanticide in these terms: "The moral question for us is not whether the suffering and dying are persons but whether we are the kind of persons who will care for them without doubting their worth."[21] How we treat these little people is not a measure of their humanity but of our own.

21. Ibid.

11

The Legacy of Abortion, Part 3: Euthanasia

Projecting from one end of the age spectrum to the other, we see euthanasia for the elderly as the counterpart to abortion for the very young. There is no moral distinction between the two. Quality-of-life proponent Joseph Fletcher agrees: "To speak of living and dying, therefore . . . encompasses the abortion issue along with the euthanasia issue. They are ethically inseparable."[1]

Those who take comfort in the fact that euthanasia is not practiced at present in America are leaning on a slim reed. Infanticide is euthanasia for newborn children. Many of the disabilities that make infants targets for infanticide are also found in older people as a result of disease, injury, or the aging process. Disabled adults understandably are alarmed. Asks Anne Finger in the February 1984 issue of *Off Our Backs*, "If disabled people aren't considered full human beings at birth, with the same rights as the nondisabled, when do we become equal? When do we stop receiving 'appropriate'—i.e. second-class—medical care and start to receive equal medical treatment?"

ECONOMIC PRESSURE

The quality-of-life reasoning used to support euthanasia may not in itself be sufficient to overcome the revulsion most people

1. Joseph Fletcher, "The 'Right' to Life and the 'Right' to Die," *Humanist* 34, no. 4 (July-August 1974):15.

feel toward killing elderly people. Economic pressure, however, may well be.

"Aging Population Could Cripple American Economy in Fifty Years." That was the headline in the *Physicians' Washington Report*, March 1980. The brief article began, "According to a long-range forecast, the rapidly aging U.S. population could cripple the economy of the nation unless steps are taken to soften the burden."[2]

The issue is a very serious one. Within fifty years there will be one retired individual for every two people in the work force. Currently, five people pay into Social Security for every one receiving benefit, and the system already flounders regularly for additional funds. Thirty-eight percent of the federal budget is spent on retirement and health benefits. There is no way the system will be able to support the increasing numbers of elderly people.

Three factors contribute to the crisis. The first is the aging of the "baby boom" generation born after World War II. The second is the skyrocketing cost of medical care. The third is the rapidly dropping birth rate, due in part to abortion.

THE DUTY TO DIE

In 1967, when the American Euthanasia Society changed its name to the Society for the Right to Die, euthanasia proponents began advocating the practice as a cherished right. Economic considerations, however, have transformed the rhetoric of euthanasia so that today more and more is said about the *duty* to die.

The first prominent public official to overtly adopt this line of reasoning was the governor of Colorado. On March 27, 1984, Governor Richard Lamm, in a speech before the Colorado Health Lawyers Association, charged that elderly people who are terminally ill have "a duty to die and get out of the way." Providing them with full health care would turn the United States into a "second-rate economic nation. . . . The average age of America will be the average age of St. Petersburg, Florida," he said. "It's the graying of America. You've got incredible implications."[3]

Lamm maintains that the solution to health care costs is a drastic "reform" of the health care system. Rationed health care would be a significant part of this. According to Lamm, "Lamm's

2. *Physicians Washington Report* 2, no. 9 (March 1980).
3. "The Elderly Terminally Ill 'Have A Duty To Die,' Lamm Says," *Denver Post*, 28 March 1984.

iron law of history is [that] limited resources make hard—and sometimes even tragic—choices not only necessary but inevitable." That may sould cruel, but for Lamm and others there is significant benefit. "I'd take the money we could save in reforming the health care system and put it into . . . restarting America's industrial engine and in the education system," he said.[4]

Understandably, Governor Lamm's remarks were greeted with protest. Colorado pro-life leader Earl Dodge charged, "Governor Lamm is trying to bring pressure upon those who are seriously ill to reject medical care as a duty to society."[5]

Robert Robinson, a lobbyist for the Colorado Congress of Senior Organizations, perhaps best captured the essence of Lamm's philosophy. "To say that we have a duty to die and get out of the way brings me back forty years ago, when a person in Germany not only advocated that, but carried it through."[6]

Protests were to be expected. Accolades were not, but they were given anyway. Time magazine, the Washington Post, and the New York Times all reported Lamm's remarks favorably, commending him as a visionary for raising an important issue. Such support confirmed that Lamm was only responsible for saying publicly what many had been thinking privately.

STARVATION OF THE UNWANTED

Supporters of Lamm's "duty to die" position insist they refer only to the allocation of the most expensive and extraordinary means of life support, such as an artificial heart. In practice, the medical establishment's "duty to die" proponents make no such distinction between ordinary and extraordinary care.

Less than two weeks after Governor Lamm's broadside against care for the elderly ill, the New England Journal of Medicine ran an article developed two years before under the auspices of the Society for the Right to Die. Entitled "The Physician's Responsibility Toward Hopelessly Ill Patients," the article carried a broad endorsement of treatment withdrawal for elderly patients who are terminally ill, including the denial of food and water, "naturally or artificially administered." To those doctors who are inclined to continue aggressive treatment of a terminal disease

4. Ibid.
5. "Embattled Lamm Clarifies 'Duty to Die' Remark," Denver Post, 31 March 1984.
6. "Governor Lamm Asserts Elderly if Very Ill, Have 'Duty to Die,' " New York Times, 29 March 1984.

because this may prove effective, the article cautions, "The rare report of a patient with a similar condition who survived is not an overriding reason to continue aggressive treatment."[7] Medical judgment today is influenced by new factors including "monetary costs to society."[8]

The ten physicians who wrote the article stopped short of arguing that doctors have a duty to assist patients in committing suicide, "for this is contrary to the law." However, they went on to argue that the desire for suicide is not necessarily "irrational"[9]

The authors suggest that resistance to starvation among "family, friends, and staff" may be broken down if they are taught that "many patients in a terminal situation are not aware of thirst or hunger."[10] If a "severely and irreversibly demented patient" stops accepting oral food and fluids, then it is "ethically permissible" to avoid any further attempts to hydrate or nourish the patient. For "elderly patients with permanent mild impairment of competence," any emergency resuscitation or intensive care should be administered "sparingly."[11]

The argument that the physician's chief task is to make the patient comfortable and that food and water are not necessary for comfort in many cases, twists the language of human care into justification for starvation.

On June 2, 1983, the *Toronto Star* reported the remarks of Harvard University heart surgeon Dr. Dwight Harken, made before an international medical conference in Edmonton, Alberta. "Society can no longer afford the best possible treatment for everyone," said Harken. "We should let the helpless cases slip away." According to the *Star*, Harken was referring to the starvation of 300,000 North American "human vegetables."[12]

On November 2, 1983, the *Washington Post* featured a major news article entitled "Two Doctors Take Controversial Stand on Feeding Those Near Death." Dr. Joanne Lynn, medical director of the Washington Home Hospice for terminally ill patients, and Dr. Anne Fletcher, director of the Children's Hospital intensive care nursery, both argue that doctors should not feel obligated to provide food and nourishment to terminally ill patients where

7. John Dearfield, et al., "The Physician's Responsibility Toward Hopelessly Ill Patients," *The New England Journal of Medicine*, 310, no. 15 (12 April 1984):956.
8. Ibid.
9. Ibid., p. 957.
10. Ibid., p. 958.
11. Ibid., p. 959.
12. "Let Hopeless Cases Starve to Death: MD," *Toronto Star*, 2 June 1983.

those are artificially administered (e.g., intravenously).

Dr. Lynn acknowledges that in her own medical practice "she has authorized the withdrawal of artificially administered food and water from about 6 to 12 patients a year who were dying or permanently unconscious." Writing in the October 1983 issue of the *Hastings Report*, she argues that withholding food and water should not be strictly limited to those who are very near death. She writes, "Even patients who might live much longer might not be well served by artificial means to provide fluid and food."[13]

In a strange twist in logic, Dr. Lynn maintains she is not arguing that physicians have an obligation to withhold or withdraw food, only that "in some cases" they are not obligated to provide it. By refusing to label the practice as an obligation, she serves notice to her colleagues that she is not going to impose her beliefs on them, but by arguing that starvation is acceptable, she in effect argues that it is right.

Reporter Benjamin Weiser indicates that interviews with a number of physicians confirmed they share these opinions but are not so bold in putting them forth. Said one doctor, "I guess the surprising thing is that somebody's willing to put it in print." The published declarations of Dr. Lynn in particular may prove as significant in advancing euthanasia as Duff and Campbell's article was in advancing infanticide.

LIVING WILLS

Growing support for euthanasia within the medical profession is not occurring in isolation from related developments in courts and legislatures. An analysis of the cases and laws bearing on the euthanasia question would be very lengthy and technical. Only a brief outline is supplied here.

Currently fifteen states and the District of Columbia have passed "living will" or "Death with Dignity" laws. The first state to do so was California in 1967; Virginia is the most recent (1983). The concept of the "living will" was developed and is now promoted by the Society for the Right to Die.

A living will is a document drawn up and signed by an individual while competent and in reasonable health. It directs physicians on what care should be provided, withheld, or withdrawn as the signer approaches death. Statutes providing for living wills

13. "Two Doctors Take Controversial Stand on Feeding Those Near Death," *Washington Post*, 2 November 1983.

are generally described as "Death with Dignity" laws or "Natural Death Acts."

Living wills are promoted by appealing to people's fear of medical technology in the face of death. No one wants to be subjected to endless medical treatments and procedures that neither cure, heal, or relieve pain and suffering. The argument for living wills is that these secure for patients the right to refuse medical care that only prolongs the dying process, along with its suffering.

In the midst of efforts to promote legislation, one vital fact is often confused or left out of debates altogether. Patients *already have the right to refuse medical treatment.* This is well established in the common law tradition of the United States. No one can be forced to receive medical care.

In addition, arguments for living wills presume that doctors are without error in their medical diagnoses, so that when they say a condition is hopeless, there is no point in pursuing further treatment. In fact, physicians do make mistakes. A recent study of 300 autopsies by medical personnel at Boston's Brigham and Women's Hospital and Harvard Medical School revealed that one in four diagnoses had been wrong. According to the *New York Times,* "About ten percent of the autopsies revealed a condition that, if recognized before death or treated accordingly, could have prolonged life."[14]

Living wills do not increase patient rights at all. In their least damaging form, the laws have had little immediate effect. In a number of states, however, including Arkansas, Virginia, and California, the laws actually serve to restrict patient rights. For those comatose or incompetent patients who never signed a living will, provisions are made for a third party to decide whether they should be given life-sustaining treatment. This creates the potential for severe conflict of interest. What if Mrs. Jones or the children have long resented Mr. Jones and look forward to his estate? In addition it can create a predisposition among physicians not to treat. The chief question may no longer be how to treat the patient, but whether to treat. This represents a marked departure from the sanctity of human life position with its emphasis on compassion and care for the helpless.

The object of these bills is to introduce legislatures to the concept of passing laws that influence how and when people die.

14. "Autopsies Show 1 in 4 Diagnoses Were Wrong," *The New York Times,* 28 April 1983.

They can only be viewed as precursors of explicit euthanasia legislation in the future.[15]

EUTHANASIA AND THE COURTS

Court actions that relate to euthanasia have generally been limited to terminally ill patients, but not always. The first case involved Karen Ann Quinlan, a twenty-two-year-old woman in a permanent coma. Believing her death was imminent, her family sought and received permission from the New Jersey Supreme Court to remove her from a respirator and so to hasten her death. Miss Quinlan confounded everyone by continuing to breathe unassisted. She will soon be entering her seventh year of life in a coma.

The most significant part of this case, however, involved the reasoning of the court. Arguing from Karen's constitutional right to privacy, the court ruled she had a right to refuse medical treatment. Since her coma prevented her from doing this, the court then ruled that her guardian could "exercise . . . the choice" for her and thereby "prevent destruction of the right" to refuse care.[16]

That logic is twisted and dangerous. When in the name of a patient's rights another person can deny her treatment, euthanasia becomes a distinct possibility under the law. By constitutionalizing and privatizing the right to refuse care, the court effectively placed the decision beyond public scrutiny or oversight.

In a very different case, involving the removal of a respirator from a comatose patient, a New York State court directly compared the value of a comatose patient near death to the value of a fetus. The implicit logic is frightening. Since it is legal to dispose of a fetus, it ought to be legal to dispose of an old man.

> Indeed with *Roe* in mind it is appropriate to note that the state's interest in the preservation of the life of the fetus would appear to be *greater* than any possible interest the state may have in maintaining the continued life of a terminally ill comatose patient.[17]

From a sanctity of life perspective, the issue in this case was not whether the patient's respirator should have been removed.

---

15. "Questions and Answers About the Living Will," *Euthanasia News* 1 (August 1975): 3.
16. *In re Quinlan,* 70 NJ 10 (1976), pp. 41-42.
17. *Eichner* v. *Dillon* and *Storar* v. *Storar,* 52 NY 2d 363, 438 NY 2d 266 (31 March 1981).

The individual, eighty-three-year-old Brother Fox, had repeatedly indicated before proceeding to surgery that he wanted no extraordinary measures used to sustain his life in the event of massive complications. Since he suffered a heart attack along with massive brain damage, His common law right to refuse medical treatment should have been honored. There is reason to question whether the case should even have come before a court. The critical issue was the premise of the court in reaching its decision. Brother Fox had no value.

COURT APPROVED STARVATION

Two important cases have recently surfaced where the issue is not so confusing as when a decision is made regarding a respirator. The issue is whether or not patients should be fed.

The first case involved the death of Clarence L. Herbert. Following a heart attack and brain damage during surgery, Mr. Herbert was comatose. After three days, two physicians, with the family's approval, disconnected Mr. Herbert's respirator. Surprisingly, he continued to breathe on his own. Food and water were withdrawn two days following. After languishing six days, Mr. Herbert died. The two physicians were charged with murder, but the charges were dismissed by the Los Angeles Municipal Court. Judge Brian Cohen ruled the doctors "had acted properly and in accordance with the best medical judgment."

A successful effort to reinstate murder charges against the physicians was subsequently vacated by a California appellate court panel. The judges ruled that the physicians' "omission to continue treatment under the circumstances, though intentional and with knowledge that the patient would die, was not unlawful failure to perform a legal duty." They maintained that the "issue must be determined against a backdrop of legal and moral considerations which are of fairly recent vintage and which as a result have not, in our opinion, been adequately addressed by the legislature."[18]

Quality of life considerations obviously prevailed. Providing nourishment to the patient was a "treatment" that could be withheld. Accordingly, the starvation of Clarence Herbert was acceptable medical care.

The second case involves an incompetent eighty-four-year-old woman named Claire Conroy. Depending solely on a feeding

18. *American Medical News*, 28 October 1983, pp. 1-2.

tube for food and water, the lady was "not brain dead, not comatose, and not in a chronic vegetative state." She had no terminal illness or fatal condition. On February 2, 1983, her nephew, serving as her legal guardian, requested and received court permission to remove the feeding tube. The court acknowledged it was giving the approval of the law to starve this woman to death.

> Her life has become impossibly and permanently burdensome for her. Prolonging her life would not help her. It would be a wrong to her. The nasogastric tube should be removed, even though that will almost certainly lead to death by starvation and dehydration within a few days, and even though that death may be a painful one for the patient.[19]

In the name of relieving the patient of a burden, the court sanctioned her starvation. The compassion was twisted. The issue was not Claire Conroy's suffering or pain but the fact she was painfully inconvenient. This decision was overturned by the New Jersey Appellate Court.[20] In doing so it attacked the lower court's reasoning:

> We are also troubled by the trial judge's framing of the issue as whether the patient will return "to some meaningful level of intellectual functioning." Put simply, to allow a physician or family members to discontinue life-sustaining treatment to a person solely because that person's lack of intellectual capacity precludes him from enjoying a meaningful quality of life would establish a dangerous precedent that could be extended far beyond the facts of the case now before us. In our view, the right to terminate life-sustaining treatment based on a guardian's substituted judgment should be limited to incurable and terminally ill patients who are brain dead, irreversibly comatose or vegetative, and who would gain no medical benefit from continued treatment. *A fortiori*, there can be no justification for withholding nourishment, which is really not "treatment" at all, from a patient who does not meet these criteria.[21]

The case is proceeding through the courts although Claire Conroy has since died of natural causes. The final decision will

---

19. *In the Matter of Claire Conroy*, Chancery Division—Essex County, Superior Court of New Jersey (Docket Number P-19083E), at 1; reported at 188 NJ Super 523 (Ch. Div. 1983).
20. *Conroy*, Appellate Division, at 17.
21. Michael L. Budde, "Policy Issues in Termination, Administration of Medical Treatment," prepared for Right to Life of Michigan, 8 September 1983, p. 16.

be most signficant. Advocates of starvation, including Dr. Lynn, maintain that the feeding tube should have been removed.[22]

EUTHANASIA AND THE FEDERAL GOVERNMENT

Already there are indications that cost control experts in the federal government are thinking in terms of (voluntary) euthanasia as a way to save money. On June 4, 1977, Robert A. Derzon, then head of Health, Education and Welfare's Health Care Financing Administration, issued a memo on cost-saving initiatives in the health care system. One of the subject headings in the report carried the title "Change Social Values Regarding Cost-Inducing Activities." The first recommendation under the point was "Encourage Adoption of Living Wills." The cost benefit analysis of human life that is reflected here along with the willingness to use coercion may foreshadow events to come.

> Encouraging States to pass such a law or, more strongly, *withholding Federal funds without passage would serve to heighten public awareness of the use of such resources and would also lower health spending when such wills are executed. The strong response to the Karen Ann Quinlan case demonstrates that such encouragement would result in some negative public reaction.*
> *The cost-savings from a nationwide push toward "Living Wills" is likely to be enormous.* Over one-fifth of Medicare expenditures are for persons in their last year of life. Thus, in FY 1978, $4.9 billion will be spent for such persons and if just one-quarter of these expenditures were avoided through adoption of "Living Wills," the savings under Medicare alone would amount to $1.2 billion. (Italics added)[23]

The second recommendation Derzon made was "Reduce Unwanted Births." Under this subheading, he included the use of federal funds to pay for elective abortions. Derzon has long since left the Health Care Financing Administration. Pro-life leaders were assured the ideas expressed in the memorandum were dead. Unfortunately, this was untrue.

On April 9, 1984, Dr. Otis Bowen, chairperson of the Advisory Council on Social Security, testified before the Senate Committee on Finance. He provided the committee with a report con-

22. "Two Doctors Take Controversial Stand on Feeding Those Near Death," *Washington Post,* 2 November 1983.
23. Copies of the Derzon memo are available from US Coalition for Life, Box 315, Export, PA 15632.

taining twenty-six recommendations to keep the Medicare program solvent. The causes for insolvency were given as "the escalation of health care costs and an increasing elderly population.[24] Among the recommendations unanimously endorsed by the Advisory Council was the adoption of living will legislation by all fifty states. With a legal basis for withholding medical care from patients in their last days of life, the Medicare program could save billions. Bowen commented, "Eleven percent of Medicare expenditures are spent in the last forty days of life and some twenty-five percent of Medicare expenditures are incurred by patients in the last year of life."[25]

DO NOT RESUSCITATE

On August 25, 1983, the Veterans Administration's Department of Medicine and Surgery issued "Guidelines for 'Do Not Resuscitate' (DNR) Protocals within the VA." In a slippery-worded circular, the Deputy Chief Medical Director dealt with the question of issuing "Do Not Resuscitate" orders for patients who suffer cardiac arrest. Ostensibly the purpose of the document was to provide guidelines for how these orders, *when requested by the patient,* are to be carried out. In the absence of such orders, VA policy is that CPR be administered to every patient.

So far so good, perhaps. But the document goes on to undo the very policy it is supposed to uphold. In the event such a request has *not* been made by the patient, the guidelines concede that doctors can determine independently to withhold resuscitation.

> However, it is acknowledged that there will be those cases where, in the exercise of sound medical judgment, a licensed physician who knows the patient may appropriately give an instruction not to institute resuscitation at the bedside of a patient who has just experienced an arrest. . . . It may be appropriate to communicate these concerns to physicians responsible for the immediate care of the patient, in the absence of the physician who knows the patient.

The guidelines move on to specify that if the patient is not competent or conscious, "the decision should be reached after consultation with the patient's surrogate, or in the absence of such an individual, appropriate family member(s) and the physi-

---

24. Statement by Otis R. Bowen, M.D., chairperson of the Advisory Committee on Social Security, before the Senate Committee on Finance, 2 April 1984, p. 2.
25. Ibid., p. 12.

cian." If it happens that a physician cannot comply for reasons of conscience, then "that physician should arrange to transfer the patient's care to another physician . . . who can so comply."

It should be clear that these guidelines do not regulate DNR orders in any neutral fashion, but contrary to VA policy they encourage their use among patients who have not requested them.

In the conclusion to the guidelines a prohibition is issued. "Under no circumstances should DNR orders be written where they are in compliance only with a request for "assisted suicide" or voluntary euthanasia. 'Do Not Resuscitate' does not mean that the medical staff will take any affirmative steps to 'hasten the patient on his/her way.' " These words offer little comfort. It is hard to understand how the guidelines can prevent abuses when they give every appearance of making a way for them.

These last examples of agitation in the direction of euthanasia are unique in that they represent a "federalizing" of the issue. In other words, the effect of decisions made on these levels is national in scope, and citizens at the local or state level are afforded little opportunity for input. This is not representative government.

The final chapters of Deuteronomy describe the foreign nation that would invade Israel because of her unrighteousness. It would be a cruel and ruthless nation, "a nation of fierce countenance who shall have no respect for the old, nor show favor to the young." Christians in America today must face the disturbing fact that this characterization comes far too close to describing their nation as well.

12

Overcoming the Violence

A couple of years ago, I finally had my opportunity to speak to students at one of the leading evangelical seminaries in the United States. I was not there to lecture in the formal sense, rather to inform students of the status of abortion and what they could do to foster support for the right to life.

I knew the facts of abortion would be hard to take (they always are), but in general these inspire action rather than despair. Especially with theological students who knew the promises of God, I expected a positive response.

Halfway through my remarks, however, a young man clutching his lunch sack stood up and exclaimed, "It's no use! There's no way to stop it." He left, presumably to wait for the rapture.

The group was stunned, and I was dumbfounded. At that moment I would have settled for the rapture, a fire drill—anything to get me out of there. Nothing happened, and I was left to confront a sea of confused expressions, some bewildered and some sheepish.

I certainly understand feeling helpless in the face of abortion. Most people view the problem as stemming in large measure from a ponderous Federal government that is largely hostile to Christianity. How can we possibly bring the practice to a halt?

As a leader in the pro-life movement, I have lost sleep over many things—like phone bills, payrolls, and our singlehanded financing of the local Post Office. Never have I questioned the victory of justice for the unborn or other victims of violence. The Word of God is simply too clear, leaving no room for doubt. God is a Father to the fatherless, the vindicator of the oppressed. I will not give way to fear. People can attempt to play God with the lives of other human beings, but He is not mocked.

One of the most glorious chapters in the history of the church deals with the manner in which God has used His people to overcome injustice and to care for the weak. When I consider the ways in which Christ is working through believers today to save lives and stop abortion, I can only be encouraged.

One fallacy often crops up in thoughts about abortion: the immediate origin of the problem appears to be Washington, D.C. (i.e., the Supreme Court); therefore the solution must also come from Washington, D.C. That is untrue.

Government is one species of bureaucracy. As with any bureaucracy, government is reactionary by its nature. It will not change unless it has no other choice. Whether the option of destroying life is removed depends on what happens in communities across the country. The problem of legalized abortion may have originated in large measure in Washington, but the solution will come as people band together to resist abortion and affirm the sanctity of human life.

STEP ONE: EDUCATE THE PUBLIC

In order to bring an end to the destruction of human life, two things must occur. First, public indifference or acceptance toward abortion and related violence must be replaced by public abhorrence. Millions of people have made the transition already. This largely is a result of education accomplished at the grass-roots level, despite a hostile press.

The nature and consequences of abortion must be taught, but so must the nature and value of human life. Our message is fundamentally positive and hopeful. It is based upon a high regard for individuals and the recognition of our social obligation to love. At the same time, it is forthright. As a former abortion clinic director recently confided, "There's a hard truth in abortion, and it must be told." Abortion is a particularly brutal form of violence that should be exposed.

In addition the myth that abortion is a social necessity must be replaced with the truth that alternatives exist and are better, much better, for everyone involved. Because experience is a good teacher of these lessons, the challenge is clear to provide services in alternatives to abortion on a massive scale. As people are exposed both to the tragedy of abortion and to the fulfillment that comes in carrying a child to term, they acquire knowledge that clichés and slogans cannot touch.

As men and women increase in their understanding of these things, they grow in their commitment to protect human life. Our leaders must see signs of this commitment before they will change public policy. Voting patterns are forceful illustrations. Public protests are not overlooked. Personal correspondence and meetings with officials are effective demonstrations of concern and the accountability that follows from it.

STEP TWO: CHANGE THE LAW

These considerations lead us directly to the second thing that must occur in order to protect human life. The force of law and the weight of government must again come down on the side of the innocent, to guard them from violence.

The Supreme Court has spoken on abortion, but this by no means is the last word from the Federal government on the matter. In fact it probably is not the last word from the Court itself. On at least 120 occasions in the past, the US Supreme Court has reversed itself on a variety of issues. The procedure is simple. The Court may overturn a prior decision by accepting a related case and issuing a contrary opinion.

JUDICIAL APPOINTMENTS

As a staunch proponent of permissive abortion, the Court appears a formidable opponent, but a closer examination reveals some encouraging facts. Currently, three of the nine justices support a reversal of *Roe* v. *Wade.* Those three justices happen to be the youngest members of the Court. They are led by the first woman in US history to be appointed justice, Sandra Day O'Connor.

With one exception each of the remaining justices is seventy-four years of age or older. The replacement of at least two of these members in the next four years is likely. If the President during that period is committed in his opposition to abortion and appoints justices who share his views, then the necessary majority will exist on the Court to overturn *Roe* v. *Wade.* The next election will be critical.

Besides appointments, other ways exist to influence the decisions of the Court. In recent years, the Court has been extremely sensitive to the political conditions throughout the country. Their opinions have reflected this. The cynical adage of former Justice Oliver Wendell Holmes is a fit description of the Court's approach to truth: "Truth is the majority vote of the nation that can lick all the others."

When the public registers a large-scale protest against its decisions, the Court is forced to listen. When its opinions are out of harmony with Congress and the White House, it generally is inclined to modify them. This is one reason campaigns to change the law are so important.

After a successful legislative drive in Congress by Senator Jesse Helms and Congressman Henry Hyde to stop abortion funding, the Court restrained itself on the question of tax funded abortions and ruled that the right to abortion does require the Federal government to subsidize abortions for women who cannot afford to pay for them. As opposition to abortion increases around the nation and is reflected in Congress, the Court's sensitivity will increase as well.

CONSTITUTIONAL AMENDMENTS

The other two avenues of overturning the Supreme Court's abortion decision involves amending the Constitution. Just as the Thirteenth Amendment overturned the *Dred Scott* decision and prohibited slavery, so an amendment guaranteeing the right to life of all human beings from their conception will overturn *Roe* and prohibit abortion. Article V of the document provides for amendment procedures.

> The Congress, whenever two thirds of both Houses shall deem it necessary, shall propose Amendments to this Constitution, or, on the Application of the legislatures of two thirds of the several States, shall call a Convention for proposing Amendments, which, in either Case, shall be valid to all Intents and Purposes, as Part of this Constitution, when ratified by the Legislatures of three fourths of the several States, or by Conventions in three fourths thereof, as the one or the other, Mode of Ratification may be proposed by the Congress; Provided . . . that no State, without its Consent, shall be deprived of its equal Suffrage in the Senate.

In order to amend the Constitution, two-thirds of both houses of Congress must pass a constitutional amendment resolution.

Upon passage, the resolution must then be ratified either by three-fourths of the state legislatures or by three-fourths of the state conventions called for that purpose. Congress determines which avenue of ratification is to be followed as well as the time frame for ratification. Usually this is seven years.

The other means of amending the Constitution differs from the first in the way in which the amendment is proposed. If two-thirds of the state legislatures call for a national constitutional convention to draft a particular amendment, then Congress is bound to convene an assembly for this purpose. The resulting amendment resolution is then subject to ratification by three-fourths of the states, either through the legislatures or through state conventions.

To date all constitutional amendments have originated in Congress rather than in constitutional conventions. A primary reason for this is that Congress is most reluctant to surrender its prerogative of proposing amendments. When drives for a constitutional convention have gathered substantial support from the states and appeared likely to succeed, Congress has felt compelled to respond with an amendment resolution, making any further drive for a convention unnecessary.

Currently twenty of the necessary thirty-four states have called for a constitutional convention to draft an amendment on abortion. If the number reaches thirty Congress will begin to stir responsively.

Amending the Constitution is difficult. Since the charter was ratified in 1787, only twenty-six amendments have been added. The first ten of these were the Bill of Rights and one (the Twenty-First Amendment) was the repeal of another (the Eighteenth Amendment, "prohibition"). That leaves fourteen amendments enacted successfully during the mainstream of American history. This is in spite of the fact that over ten thousand constitutional amendments have been introduced in Congress over the years.

Tremendous dedication is required if the Constitution is to be amended. Nevertheless, this is necessary in our day. Given the imaginative interpretations of law and redefinition of rights that absorb so much of the Federal judiciary's time, we must make explicit within the Constitution the right to life.

THE COMPROMISE AMENDMENT

In 1981, despair of ever accomplishing this led the US Catholic bishops to propose a compromise constitutional amendment. As-

suming that an amendment would garner more votes if it abandoned the right-to-life principle, the bishops' proposal sought
only to empower state legislatures to deal with the question of
protection for the unborn. As a states' rights amendment, it
would not recognize the right to life for the unborn, but it would
make the protection of unborn children a legal option. If a majority of legislators in a state opposed abortion, abortion could be
illegal. If they favored abortion, then abortion on demand would
continue. Known as the "Hatch Federalism Amendment," this
proposal was sponsored in the Senate by Orrin G. Hatch.

As we've already seen, a state's rights compromise was attempted as a solution to another issue of justice, slavery. It failed
to resolve that conflict either in Congress or in the states because
it left unaddressed the question of justice. A state's rights amendment in the matter of abortion would fail just as badly, and for
the same reason. An issue of justice cannot be treated as just
another political problem that yields to pragmatic compromises.
The lives of people are at stake. Lord Acton, the nineteenth-
century British political thinker, rightly characterized arrangements where rights may be withheld by legislatures as "tyranny
of the majority."

Proponents of the bishops' compromise on abortion argued
that protection as an option for a state is better than no option at
all. As a theory this was irrefutable, but it was beside the point.
Any time individuals or movements offer to abandon the principle they have stood for, politicians view this for what it is, a sign
of weakness and a lack of resolve. In the case of slavery, it was
not the abolitionists who offered to compromise the freedom of
black slaves. Quite accurately, members of Congress took the
bishops' recent offer as an indication of their desire to dispense
with the abortion issue as a political question in order to move
on to other matters. The result in Congress was extraordinary
determination to defeat rather than to pass the proposal.

No constitutional amendment, no matter how emasculated,
had any chance of passage, let alone ratification. Rather than
garnering more votes than a strong amendment, the weakened
proposal, after being weakened still further, failed to garner a
simple majority in the Senate. By a vote of 49 to 50, the so-called
"Hatch Federalism Amendment" went down to defeat. This was
far short of the 67 votes necessary for passage.

Even before the defeat, the bishops made clear through a
much-publicized pastoral letter that their next "pro life" emphasis would be nuclear weapons. Within six months of the vote,

Archbishop Joseph Bernardin, principal author of the pastoral letter and recently named head of the bishops' pro-life committee, declared that the pro-life agenda had been expanded beyond abortion to include opposition to nuclear weapons and to capital punishment. It also included support for poverty programs and, because of concern for human rights violations, opposition to the Reagan administration's policies in Central America. All these together, from abortion to foreign policy, are now to be viewed as a "seamless garment."[1]

Thousands of pro-lifers, both Catholic and Protestant, were stunned by what was taking place and refused to submit in support of the state's rights proposal. They appealed to pro-life leaders in Congress for support.

On June 28, 1983, when Senator Hatch's amendment was debated for an hour and defeated, one man in the Senate, Jesse Helms, stood firm and refused to surrender the right-to-life principle. Because of his courageous witness, the Congress was put on notice that the standard of protection for the innocent would not be abandoned. The integrity of the pro-life message in the political arena was preserved because of one man. Following are excerpts from his remarks on the Senate floor.

> As I said yesterday, the unfortunate fact is that S.J. Res. 3 [Senator Hatch's amendment] does not advance the principle that human life is inviolable. Instead, it surrenders forever this principle in exchange for the illusory hope that some lives may be saved. . . .
> . . . S.J. Res. 3 would institutionalize in the text of the Constitution the idea that abortion is a matter of choice for the governing authorities. Moreover, it would thereby undercut the correct understanding that the fifth and fourteenth amendments protect all human "persons" including the unborn. In short S.J. Res. 3 runs contrary to the animating moral principle of the prolife movement that no government ever has the authority to sanction the destruction of unborn human life.[2]

Constitutional amendments are passed and then ratified by groups of determined people who refuse to abandon what they know to be true. If compromises must come, let them come from the politicians, not from those who defend innocent people or from those who identify with the Lord Himself. Never from Christians.

1. *Washington Post*, 10 December 1983. See also *New York Times*, 7 December 1983.
2. US, Congress, Senate, *Congressional Record*, 129 S 9307 (28 June 1983).

We don't accept relativism in our personal conduct. We reject it in our professional endeavors. It should have no place in our political commitments, either. Justice is secured not by retreating from principles of justice, but rather by advancing them among our leaders and our countrymen.

CONCLUSION

There is no question that we are a number of years away from amending the Constitution. Action within the Supreme Court itself is more likely in the next five years. Regardless, no advances of any sort can be made apart from strong, local efforts to overcome abortion within communities. Although it may be legal, it can still be rendered illegitimate in a variety of ways. In this way we can build toward a consensus on this issue. The succeeding chapters deal with the duty of Christians in bringing this about with specific forms of witness and ministry.

13

The Responsibility
of the Church

It was Sunday afternoon, and I was exhausted. After two weeks
of work away from home, I faced another week in a different
city. My plane had just arrived in Phoenix, where I would train
volunteers to work in a new Crisis Pregnancy Center.

As I was greeted at the airport, the news came through smiles,
"We've arranged for you to speak in a church tonight!" I held on
with grim determination and began fumbling through my notes
trying to find something I could bless the saints with.

As we arrived at the church, I noticed in the lawn beside the
sanctuary a tombstone. It was not part of a cemetery associated
with the church but a lone piece of granite, lying flat in the grass.
I walked over to take a look. It said, To an Unborn Child.

I entered the church and awaited my opportunity to speak.
The pastor rose and greeted the people. Then he asked how many
had participated in the "Family Festival for Life" the previous
day. This was a fund-raising family event for the new Crisis
Pregnancy Center in the area. More hands shot up than I could
count, and the rest of the congregation applauded. I was over-
whelmed.

In those moments, my Lord refreshed me and confirmed again
what I know from the Word of God to be true and what I know
from my experience to be happening. God, by His Holy Spirit, is
writing the truth about human life not on tablets of mere stone

but on the tablets of human hearts. Around the United States, thousands of Christians are rallying to protect unborn children. Their action is not motivated by any political ideology, and it is not understood as something done in addition to the Christian walk. It is being done in Jesus' name and for His glory.

These Christians understand that abortion is fundamentally an attack against God. The authority of His Word is denied so that His creatures may be destroyed. Those Christ identified with most directly have become the victims of intolerable violence—weak, defenseless human beings.

To those who rally to protect and nurture them, Jesus says, "To the extent that you did it to one of these brothers of Mine, even the least of them, you did it to Me." To those who do nothing, He says, "Truly I say to you, to the extent that you did not do it to one of the least of these, you did not do it to Me" (Matthew 25:40, 45).

There is no question that God's Word calls us to heroic efforts to protect weak, defenseless people who are threatened with violence. "Deliver those who are being taken away to death, and those who are staggering to slaughter, O hold them back. If you say, 'See, we did not know this,' does He not consider it who weighs the hearts? And does He not know it who keeps your soul? And will He not render to man according to his work?" (Proverbs 24:11-12).

It is a matter of justice and a matter of love.

STANDING FOR RIGHTEOUSNESS

Christians have an obligation to expose lies and forward truth. Most Christians would agree that is the case when the debate centers upon the core truths of salvation or the authority of Scripture. But other categories of truth, portions of God's Word, are under attack as well. Those committed to the whole counsel of God should be prepared to defend every jot and tittle, such as the law of God "Thou shalt not kill."

Our secular society has long since passed over the doctrines of Scripture that relate to Christ and salvation. But a broad ethical and legal consensus based upon God's law has only recently disintegrated. The result in our day is a vitriolic attack on the moral truths of the Bible, especially the sanctity of human life. The debate is often legal in nature and occurs in legislatures rather than in ecclesiastical assemblies. The editorial pages of our nation's papers present a more likely forum for the airing of issues than theological volumes tucked away on bookshelves.

Regardless of the setting, however, it is the truth of God's Word that is under attack, and Christians loyal to the Author should feel challenged to respond.

> Blessed are those who have been persecuted for the sake of righteousness, for theirs is the kingdom of heaven. Blessed are you when men revile you, and persecute you, and say all kinds of evil against you falsely, on account of Me. Rejoice, and be glad, for your reward in heaven is great, for so they persecuted the prophets who were before you (Matthew 5:10-12).

The age of the Old Testament prophet is past. The prophets, Jesus taught His disciples, "were before you." But the prophetic function of standing for righteousness has not disappeared. It was preserved in the ministry of Jesus and passed on to His disciples. As a result they stand in the tradition of the prophets and can expect similar treatment to that which befell their predecessors.

There is only one other option Jesus gives His disciples. It is found in the succeeding passage where Jesus illustrates what it is to stand for righteousness: "You are the salt of the earth; but if the salt has become tasteless, how will it be made salty again? It is good for nothing any more, except to be thrown out and trampled under foot by men" (Matthew 5:13).

If we do not face persecution for our witness and work, we will face ridicule for our indifference and apathy. Either we are going to stand for righteousness, or men will walk all over us as though we were worthless salt.

Every Christian and every church makes a decision either to apply the truths of Scripture to society and work to see righteousness advanced, or else to shrink back, condemning what is taking place without working for biblical solutions to the desperate problems that do exist. The former leads to severe criticism. Even the Constitution is invoked to disqualify our work and witness. The latter leads to outrageous stereotypes and the characterization that we are mean-spirited, unloving, and self-righteous.

WHAT IS AT STAKE

Few times in American history has an injustice as grave as abortion occurred. Nonetheless, violence is now sanctioned, and unwanted human beings by the millions are being exterminated.

The church must respond. Its integrity and the credibility of its message are at stake. The proclamation of the gospel of Jesus Christ presupposes that the commands of God (His law) are a good and perfect standard by which men and nations are judged. It presupposes as well the failure of men to obey. When the church fails to bear witness to the good commands of God in a society that rejects them, it accommodates the sinfulness of man rather than the holiness of God. This directly affects the preaching of the gospel. Divine mercy is perverted into cheap grace.

Over the centuries, it has not been the easy sayings of the Bible that have resulted in the persecution and death of Christians, rather the hard sayings that reveal the condition of men, the content of true righteousness, and the uniqueness of Jesus as the one true Lord—both Savior and Judge. Nevertheless, from God's declaration of promise to Abraham (Genesis 18:19) to the Lord's Sermon on the Mount, God has revealed His expectation that His people stand for righteousness.

In our society, which has widely adopted the view that all truth is relative to the individual and that no truth is absolute, the perverse conviction has grown that commitment to principle necessarily involves a disregard for people. This topsy-turvy view of truth in relation to the welfare of people is self-defeating when it is the good of people that is being sought: "I call heaven and earth to witness against you today, that I have set before you life and death, the blessing and the curse. So choose life in order that you may live, you and your descendents [literally, seed]" (Deuteronomy 30:19).

After giving to His people the truth regarding Himself and how people were to behave in society, the Lord summed up the whole of obedience to His law in two words: choose life. When societies embrace God's law as the basis for their own laws and public policy, peace and order result. Justice is established and the innocent are protected. When individuals follow God's precepts, life goes better for them.

The society that rejects God's law rejects mercy, justice, and faithfulness (Matthew 23:23). It "chooses death." Right conduct is soon sacrificed as injustice replaces justice, and cruelty substitutes for compassion. The welfare of human beings suffers, and sometimes, as with abortion, violence is unleashed so that human beings may be killed. The society that rejects God has turned on itself.

God's precepts of justice restrain evil. Lawlessness unleashes pain, suffering, and death. It always produces casualties. As

Christians we are charged to resist the lawlessness of abortion or face Divine rebuke.

Like a trampled spring and a polluted well
Is a righteous man who gives way before the wicked.
(Proverbs 25:26)

LOVE YOUR NEIGHBOR

Throughout the Word of God, we are taught to love God and as a consequence to love our neighbors. Flowing directly from our relationship with God, love defines our social responsibility. We can hardly avoid this in reading the New Testament, where the Levitical passage "love your neighbor" is the most-quoted Old Testament Scripture.

Our relationship to God is directly indexed by how we treat or regard our neighbor. When we love God, we love our neighbor. When we hate God, we destroy our neighbor. When we're indifferent toward God, we're indifferent toward our neighbor. And who is my neighbor? Anyone within reach of my help.

There exists no substitute for our actively seeking our neighbor's good. Being "tied up" with religious observances and spiritual exercise proves no excuse before God. In the Old Testament God repeatedly rebukes Israel when, in the midst of intense religious activity, weak defenseless people are treated unjustly, and no one will defend them. In the mind of God, the peoples' concern for justice and mercy rather than their practice of God-ordained religious ritual revealed their heart toward Him. On this basis He judged Israel.

Jesus upheld and reinforced this standard. On two occasions he directly invoked the admonition of the prophet Hosea, "I desire compassion, and not sacrifice" (Matthew 9:13, 12:7; Hosea 6:6).

Love obliges us not only to care for neighbors who are the victims of injustice, but also to overcome the injustice itself so other neighbors may be spared. As an expression of Christ's love, we provide food for the hungry, care for the sick, clothing and shelter for the poor. Surely we must be prepared as well in the name of Christ's love to protect the defenseless unborn child and to secure justice for him. Indifference toward the plight of these humans is yet another inhumanity they suffer.

Confronting evil is never easy. It is difficult because evil always has a way of kicking back. It is especially difficult to attack an injustice like abortion that is widely accepted in society. In the course of opposing it, there comes opposition in return and the charge that we have fallen out of step with the twentieth century. No one except the bumpkin or the self-righteous can enjoy such criticism with the social isolation that accompanies it.

Nonetheless, if opposing evil is right, then it is something we should do. And for Christians there is the promise of comfort and *peace* through the Holy Spirit (2 Corinthians 1:3-5). There is as well the promise of triumph in Jesus Christ (Romans 8:31-39).

The Word of God teaches clearly that for Christians the issue is not whether the victory of righteousness is secure, but rather their persistence (Matthew 28:18; Ephesians 1:20-22. See Matthew 24:13; Hebrews 11:27; 12:1-2). Perseverance in overcoming evil is God's challenge to His people (2 Timothy 2:3; 4:5; James 1:12; 5:7-11). This is especially evident from the book of Revelation in Jesus' messages to the seven churches (Revelation 2-3).

Persevering faith is living faith, faith that expects God to deliver the afflicted and accomplish justice. In Psalm 27:13 King David wrote, "I would have despaired unless I had believed that I would see the goodness of the Lord in the land of the living." This is faith for our day as well.

CONCLUSION

Determination and confidence in our witness comes from the knowledge that our labor for the Lord is never in vain (1 Corinthians 15:58). There will come a day when we stand before Christ, and our labor done in His name will add to the weight of His glory. Before that day arrives, before our labor's impact is fully known, we have God's promise of fruitfulness now. As we conduct our lives and order our speech with authority as God's children, our Lord's redemptive power will be poured out upon this generation. Christians really can make the world a better place in which to live.

14

Objections to Involvement Considered

For many years I have worked with Christians to bring an end to abortion. I have learned that any number of concerns keep them from involving themselves. I can identify with some who raise objections, because at one time I had some myself.

When I agreed to serve as the executive director of the Christian Action Council, I was newly graduated from a fine seminary. The seminary experience comprises the good things of evangelicalism along with its cultural biases and prejudices. So my head was full of wonderful ideas and hopes that come from an intensive education in the Word of God. At the same time, I had some confusing feelings and attitudes.

Was valid ministry possible outside the setting of a local church? Was an attempt to advocate the truth before my culture appropriate? Should I as a Christian stand for the justice of God as well as for His mercy in Christ?

Gradually, I came to realize that Jesus Christ is Lord of all. He's not just "my Lord," "your Lord," or Lord of the church. Rather He is Lord over every principality, power, creature, and thing. As a result His Word is authoritative over every decision, in every situation, on every issue, in every life. If temporal authorities or institutions war against Christ and reject His authority over them, then it is right that His disciples oppose them and work to overcome the evil they promote. We exalt Christ as Lord not only by worshiping Him as Lord but also by applying biblical truths to our lives and to the operations of society.

Objections to involvement in the struggle to resist abortion and related violence should not be lightly dismissed. They deserve careful consideration.

OBJECTION 1: SEPARATION OF CHURCH AND STATE

On a number of occasions pastors or Christian leaders have told me they will not participate in efforts to protect unborn children because they believe in the separation of church and state. Their fear seems to be that Christians go beyond their civic duty or moral responsibility and enter a forbidden zone of activity when they attempt to influence the state.

"Separation of church and state" is a slogan; like any slogan, it can be used to encapsulate a truth or conceal a lie. Many people on hearing the phrase assume some hallowed precept in the US Constitution is being quoted. In fact it never appears there.

The first amendment to the Constitution, Article 1 of the Bill of Rights, deals with the freedom of religion along with freedom of the press and the freedom of citizens to assemble.

> Congress shall make no law respecting an establishment of religion, or prohibiting the free exercise thereof; or abridging the freedom of speech, or of the press; or the right of the people to peaceably assemble, and to petition the government for a redress of grievances.

Two clauses make up the section on religion, the "establishment clause" and the "free exercise clause." These reflect two concerns of the framers.

The "establishment clause" forbids the federal government (Congress) from elevating one religion to the status of an official national religion, for this would be to the detriment of others. The inclusion of this in the Bill of Rights was necessary for the ratification of the Constitution by all thirteen states. A number had already established state churches within their jurisdictions. They feared the federal government might attempt to interfere with their policies and force them to embrace a national church. The former colonists' memories of the British Crown's special sanctions for the Anglican Church and against other faiths were too vivid to forget. The new government must not repeat the abuses.

The "free exercise clause" forbids the government (Congress) from suppressing or interfering with religious expression. This is not unqualified; people may not do anything they wish in the name of religion, such as killing others. Nonetheless, God-fearing people have the freedom to practice their faith within the United States, and no federal edict may contradict this. The motivation behind the free exercise clause was to protect churches from state interference and regulation as well as preserving the freedom of conscience. The assumption was that the exercise of religion was good for men and society, and that Congress should be favorably disposed toward it.

This is well illustrated by actions taken by the Congress in 1787, when it was composed largely of men who had served as delegates to the Federal Convention in Philadelphia where the Constitution was drafted. In 1787 and again in 1789, the Congress passed the Northwest Ordinance. These laws partitioned the frontier in what is now the Midwest into sections for settlement by the westward-bound pioneers. They required that land be set aside for education. They provided as well the rationale behind the law.

> Religion, morality, and knowledge being essential to good government and the happiness of mankind, schools and the means of education shall forever be encouraged.[1]

Those who set a course for this nation and enshrined that course in the Constitution believed religion (recognized then as Christianity in its various expressions) is quite simply good for people and good for the government, promoting right conduct and social order. The government should encourage it, and public education should teach it.

The phrase "separation of church and state," was first used in a letter written by Thomas Jefferson to a group of Baptist ministers in 1802.[2] In it he described the Constitution's guarantee of religious freedom by writing that the Constitution had erected "a wall of separation between church and state." His point was to assure this group of ministers that the church would forever be protected from the government.

1. Ordinance of 1787, 13 July 1787, Art. 3; reprinted in *Documents Illustrative of the Formation of the Union of American States*, 52 (1927).
2. John W. Whitehead and John Conlan, "The Establishment of the Religion of Secular Humanism and Its First Amendment Implications," *Texas Tech Law Review* 10, no. 1 (Winter 1978):4, n. 15.

Like other framers of the Constitution, Jefferson felt strongly that religious knowledge is a healthy influence on society and government. On this basis he encouraged religious instruction at the University of Virginia, which he founded in 1819. He explained his position in light of his "wall of separation" language:

> It was not . . . to be understood that instruction in religous opinion and duties was meant to be precluded by the public authorities, as indifferent to the interests of society. On the contrary, the relations which exist between man and his Maker, and the duties resulting from these relations, are the most interesting and important to every human being, and the most incumbent on his study and investigation.[3]

The Constitutional "wall of separation between church and state" is a hedge against state attempts to control the practices of church bodies or the faith of their adherents. This guarantee of religious freedom was never intended to prohibit religious people's exercising free speech and influencing the state. In fact, that was occurring, and the assumption was that that kind of influence *should* occur.

Today "separation of church and state" is used to connote a very different message that is completely contrary to those rights embodied in the First Amendment. Because of the slogan's past association with the First Amendment guarantee of religious freedom, the new message tends to be accepted without proper scrutiny.

With society's acceptance of a totally secular approach to law and public policy, religion has acquired a hostile audience. Many view the Christian viewpoint as an antiquated and false view of life. Under the banner of the separation of church and state, an antagonistic press, along with groups such as the American Civil Liberties Union, now argue that Christians may not influence law and social policy because their religious convictions motivate them and influence the proposals they support.

These critics invoke the First Amendment as justification but never quote it, of course. For they are trying to deny to an entire class of people access to the democratic process by appealing to the portion of the Constitution that guarantees such access. It is one thing to charge that Christians have nothing to say. It is quite another to charge they have no right to say it or that the government must not listen.

3. *The Writings of Thomas Jefferson*, Paul Leicester Ford, ed. Memorial Edition (New York: G. P. Putnam's, 1904), pp. 414-17.

Nevertheless, over the last ten years, the ACLU has repeatedly construed the abortion issue as a First Amendment matter, denouncing the involvement of Christians in efforts to stop it. They argue that any law prohibiting abortion or the use of federal funds for abortion represents an "establishment of religion" because their passage is motivated by a religious belief in the sanctity of human life. This is a dangerous argument since laws against murder, theft, and other crimes result from a similar motivation and are grounded in the same religious moral code. Should they be unconstitutional too?

This is also a frivolous argument. The ACLU brings religious leaders to testify before Congress whenever hearings are held on the prohibition of capital punishment. On such occasions the sanctity of human life is repeatedly invoked.

The ACLU's appeal to the First Amendment in support of abortion extends to the "free exercise clause." They argue that procuring an abortion is a religious matter for some, and therefore attempts to prohibit abortion violate the free exercise of those individuals' religion. In fact their attorneys have gone further and charged the government has a (sacred?) duty to fund abortions for such women when they cannot afford to pay for them. On this view, abortion is a religious rite the government is uniquely obligated to subsidize.

At least one Federal District Court judge sustained this point. Judge John Dooling of Brooklyn made the following declaration in support of his decision that the government is obligated to fund permissive abortion under Medicaid.

> A woman's conscientious decision, in consultation with her physician, to terminate her pregnancy . . . is an exercise of the most fundamental of rights, nearly allied to her right to be, surely part of the liberty protected by the Fifth Amendment, doubly protected when the liberty is exercised in conformity with religious belief and teaching protected by the First Amendment. *To deny necessary medical assistance for the lawful and medically necessary procedure of abortion is to violate the pregnant woman's First and Fifth Amendment rights.* (Emphasis added)[4]

Hostility toward the truths of God's Word is not new, nor is hostility toward His people. Few Christians are aware, however, of how this is being worked out in the abortion debate under the banner "separation of church and state."

4. *McRae v. Secretary of HEW,* US District Court, Eastern Division of New York, 76 C 1804.

In 1980 the Supreme Court heard arguments in a case involving the constitutionality of laws prohibiting the use of federal funds for abortion under Medicaid. At one point, Justice Potter Stuart had the following exchange with ACLU attorney Rhonda Copeland.

Justice Stuart: "Is it permissible for religiously motivated people to lobby?

Ms. Copeland: "To some extent."

Justice Stuart: "You mean as long as they don't succeed."[5]

The new prejudice that is acceptable in elite circles today is prejudice against religious people who believe in the fundamental moral precepts revealed in God's Word. Frequently I have been told that I am trying to impose my morality on others, when in fact just the opposite is occurring. We don't claim that secular people cannot influence public policy unless they speak as Christians. But the argument is made that "religious" people cannot influence public policy because they do so as "religious" (read Christian) people. Only if we speak as totally secular people should our voice be heard. This is where the imposition is occurring and true freedom is threatened. Everyone has a right, whether creedal or creedless, to persuade society and influence government to adopt his viewpoint on any issue.

If the Constitution of the United States and laws throughout the nation were to prohibit Christians from expressing their belief in the sanctity of human life, confronting the government with the injustice of abortion, and speaking to the conscience of our society, we would have no choice but to violate those laws. We serve one Master, and He tells us to defend the least among us. The "separation of church and state" is hardly a justification for noninvolvement.

OBJECTION 2: "I DON'T GET INVOLVED IN POLITICS"

Several years ago while in Chicago, I conducted a Bible study for the elders of a very fine evangelical church. When I announced the study would be in Amos, one of the elders turned to an assistant pastor and asked where Amos was. The young man quipped, "In the clean part of your Bible." Sure enough, those pages were as clean as the day they were printed.

The study focused upon the responsibility of God's people to speak to issues of righteousness in their society, and I decided to

5. *Action Line* 4, no. 4 (1 June 1980).

apply this lesson to the matter of abortion. Afterward the assistant came up to me and said, "I agree with you totally that abortion is wrong, but I don't get involved in politics. I just preach the gospel."

The remark summarized well the longstanding prejudice of many Christians toward political involvement and the assumption that a contradiction exists between Christian duty and political involvement. But if the "clean parts" of the Bible were studied more, Christians would recognize the prophetic task they have in any society in which they find themselves.

Most Christians heartily approve of the role the Bible played in shaping the values and policies of this nation. Their hearts are full of gratitude for the rights they enjoy as a result of the application of biblical principles to temporal laws. With considerable pride, they point to the United States as a nation that was founded upon belief in God as the sovereign Lord and Creator.

All of those sentiments are as they should be. God's Word speaks to the state in very definite ways, defining its duty to protect the innocent and punish the guilty. The Bible as well teaches the dignity of the individual before God and establishes a standard of justice whereby the weak have rights, too, even if they can't defend them. When John Wycliffe translated the Bible from Latin into English in 1382, he declared in a preface the noble purpose behind his effort: "This Bible is intended for the government of the People, by the People, and for the People." Few individuals know the alleged origin of this phrase, and fewer still recognize the Book that makes this hope a reality.

God's Word had a tremendous impact on the formation of the United States, because for generations Christians had taught its relevance to the affairs of state. The heirs of this teaching accepted their responsibility to speak to issues of the day, finding biblical solutions to thorny legal and social questions.

When Christians today refuse to participate in representative government and complain that this nation is following an evil course, they bear a portion of the responsibility. When Christians fail to vote and interact with their elected representatives, complaining that politics is corrupt and nasty business, they serve only to keep politics corrupt and nasty.

Preaching the gospel is more important than voting or writing a legislator, visiting a congressman, or running for the school board. In all my years of activism, however, I have never been forced to choose between them. I vote, I write letters, I meet with legislators. None of those activities hinders me from preaching Christ and communicating the gospel. Over the course of time, in fact, my "political involvement" has presented me with many opportunities to speak of Christ with people I would never have otherwise known.

Politics is nothing more than the art of government. Wherever decisions are made to govern and influence society, the truths of God's word should be upheld. This is a duty for Christians to perform whether in the politics of the state, the politics of the workplace, or the politics of the church. When government is based upon biblical standards, the governed are taught to fear God and respect men. This is not preaching the gospel, but it does serve to prepare hearts for the message of Christ.

It was politically significant that God brought Paul to Rome to appear before Caesar (Acts 28:19). It was politically significant that under Paul's ministry, members of Caesar's household became Christians (Philippians 4:22). It was politically significant that by the end of the first century A.D., members of Caesar's family were believers,[6] and that by the beginning of the fourth century A.D., Caesar himself was a Christian. As men and women in positions of influence came to faith in Christ, they began to apply His truths where they could, ending injustice and demonstrating the mercy and righteousness of their God. There is no shame in it.

I often wonder at the reluctance of Christians to bring the truth they know to bear upon society when those who reject it are so militant in their involvement. Perhaps this is due to some sort of fatalism—that after all, it doesn't matter what we do because all the world is in the hands of the Evil One.

I have never accepted this view because it is contrary to the Bible. The New Testament is a briefing book for Christian soldiers, not an excuse for Christian cowardice. News of Satan's strongholds in the earth should not send us whimpering to our sanctuaries. On the contrary, this information tells us where the enemy camps, where the next battle should be fought. Jesus promises every generation of His disciples that the gates of hell cannot withstand their charge (Matthew 16:18). We have every reason to advance against the kingdom of darkness with boldness and love.

The apostle Paul repeatedly uses military imagery to depict the Christian walk (2 Corinthians 10:3-5; Ephesians 6:10-20; 2

---

6. F. F. Bruce, *New Testament History* (Garden City, N.Y.: Doubleday, 1972), pp. 413-14.

Timothy 2:3-4). Throughout the book of Acts we see many examples of militant Christian faith. It is never disrespectful but always firm. The apostles were willing to confront and resist authority, to venture into the most hostile environment imaginable for the glory of Christ, to bring His truth to bear wherever they might. We should be no less militant in matters pertaining to the righteousness and love of our God in this day.

OBJECTION 3: ABORTION IS TOO CONTROVERSIAL

I had been invited to speak by an assistant pastor of one of the largest evangelical churches in Georgia. The denomination associated with the church boasts one of the strongest official statements of any against abortion. I assumed I was among people who shared my convictions.

Soon after my arrival I was informed that I would be given three minutes in the Sunday evening service rather than twenty-five. My message was to consist of a very brief introduction to the work and witness of the Christian Action Council.

Eventually an explanation was forthcoming. I was told the decision had been made not to raise the abortion issue in the church. Many leading citizens in the community were part of the congregation, including at least one physician who favored abortion. Abortion was just too controversial.

I was shocked. I might have expected this had I been in a liberal church that supported abortion.

When my opportunity came to speak, I crammed as much information on abortion as is humanly possible into three minutes. People looked receptive, and I offered to meet with anyone after the service to answer questions.

The head pastor took the pulpit and thanked me for the information. Then, as if to assure that peace would reign, he said, "Abortion is a serious problem in this country. But we can be grateful that no abortions are performed in our town."

There were no abortion clinics in the community at that time, but that did not mean abortions weren't being performed. Within twelve months, however, two clinics were operating there, one within sight of the congregation as they entered their church for Sunday morning worship. The salt had proved tasteless. Fearing no protests, the abortionists moved in.

I fear when preachers of the gospel refuse to declare grave sin as wickedness. In order to avoid causing offense to men, they offend God, compromising His truth and obscuring His holy character. Indeed the gospel itself is compromised as men are lulled into a false sense of security before God. While approving the destruction of those He creates in His image, they presume to walk in His favor. God's grace is not lawless:

> Not everyone who says to Me, "Lord, Lord," will enter the kingdom of heaven; but he who does the will of My Father who is in heaven. Many will say to Me on that day, "Lord, Lord, did we not prophesy in Your name, and in Your name cast out demons, and in Your name perform many miracles?" And then I will declare to them, "I never knew you; Depart from Me, you who practice lawlessness." (Matthew 7:21-23)

I can certainly sympathize with the concern of ministers in dealing with abortion when members of their congregation have had abortions. Since at least 10 percent of women of childbearing age have had one abortion, I assume that whenever I speak before groups, men and women are present who know firsthand what abortion is like. For the women and families involved, there is always pain and regret, and no one should seek to add to those. That pain and regret, however, are yet another reason churches must deal with the issue, taking a firm stand against the violence.

We are uniquely equipped to do this. At once we can present the gospel of Christ's love and forgiveness to hurting people and teach what the Bible says about human life to those who may be confronted with a crisis pregnancy in their own lives or relationships.

How much pain and grief are avoided when Christians learn God makes no mistakes in creating human beings, or that human life in the womb is sacred to Him! I have long since discarded the notion that good Christian families aren't involved with abortion, because many are. Often I am approached by people in great distress asking why they had never been taught that abortion is wrong. It is a joy for me to lead them out from under the condemnation they feel, but I grieve that they were not warned. Controversial or not, the issue must be addressed.

OBJECTION 4: "WE'RE PURSUING THE BEST THINGS"

The tour of the church property was completed. It was big. The budget was large, and membership was growing steadily. I was impressed and hopeful. I had been sent on a good-will mission for one of our Crisis Pregnancy Centers. My job was to pursuade the pastor that the CPC was worthy of the church's mission support. I was about to be disappointed.

"I'm sorry," he said, "but you have to understand we want to be involved not just in good things but in the best things. My first priority is to save souls, not the lives of unborn infants who are going to heaven anyway." I appreciated the honesty in his reply to my request. Reaching out in Jesus' name to women with crisis pregnancies was not a priority. There was no room in the church for this kind of ministry. The violence of abortion could be tolerated because the victims of the injustice ended up with the Lord. I was tempted to ask how he felt about the murder of Christians.

In touring the facility, I had been shown the plans for a new building project. Another big edifice would soon be erected for the Body of Christ. No support, however, could be found for a gospel ministry that included providing material assistance to frightened, broken people.

I am not surprised that among churches using a budget/membership index to measure success there is no time to reach out to people possessing nothing, requiring large amounts of personal attention, and offering very little in the way of return on the church's investment of time and resources. Nevertheless, it saddens me greatly and breaks with a tradition of mercy that has given the church a noble heritage.

Historically, American churches have sent missionaries to remote places throughout the world with the understanding—it has ample precedent—they are to serve rather than to be served. They are to sacrifice their lives with no expectation of reward or adulation. These courageous people have done just that. In addition food, shelter, clothing, medical care, tools, and instruction have been provided as free love-gifts to everyone in need, not as rewards to those who prove receptive to the gospel. As a result, as the gospel has been preached, millions have embraced the Savior.

Among many American churches today, a different orientation has developed. With the exception of token financial or personal involvement in ministries to the downtrodden (the urban poor, prisoners, the elderly), only those ministries that serve to increase church numbers are acceptable. If a doctrine of Scripture is controversial or unpopular, you will not hear it from the pulpit, and if a redemptive ministry comes along that requires a true sacrifice on behalf of others, little place can be found for it.

As far as numbers and influence are concerned, Jesus' ministry was unimpressive. Our Lord wasn't interested in courting the rich or in attracting great multitudes of followers. He concentrated His efforts on the lowly, caring for them like a shepherd tending soiled, injured sheep. His care for others was not contingent upon their bowing before Him as Lord of the Universe. Neither should ours be. Our integrity as Christians is at stake and so are the souls of countless mothers and fathers.

OBJECTION 5: "I DON'T KNOW WHAT TO DO"

Every day in our office, a sack of letters arrives. Many record the agony that is felt by Christians as they realize for the first time what legal abortion means. Very often they express frustration over what to do. They don't know how to be effective in turning back such a monumental injustice or how they can actually help women facing unplanned pregnancies.

When God commanded Zechariah to rebuild the Temple, the prophet obeyed. The task was immense, and the resources were so few. The labor appeared as folly to many, and they scoffed at Zechariah. Through this man of God, the Lord responded, daring the scoffers to approach Him directly: "Who has despised the day of small things?" (Zechariah 4:10). The Temple was rebuilt, and those who scoffed were put to shame.

CONCLUSION

God uses ordinary people to accomplish extraordinary things for Him. He blesses the efforts of those who trust Him. He looks for people through whom He may be glorified. There is a great deal Christians can do to stop abortion and related violence.

15

Faith with Works, Part 1: What Your Church Can Do

Armed with the truth of God's Word and the love of Christ, churches are uniquely suited to address the human tragedy of abortion. Without disrupting other vital ministries, churches can effectively deal with the problem of abortion both within their congregations and throughout their communities. People who have suffered abortion can be brought to forgiveness and the knowledge of Christ. Those who face abortion can be taught the better way of choosing life and assisted in doing so. Young adults and others can be directed from the Word of God into an understanding of sexuality and marriage that is both positive and persuasive so they are spared altogether the pain of a crisis pregnancy. Leaders within the community can be taught from Scripture that they are accountable before God to protect the innocent, including the unborn. Finally, they can be encouraged to do so.

FROM THE PULPIT

> The preacher who is the messenger of God, is the real master of society, not elected by society to be its ruler, but elect of God to form its ideals and through them to guide and rule its life. Show me the man who, in the midst of a community, however secularized in manners, can compel it to think with him, can kindle its enthusiasm, revive its faith, cleanse its passions, purify its ambitions, and give steadfastness to its will, and I will show you the real master of

161

society, no matter what party may nominally hold the reigns of government, no matter what figurehead may occupy the ostensible place of authority.[1]

There is no question that the preacher can be a powerful influence on his own congregation and on the standards of his community if he is willing, unashamedly and without compromise, to proclaim the Word of God. Preachers are not ordinary men. They are men called and empowered by God's Spirit to be His spokesmen. Those who clothe themselves with humility and proclaim fearlessly the whole counsel of God fulfill their mission and bring glory to Jesus Christ.

The temptation to "peddle" the Word of God always exists, of course—to make the hard words of God soft or to ignore the controversial ones. On several occasions colleagues in ministry have confided they fear for their jobs if they preach in a straightforward way on abortion. Perhaps they are right. But what sort of job do they have if it requires silence on any portion of God's Word? It is not ministry in Christ's name, no matter how often the claim is made, no matter how fast the congregation is growing. Preachers among all people cannot serve two masters. If we bow to fear or intimidation, we forfeit our authority as God's children and grieve the Holy Spirit, who came that we might know the truth and have the courage to die for it. Inadvertently we serve the murderer and liar, Satan.

The preacher is obliged especially to uphold those truths that are deliberately ignored or assaulted. Through this witness he fulfills the commandment of God to "[convince] some, who are doubting; save others, snatching them out of the fire" (Jude 22-23). This is the faithfulness in an evil day.

> If I profess with the loudest voice and clearest exposition every portion of the truth of God except precisely that little point which the world and the devil are at the moment attacking, I am not confessing Christ, however boldly I may be professing Christ. Where the battle rages, there the loyalty of the soldier is proved, and to be steady on all the battlefield besides, is mere flight and disgrace if he flinches at that point.[2]

No point of God's truth is more directly under attack in our day than the sanctity of human life. This is not an academic

1. Charles Sylvester Horne, lecture, Yale University, 1914.
2. Martin Luther, quoted in Francis A. Schaeffer, *The God Who Is There* (Downers Grove, Ill.: Inter-Varsity, 1968), p. 18.

matter. The result is the destruction of human beings on a scale that no one can imagine. Singer Annie Herring's release is one attempt to capture the horror of it: "My God, They're Killing Thousands!"

Much biblical teaching bears directly on the sanctity of human life: The creation of man in God's image; the judgment of God against violence; the involvement of God in creating human beings before birth; the incarnation of Jesus Christ. Men of the Word have much to draw from in defending the sanctity of human life.

In addition the Word of God provides extensive teaching on how God's people are to respond to injustice that results when the value of human beings is denied: Stand for righteousness; love your neighbor as yourself; rescue the defenseless; comfort the afflicted; pursue justice; deliver those in distress; obey the law of God over the laws of men. The major part of obedience rests not in proclaiming the truth but in putting that truth to work.

The result of faithful, consistent preaching has always been changed lives. As believers have been edified and instructed in their duty before God, they have taken the truths they know and applied them whenever and wherever they had opportunity to do so—as parents, as employers or employees, as public officials, as citizens, as workers in ministries outside the church. With the Bible as their guide, they have devoted their training, backgrounds, and skills to solving human problems. Through these efforts Christ's love has been evident, and opportunities to share the gospel have multiplied. Christian attorneys, doctors, social workers, legislators, teachers, engineers, and a host of others are qualified to advance the cause of Christ in unique ways in their society. The preacher has the privilege of discipling them from the Word.

Many pastors fear "politicizing" the pulpit or their broader ministry, and I share their concern for a variety of reasons. Some are very practical. Denouncing or endorsing candidates for public office destroys the pastor's ability to confront them from the law of God or to share Christ's love with them. This is just as true for candidates they support as for those they oppose. The politician regards preachers *only* as a political asset or liability if they relate to him politically. They represent a bloc of votes and nothing more.

It is true that most politicians on most issues respond only to political pressure, basing their decisions on how those will affect their standing with voters or the elites they want to impress. Christian citizens should be wise to this; it is part of life. But the work of the pastor in regard to public officials is not defined in terms of political pressure.

The pastor's job is one of instruction, encouragement, and confrontation from the Word of God. His demeanor should be characterized by humility, not belligerence. His motivation must be love for his holy and righteous God, not anger toward the individual. In order to execute the ministry of the Word, he must be willing and prepared to confront secular authorities over the injustices they support and to call them to repentence around the gospel. They must be prepared as well to praise authorities for their just decisions, drawing attention to the Source of justice. These tasks as much as prayer are part of biblical ministry, not politics. Martin Luther summed up well this responsibility of the preacher in terms of a mother cat's duty to clean her offspring:

> We should wash the fur of the magistrate and clean out his mouth whether he laughs or rages. Christ has instructed us preachers not to withhold the truth from the lords but to exhort and chide them in their injustice. Christ did not say to Pilate, "You have no power over me." He said that Pilate did have the power, but He said, "You do not have this power from yourself. It is given to you from God." Therefore He upbraided Pilate. We do the same. We recognize the authority, but we must rebuke our Pilates in their crime and self-confidence. . . . We must confess the truth and rebuke the evil. There is a big difference between suffering injustice and keeping still. We should suffer. We should not keep still.[3]

There always exists the temptation to defer to the wealthy and powerful, whether in our congregation or our community. Those whose impact for good or evil is broadest in society are often the very ones we are least willing to evangelize, encourage, or admonish. James addresses this problem in particular as it relates to church life. Especially within the Body of Christ, failure to teach and admonish brings disgrace on a church, not to mention embarrassment.

Having traveled throughout the United States for several years, I am amazed at the way God has blessed the ministries of men who are humble in themselves but willing to uphold the truth about abortion no matter how hostile the reaction may be.

---

3. Roland Bainton, *Here I Stand: A Life of Martin Luther* (New York: Abingdon, 1950), pp. 244-45.

In Washington State, a very dedicated young pastor was planting a church when he was confronted with the opportunity to take a strong public stand against abortion. He could have deferred out of fear for how this would affect the growth of his young fellowship. The church growth books he had read said that taking a stand on a controversial issue is bad. He followed his conscience and the Word of God, however, instead of the manuals. From the Bible, He began speaking out against abortion in totally secular assemblies. Today he attributes half the church's membership to his public witness.

Men and women are looking for clear direction from the Word of God. They are hungry to hear preachers who have the courage to proclaim the righteousness of God and the lordship of Jesus Christ, not in abstract ways but in terms of the issues and struggles they face daily. May God raise up mighty men who love Him, like the sons of Issachar, "men who understood the times, with knowledge of what . . . [to] do" (1 Chronicles 12:32).

IN THE PEW

In many Bible-believing churches, the form of government is such that the congregation hires and fires the pastor. As a result, some pastors express reluctance to preach on matters to which the Bible speaks when they feel no support from the congregation to do so. Church members can do a great deal to encourage their pastor to be strong and forthright in declaring the value and dignity of human life. With their prayers they can undergird his ministry. With their words they can let him know that his sermons and teaching in opposition to abortion are appreciated. In addition they can supply him with a good fact-filled literature on the abortion question. As one who pastored a church, I know how much I appreciated receiving concise, accurate information from the members. The pastor's schedule is often so busy he has no time to research a matter like abortion.

IN THE WORSHIP SERVICE

Worship services can be developed around any of the great truths of Scripture. The sanctity of human life is one of those. A service in which we give praise to God for creating us in His image is a powerful teaching experience as well. We cannot learn about man as a creature formed by God without growing in our hatred of violence. We cannot confess with David that God knit us in our mothers' wombs without increasing our regard for the unborn child. We cannot appreciate the incarnation of Jesus Christ without realizing how valuable human life is.

The Christian Action Council helped several thousand churches develop a "Sanctity of Human Life Sunday" on January 22, 1984. This was the eleventh anniversary of the Supreme Court's abortion decision. Through this experience we discovered how great the impact can be when Bible-believing churches in a community celebrate the sanctity of human life on the same Sunday. The coordination of worship had a dramatic effect in many towns and cities as the truth was clearly and boldly proclaimed. The event was covered in the press. Many people heard the truth about human life for the first time. They also heard about Christ. Christians were encouraged to see that fellow believers shared their convictions. Commitments resulted to establish ministries to women with crisis pregnancies and to actively resist abortion locally.

IN PASTORAL MINISTRY

Most of the ministries the church can undertake to halt abortion are preventive. But what of the people who have participated in abortion and now experience the violence every day of their lives? Ministry to these victims is a challenge that can be met only with compassion and the gospel. Only through Christ's love and forgiveness can men, women, and couples be delivered from the guilt, pain, and anger that follow in the wake of abortion.

Biblical ministry in this area is the opposite of its secular counterpart. Secular counseling leads a woman to accept her abortion and look for ways to grow through the experience. There is no resolution of the guilt she feels, only rationalization. Behavior modification therapy may be used to change destructive behaviors that have developed in an effort to deal with guilt. At best the approach is superficial and limited.

In order to minister effectively to the woman who has gone through abortion, she must be encouraged to express the anguish she feels. With great compassion, the minister should give her whatever time is necessary to tell her story. As the counselee trusts the minister and senses his acceptance, she is freed to express the cause of her pain directly. So often this is summed up in four words, "I killed my baby."

By providing this kind of supportive relationship where the woman is allowed to confess her abortion, she is enabled to face it herself. This is absolutely necessary before healing can begin.

Having acknowledged the truth about her abortion, the woman is able to mourn the loss of her baby. She should be encouraged to do this. As she moves through the grieving process, she instinctively moves out of the role she played in the abortion and into the role of mother. Granted, these two contradict each other absolutely. Her role in the abortion was a perversion of her maternal role. This is precisely why grieving is so important. For the mother to regain her dignity and self-respect, she must make the transition in regard to her child, accepting motherhood and repudiating her role as executioner. I am aware of no other way to recover from an abortion.

The woman's psyche inevitably forces her to accept motherhood. Unless the role of executioner is repudiated, the mother will experience a brutal conflict. Responding to her nurturing instinct, she condemns herself for the abortion. Justifying her conduct, she represses an essential part of her personality as a woman. The result is emotional strain that distorts the personality.

In order to repudiate the abortion and separate herself from the role she played, the woman coming for counsel must be released from the responsibility she bears. The Lord Jesus alone can do this for her, not a minister, family, or friends. Their acceptance is an important expression of the forgiveness Christ offers, but Christ alone can forgive.

The minister must be prepared to carefully and thoroughly present Christ's ministry so she sees that His love is boundless. He must explain Christ's sacrificial suffering and death so she understands the extent of sin's power over men. Lastly, the minister must unfold Jesus' resurrection from the dead so she recognizes the greater power of mercy and redemption that Christ alone possesses. Only when the good news has been explained and accepted can the mother in confidence turn to the Lord as her Savior. Through this work of grace, she is renewed by the same Spirit that raised Christ from the dead.

IN THE SUNDAY SCHOOL

Many churches today are studying contemporary social and moral issues in light of God's Word. The life issues—abortion, infanticide, and euthanasia—are typically at the top of the list, as they should be. This is very encouraging, especially when Sunday school classes progress beyond study to involve themselves in ministries, like a Crisis Pregnancy Center, that actually deal with the human problems.

There is another subject that must be addressed biblically, either in Sunday school or during other teaching opportunities. The subject is human sexuality, and the students should be adolescents, with their parents' approval *and* participation.

Never before has our society's understanding of sexuality been more in conflict with biblical teaching. Young men and women growing up in our churches are exposed to powerful influences that scorn Scripture's admonitions to purity, the sanctity of the marriage relationships, and the absolute condemnation of homosexuality. These influences occur as examples within the family or among friends, strong approval of promiscuity in contemporary literature, music and television programming, and federally funded sex education programs from organizations like Planned Parenthood, which are totally amoral in their approach. Sex is presented as an isolated experience of pleasure unrelated to the rest of life. Our children need direction from the Bible.

It is no coincidence that the abortion revolution in the seventies followed upon the sexual revolution of the sixties. In light of permissive sexual behavior, abortion is presented as a social necessity. Both are justified in the name of "quality of life." This is ironic in a sad way because the result has been the exploitation of millions of adults and the deaths of millions of children. These tragedies can be avoided in the lives of our children if they are taught the truth and encouraged to obey it.

In every aspect of life, biblical truth is liberating. Obedience leads to joy and true fulfillment. The Bible's teaching on marriage, the nature of sexuality, and love is inspiring and realistic at the same time. Paul repeatedly teaches that our sexuality is a force in our lives and nothing to be ashamed of. Genesis reveals that it is a gift from God and a source of human creativity. Nowhere is this more evident than in love between a man and a woman; that love can issue forth in new life. Proverbs teaches that sexual intimacy in marriage should be exhilarating and satisfying always. Paul shows that marriage is a refuge in Christ where tender affection, encouragement, and help are abundant. Our Lord teaches so vividly that true love never sacrifices others for self but sacrifices self for others.

At the same time scriptural principles are taught, young adults are curious to know how this is worked out in people's lives. Coming from broken homes, many teens have never been exposed to a healthy marriage, a stable father figure, or a happy family. Testimonies can be very useful in answering many questions. I know of no better way to convey the impact of obedience or disobedience to the good commands of God. Younger and older couples can share their experiences in marriage. Young parents can bring their baby and discuss what their love means in terms of commitment and dirty diapers. A single mother can share her experience with the class, as can a divorced person or someone who suffered abortion. Christian adults who were sexually involved outside of marriage can talk about the effects of their behavior on themselves and others.

Last, young adults need to think through the possible consequences of sexual sin or purity in their own lives. Open-ended questions are useful in leading them to consider the destructive ways sex is used in relationships. Divided into small groups they can imagine life after the relationship is over. The effects of venereal disease and unexpected pregnancy should not be overlooked, along with their impact on career and marriage goals. Positive considerations can focus on the deepest longings of students. They especially want to be loved and accepted so they can love in return. That love and the families it produces are gained only with sacrifice. This is a tremendous incentive to reject peer pressure and strive for God's best.

IN THE CHURCH LIBRARY

Many outstanding books have been published on abortion, infanticide, and euthanasia. Churches serve their people well when they include these works in their libraries. The information they contain is useful to students in classwork, to teachers and study groups within the church, and to all Christians who want to encourage righteousness in their communities.

IN THE PRAYER MEETING

Churches have a powerful weapon with which to stop abortion—prayer. Paul makes clear in Ephesians 6:10-18 that prayer is the weapon of Christian warriors who "stand firm against the schemes of the devil." Prayer is no substitute for effort but ennobles effort done in Christ's name. Through prayer Christians exercise their authority as the children of God over the affairs of men.

To understand fully what is taking place in abortion and related violence, these must be spiritually discerned. When they are, the need for prayer becomes obvious. The principalities and powers are keenly involved with the violence that is now taking place. Satan is delighted to see an entire civilization reject not only the truth of God's Word, but also the truth He places in men, that it instinctively is good to protect and nurture our children. The destruction of life is joy to the evil one; deception is his chief weapon. The end of fatherhood, motherhood, and the family are necessary for his control to increase. Eventually, the accumulated power of his dominion will be unleashed on the one group he hates the most, God's people. Christian complacency in our day guarantees Christian suffering in his.

There is no substitute for prayer. The demands of life as well as the fatigue they produce can threaten to reduce our prayer time to insignificance. We cannot avoid the admonitions in Scripture to pray without emptying our lives of the power to complete whatever mission God has for us. God desires holiness—in fact, He commands it. This is not possible apart from prayer, for this exercise of faith is the only means by which we can draw near to God. Unless we do so, we will fail to resist evil. The devil will not flee from us.

Beginning with ourselves, Christians must repent of indifference within the church and pray that God will stir up the Body of Christ throughout the land. As churches lift their complaint to God, imploring Him to vindicate the weak and establish justice, He hears those prayers. As they beseech Him for direction, He gives it. He has heard and answered similar prayers before. In *Abortion and the Conscience of the Nation*, Ronald Reagan wrote:

> I have often said we need to join in prayer to bring protection to the unborn. Prayer and action are needed to uphold the sanctity of human life. I believe it will not be possible to accomplish our work, the work of saving lives, "without being a soul of prayer." The famous British Member of Parliament, William Wilberforce, prayed with his small group of influential friends, the "Clapham Sect," for *decades* to see an end to slavery in the British empire. Wilberforce led that struggle in Parliament, unflaggingly, because he believed in the sanctity of human life. He saw fulfillment of his impossible dream when Parliament outlawed slavery just before his death.[4]

Our leaders face such pressure. Our prayers for them should include requests for wisdom, discernment, and courage. So many know the truth but are unwilling to risk their political careers in order to stand firm. For those in authority who remain commit-

4. Ronald W. Reagan, "Abortion and the Conscience of the Nation," *Human Life Review* 9, no. 2:15.

ted to the destruction of life, we can pray that God will change their hearts or replace them with God-fearing leaders.

Prayers for individual women considering abortion can turn them around. I have witnessed this repeatedly. God is mighty in power, and He delights in our coming to Him with requests that only He can fill.

IN OUTREACH MISSIONS

Virtually every church is involved in supporting missions both within the US and overseas. In home missions, many churches not only provide financial support but personnel as well. This is common in rescue mission work, prison ministries, and ministries to the elderly. In recent years, with the influx of refugees from Asia and the Caribbean, many churches have been active in helping their new neighbors get settled. They have provided them with food, clothing, temporary shelter, and lessons in English. Men and women of God have recognized these refugees as a mission field in need of Christ's love. Taking the Bible's admonition to heart, they have cared for the aliens among them. As a consequence many have trusted Christ.

As a result of the Supreme Court's abortion decision another mission field was created. It is composed of women with unexpected or crisis pregnancies. Because of the Court's judgment, social policy in the US has shifted dramatically in favor of abortion. Very little official encouragement remains to carry the inconvenient baby to term. The assumption behind the Court's decision, that abortion is a simple "termination of pregnancy," has affected the thinking of millions of people. Many women who desire to choose life find little public approval or support from family or friends. The law sides with the husband or boyfriend who shirks his responsibility as a father and pressures the mother toward abortion. There is no appeal she can make to the law except to sue for child support. Indeed it makes his irresponsibility appear very reasonable. The woman who desires to endure her crisis pregnancy and give life to her child faces condemnation as a "fool," which in the secular mind is equivalent to evil. And yet, the wisdom of the ages is on her side.

Abortion advocates will retort that the law does not *require* that abortions be performed, so no one is *forced* to get one. That is naive thinking. The law approves the destruction of human beings in the womb at virtually any time for any reason but rests the responsibility solely with the mother. Appealing to vague socioeconomic and emotional indicators, it teaches this is the preferable course to follow in a variety of situations, but again, only the mother can decide. The law endorses the abortionists' lie that trivializes the practice as something other than killing and so assaults the mother's natural awareness that she is "with child." It excuses the abortion clinic industry from telling the truth to the mother but requires that she decide what is best. The law prohibits parents from "interfering" in their teenage daughter's decision about abortion, in effect making the abortionist the final influence on her. Federal law today requires that over one hundred million dollars annually go to family planning groups, such as Planned Parenthood, which in turn promote, counsel, and in many instances perform abortions. Because of the law today, women with crisis pregnancies are forced to consider abortion and are subjected to a variety of pressures to destroy their babies. It is no wonder so many women contend they were "forced" to get an abortion.

CRISIS PREGNANCY CENTERS

There are many reasons women go through with an abortion. The main reason we find is brokenness in relationships. When the mother decides to break her relationship with her child and get an abortion, this indicates a whole series of broken relationships in her life. Precisely at that point in her life when she needs more encouragement and support than ever before, none is available. It is disturbing to realize that the life-styles of many people—men and women—are in truth styles of death and dying. They subsist on the ragged edges of life with despair as their only companion. The possibility of love is met with destruction, and Satan joyfully dances a dirge.

But not for long. Churches in growing numbers around the United States are developing Crisis Pregnancy Centers and reaching out, in Jesus' name, to women with crisis pregnancies. These ministries in alternatives to abortion rely upon the good efforts of trained volunteers under the supervision of a director. They take seriously the challenge of Jesus in Matthew 25:31-46 to reach out to those in distress with acts of mercy and compassion. Through Crisis Pregnancy Centers, women find emotional support and encouragement, the gospel of Christ's love and forgiveness, and practical assistance that is so necessary for young mothers as they prepare to give birth to a baby.

The Christian Action Council developed the Crisis Pregnancy

Center program over the course of three years, 1978-1980. In 1980 we began working with churches to open centers. Each is locally incorporated and funded. Some are operated directly under the auspices of one church. Most represent a joint ministry by several likeminded congregations in the community. In spite of early warnings we received that this ministry would prove too challenging for Christian volunteers, we have seen repeatedly that the critics were wrong. Thousands of Christian men and women are determined to stop abortion; to them sacrificing time for these ministries is a blessing.

Crisis Pregnancy Centers are steadily growing in number. In 1980, two CPCs were opened. By the end of 1981, the total reached eleven. In the following year thirteen additional centers were opened, and during 1983 the total number of established centers passed fifty. They operate in rural areas (e.g. Pine City, Minnesota) as well as urban settings (e.g. Baltimore, Maryland). The number of women seen monthly increases with the age of the center. The busiest CPCs are now seeing 150 women every month. Over 20,000 women will receive help from Crisis Pregnancy Centers in 1984.

The ministries have proved very effective. Although everyone coming to the centers for help thinks she is pregnant, we have learned that only about 60 percent are with child. Surveys have indicated that pregnant clients are split in their opinion of abortion when they come in. About half approve of abortion, and half are opposed. Because of the emotional stress they are under, those opinions are very relative. They are likely to change several times during the decision-making process. After the counseling and care of trained volunteers, 80 percent of pregnant clients are carrying their babies to term. Some embrace Jesus as their Lord and Savior, while many others turn back to Him, having rebelled against the Lord they knew. Couples are being reconciled, and whole families are coming back together.

The goal of these ministries is not only lives saved but lives transformed through the power of the gospel. It is exciting to witness the changes that occur. The following testimony came from a woman who came to the Crisis Pregnancy Center in Mountain View, California.

When I first went to the Crisis Pregnancy Center, I was in need of temporary housing. With their help I am staying with a Christian family.
Since the first time I went to the Crisis Pregnancy Center, my life

has had a 100% change for the better. I cannot say enough about the Center except I hope that more women go there and get the love and help that I received. For without their love and help and the family's help, I would not have been able to find God. To me that is the most rewarding.[5]

Most observers, friendly and otherwise, are amazed at the effectiveness of these ministries. They want to know what makes them so. To answer that question clients at one center were asked what was most helpful to them. It was thought perhaps that the services being offered were the key factor. These are extensive, ranging from free pregnancy testing and video education on prenatal development and abortion, to maternity clothes, baby clothes, childbirth classes, housing arrangements, referrals for medical care, adoption, or public assistance. According to the clients, however, the services were not the most important part of the center. Rather, it was the love and acceptance they felt from the people who worked with them. For many clients, their only source of love and encouragement were the Christians working with them. Christ's love and compassion in His people were making the difference.

I have given many examples of the pain women experience as they go through abortion. Although it would be fiction to say that choosing life in a crisis pregnancy is easy, it is accompanied by much fulfillment. Self-respect that was lost is regained, along with a tremendous sense of satisfaction. This is well illustrated in the following testimony received from a woman who was helped by the King County Crisis Pregnancy Center in Seattle, Washington.

I've never regretted my decision to give birth to the baby. In general my pregnancy has been a time of heightened awareness and extremely emotional, which can be very fulfilling. My senses are more alive, like my whole being is invigorated with meaning and usefulness. Being vulnerable has been good. I've learned that pain is a reality and working through deep pain can often bring deeper healing.

One of the neatest discoveries was that intimate identification with the child and acceptance of his life and worth have increased my self-esteem. As I decided the baby had a right to live and a future of hope, I discovered this belief applied to me as well.

I've experienced a sort of accelerated maturity in these last few months. I've faced many needed changes in my life and dealt with

5. Testimony on file with the Christian Action Council.

them. . . . Also, there's been a lot of grieving and confusion, but there's been a lot of time to explore the emotions and find peace and new directions. For me the nine months have been a break between past and future, a time to fully concentrate on life's value and potential.

The whole experience has given me more respect for the Creator, God, and ultimate joy in participating in a creative act.[6]

In the spring of 1983, the Christian Action Council sponsored interviews with dozens of women who had faced unexpected, difficult pregnancies. The grief of those who aborted contrasted sharply with the joy of those who chose life. A radiant young woman, five months pregnant, made the following remarks about her decision to carry her child to term:

When I finally decided that this was what I had to do, it was very clear to me, and I wasn't afraid any more. I felt important, and I felt that this little life would be taken care of.

I feel wonderful, I really and truly do. I'm not saying that I don't have problems and that there aren't things wrong. But I've never felt so sure that I was doing the right thing before in my life. And the feeling that I am carrying another little life and making sure that someone else comes into the world, it's really an incredible feeling. It's new.[7]

The growth of Crisis Pregnancy Centers around the country is phenomenal. As more and more churches become involved in direct ministries providing alternatives to abortion, the abortion rate will visibly begin dropping in the United States. Although ministry alone will not change the law or eliminate the death ethic that threatens us all, it is dramatic proof that God's Word is living. In spite of the corruption that characterizes secular authority in the United States, God's redemptive purposes are not thwarted. "Be astonished! Wonder! Because I am doing something in your days—You would not believe if you were told" (Habakkuk 1:5).

SHEPHERDING HOMES

Regardless of how many efforts are made to bring families and couples back together, many women are rejected and left alone when they decide to carry their babies to term. They need not

6. Interview on file with the Christian Action Council.
7. From *Understanding Pregnancy Alternatives,* an educational film developed by the Christian Action Council.

only our love and respect but part of our very lives. Many churches work with the Christian Action Council and others to develop Shepherding Home Ministries in which families open up their homes to receive women during the course of their pregnancy and sometimes beyond.

Housing ministries are always challenging and should not be romanticized. They require a great deal of supervision, but when the planning has been carefully done, they are very fruitful. Many pregnant teens have never known the security of a father's love or strong family relationships. Living with a Christian family not only solves an immediate housing problem but serves as a powerful educational experience.

Part of Christian family living is church life, of course, which is why cooperation from the entire congregation is necessary for a Shepherding Home Ministry to work. Too often Christians have condemned unwed pregnant women as they come to church. Their swollen bodies have been treated as a sign of dishonor. I suspect that if the bodies of all who have been involved in some form of sexual sin were to swell, there would be a lot of swollen bodies in a lot of churches. The point here is not to insult anyone but to warn against hypocrisy.

When a young woman walks down the church aisle with her stomach swollen by the child within, this sign of pregnancy is a sign of honor. She is resisting the pressure of our day to destroy her child, and she is choosing life. God is involved dramatically with her, and we cannot deny it. Accepting and caring for her in no sense represents support for fornication or adultery. Jesus didn't hesitate to care for harlots. We shouldn't hesitate to help scared girls who made a mistake.

ADOPTION

On many occasions people have suggested that adoption is the solution to abortion. Since women don't want their children, they may simply arrange to have them adopted. This is a simplistic view. Few women get abortions because "I don't want this child." When they are assisted and encouraged to carry their babies to term, the vast majority raise and love their babies. Virtually all married women who elect to carry their babies to term will parent them. Over 90 percent of teenagers who carry their babies to term similarly raise their children. For single women in their twenties or thirties, the decision to give birth to a child usually includes raising the child.

The emotions associated with a crisis pregnancy are complex and often contradictory. It may seem incongruous that a woman considering abortion can in a matter of weeks become fiercely determined to raise her baby, but it happens all the time.

As a result of abortion in America the number of babies who are available for adoption has dramatically fallen. Consequently, demand for babies by adoptive couples has grown. In our Crisis Pregnancy Center ministry we have had ample opportunity to witness the determination of privately hired attorneys as well as adoption agencies to secure babies for adoption. As a ministry we work to protect our clients from this kind of pressure and harrassment. At the same time we rejoice with clients who, because of their own initiative and love for their babies, decide to release them for adoption.

Adoption can be a vital ministry even if in a different way from what many people expect. We affirm that all human life is sacred, that we must apply "love your neighbor" to everyone. With this admonition in mind there are many babies available for adoption today; they cry out for the love of parents just like other infants. The problem is that barriers exist that keep them from being adopted. There is no reason those barriers should not be torn down in the name of Christ.

The barriers are in many instances bias and prejudice; in some cases they are laws. Some of the children we are talking about have mental or physical handicaps. Some are members of racial minorities in a predominantly white society. Others come from foreign lands and, being a little older, have never learned English.

It would be improper to assume that a particular family should adopt anyone, but families in our churches must be challenged to consider and pray through the possibility of adopting a child that no one else wants or is willing to love. Through this ministry of sacrifice the Christian community can model a love that overcomes prejudice and bigotry, that is fit for the entire society. One of the strong arguments for abortion and infanticide is that the children being killed are unwanted and unlovable. We can show how false this rationalization truly is.

THROUGH MINISTRIES TO SINGLE PARENTS

As the number of single parents in the US grows, the complexion of our churches is changing as well, since many of these parents are Christian people or have come to faith in Christ subsequent to their becoming parents. Since we urge women to carry their babies to term, we must be prepared to minister to them after the babies are born. Worship and Bible study are essential; knowing Christ and following Him as Lord is the essence of life for anyone. There are other ways as well that the community of God's people can serve them.

The children need exposure to father figures. Mothers need opportunities to share with each other and to encourage one another. Developing services as simple as cooperative baby-sitting are a big help. These can enable women to work who could not afford day-care expenses. In addition single parents should be included in the broader fellowship of the church and not treated as an isolated minority who live in the shadow of some former sin. As the redeemed of the Lord we are called to assist our brothers and sisters in overcoming the effects of sin.

THROUGH MINISTRIES TO THE ELDERLY

There is no basis for assuming euthanasia on a mass scale will not come to pass, unless our current efforts to change public policy are successful. This is a sober assessment but a realistic one, and there are a number of steps that need to be taken now.

First, Christians must be re-educated to their responsibilities under the fifth commandment, "Honor your father and your mother, that your days may be prolonged in the land which the Lord your God gives you" (Exodus 20:12). Traditionally Christians have understood this commandment to include the obligation to protect and shelter parents when they become enfeebled or disabled. This standard must be reasserted.

In His confrontations with the Pharisees, Jesus made clear that failure to keep the fifth commandment is inexcusable. The Pharisees taught that material help could be withheld from parents in order to support the Temple, for this was "giving to God." Invoking the condemnation of Isaiah, Jesus sharply rebuked them. "This people honors Me with their lips, but their heart is far away from Me. But in vain do they worship Me, teaching as doctrines the precepts of men" (Matthew 15:8-9; Isaiah 29:13).

True piety involves caring for parents. The apostle Paul underscored this teaching in his admonition to Timothy: "Let [children] first learn to practice piety in regard to their own family, and to make some return to their parents; for this is acceptable in the sight of God" (1 Timothy 5:4).

In addition, Christians must develop ministries of care to other elderly in their midst. Many Christians are "widows indeed," elderly people with no family to support them. Such ministries should exist regardless of the threat of euthanasia. Nonetheless, the specter of euthanasia should lend conviction and urgency to our deliberations. In view here are ministries of home care provided by the local church to those who can live very well outside an institutional setting if only they are assisted with the basic tasks of life and provided with companionship. Much of the actual work of caring for the elderly could be accomplished by dedicated volunteers, especially young people, who are trained and supervised.

Finally, Christians must develop an alternative healthcare network for the elderly. In addition to the central component of home care, this network would encompass out-patient clinics, convalescent homes, hospice settings for the terminally ill, and hospitals. Some facilities and institutions already exist, but more must be developed and coordinated at least on a regional basis.

Doctors, nurses, social workers, and others skilled in the delivery of human services must begin the planning now. My great fear is that the church will wait until it is too late to begin these ministries. The task proposed is monumental, but it can be accomplished if the Body of Christ will dedicate itself to this purpose. Certainly the resources exist, and God's people do not lack wisdom when they turn to Him for guidance.

16

Faith with Works, Part 2: Becoming a Pro-Life Activist

It may be argued that the New Testament does not provide us with an example of Christian activists reforming the corrupt policies of the Roman Empire. This is true. Neither does the New Testament provide us with examples of Christians crusading to bring about reforms in medicine, education, the arts, or the sciences.

These observations about the earliest Christians provide no basis for condemning later Christians who pursued justice and reform in their societies. The early saints were quite preoccupied with survival in a society that made sport of murdering them. Because of their intrepid witness and that of succeeding generations, Christian truth largely prevailed over pagan ideals and practices. Western society developed around biblical notions of justice and mercy, notwithstanding the corruptions of ambitious and evil men. As a result we have opportunities to influence our culture in ways the early Christians never could. At the same time Christian truth is constantly assaulted.

The battle lines have advanced. The courage of the early saints is our example. We dare not shrink from the challenges before us. If we do, we bring disgrace to our legacy and hasten our culture's return to barbarism. Sooner or later, the violence that comes will overtake the church.

You are the light of the world. A city set on a hill cannot be hidden. Nor do men light a lamp, and put it under the peck-measure, but on the lampstand; and it gives light to all who are in the house. Let your light shine before men in such a way that they may see your good works, and glorify your Father who is in heaven. (Matthew 5:14-16)

Jesus calls His disciples the light of the world because of their mission in the world. They are to witness the righteousness of God before men first and foremost by their works. They are to do this in the name of Jesus Himself. Because opposition and persecution inevitably come to those who obey, Jesus warns His disciples to resist the temptation to conceal their witness, for this would undo all that He purposes to accomplish through them. Our Lord's final exhortation is to let the truth He places in us work itself out in our lives, that people would give glory to the Father. Whether this glory is given at the time of our labor, on the occasion of an unbeliever's repentance, or at the time of the final judgment is beside the point. Christians are to be activists in their society, not for any political party or religious sect, but for the Lord Himself. As a result glory is ascribed to our God.

Christians cannot justify indifference to the evil around them any more than they can justify indifference to the state of men's souls. If we confine our work to the boundaries of that building we call the church, are we not concealing our witness from the world? Will we not answer to God for this? If the cruel violence that is taking so many lives is to stop, Christians must confront the darkness of this world with the light that is in them. They must determine to overcome the evil. This calls for a measure of sacrifice that may be new to many, but these are truly desperate times.

Christians today are working to resist abortion and related violence in a number of ways. Each task is necessary, each requires persistence and a high degree of dedication. Literally millions of people must become involved in one way or another in order to protect the least among us.

INFLUENCE THE STATE

Let every person be in subjection to the governing authorities. For there is no authority except from God, and those which exist are established by God. (Romans 13:1)

What is it for Christians to be subject to governing authorities? Surely this should not be taken to mean that the Christian's relationship to the state is one of blind obedience. If this were the case the Bible teaches Christians to commit atrocities when ordered to do so by a secular authority. There is an overruling principle in submission, which is clear from the text itself. It is the authority of God. As long as governing authorities carry out their responsibilities in accordance with the will of God, Christians are obliged to submit to them. However, when the laws of men conflict with the laws of God, the Christian must obey God and disobey the man-made law.

This priority of God's will is illustrated in the book of Acts, where Peter twice was commanded by authorities to cease preaching Christ. He resisted their authority and continued to witness to the Lord's resurrection (Acts 4:19-20; 5:29).

The principle of resistance is illustrated in greater detail in the book of Daniel. Daniel's enemies convinced King Darius to issue a decree that no man could petition any god or any man other than the king for thirty days. Daniel easily could have resisted the authorities by retiring to a private room when he wished to pray, and no one would have been the wiser. However, he knew that his duty under the first commandment, to love God totally, was broader than this. J.I. Packer has outlined the greater concern and determination of this man of God:

> It is not that Daniel . . . was an awkward, cross-grained fellow who luxuriated in rebellion and could only be happy when he was squarely "agin" the government. It is simply that those who know their God are sensitive to situations in which God's truth and honour are being directly or tacitly jeopardized, and rather than let the matter go by default will force the issue on men's attention and seek thereby to compel a change of heart about it—even at personal risk.[1]

Rather than hiding himself when he prayed, Daniel ascended to the upper chamber of his house, opened the windows toward Jerusalem, and, as was his custom, prayed three times daily. Confrontation with the civil authority was certain. Daniel's enemies were delighted with his boldness and betrayed him to the king. As a result Daniel was thrown into the lion's den, where he faced certain death. But it never came. God delivered Daniel and thereby vindicated both His servant and His servant's message. Through Daniel's witness God made Himself known throughout the land, and people came to worship Him.

1. J. I. Packer, *Knowing God* (Downers Grove, Ill.: Inter-Varsity, 1975), pp. 23-24.

When the laws of men are in conflict with the laws of God, our commitment must extend beyond personal holiness. Even if we can manage to keep our behavior pure, it is not for us to rest content. Christians should confront the authorities over unrighteous laws in order to change them and so to vindicate the righteousness and truth of their God.

Living in a democracy we have a much safer opportunity to do this than Daniel had. In order to confront the civil authorities, Daniel had to break the law and risk his life. In the United States Christians are protected as citizens when they confront their civil leaders. Participating actively in the government of the nation is a duty, not an imposition, as our secular critics have maintained. Submission in a democracy does not require silence but the active fulfillment of one's civic responsibilities.

In order to help them be effective in opposing abortion, I encourage Christians to link their individual efforts to a broader effort that involves thousands of Christian people. A united witness that is coordinated and specific to pieces of pro-life legislation or other pending matters can change public policy. Broad, diffuse appeals to protect the unborn or isolated attempts to stop infanticide have very limited impact.

This is the primary reason that pro-life organizations have local affiliates or chapters. As a pro-life movement distinctively committed to Christ, the Christian Action Council has established hundreds of local groups that share the name.

Each local group focuses its efforts on its own community, where their impact is the greatest. At the same time, these are synchronized with similar efforts in other communities or with legislative developments or policy debates in Washington, D.C., or in state capitols. The cumulative impact is considerable.

Another advantage to cooperative efforts is that credibility comes to the Christians who become involved. They are regarded not only as determined but as professional in the good sense.

One other prerequisite must be met for effective action. The more informed Christians are, the greater their impact will be. Understanding the abortion issue is critical. This includes both the substance of the issue and the politics of abortion, where the battle lines are drawn. Staying current on developments in the law, the courts, and the federal bureaucracy may seem like an impossible task, but this really is not so difficult.

Although the press provides little in-depth information on the abortion question, organizations opposed to abortion publish regular reports and updates. These serve to bridge the knowledge gap and make Christians articulate on the issues. If you are not receiving a regular update, you may write for *Action Line*, the newsletter published by the Christian Action Council.

In addition I encourage Christian people to interact directly with their legislators and other elected officials. You can do that in at least three ways: through letters; in visits; at public hearings. Each of these is a valuable opportunity to bear witness to the sanctity of human life and to the risen Lord, Jesus Christ.

WRITING LETTERS

In Congress there is a rule of thumb about letters that are received. For every citizen who writes his or her Congressman about an issue, it is assumed that several hundred other citizens feel exactly the same way but did not take the time to write. The same assumption is made for letters that are sent to the president, a governor, a state legislator, or a city official. When Christians write letters to express their opposition to abortion, the impact of that correspondence is multiplied.

Many people are concerned that their letters are read and weighed carefully rather than tossed aside. Several steps can be taken to assure that correspondence receives personal attention.

1. Be respectful and courteous.
2. Write legibly or type, keeping the letter to one page or less.
3. Express your opposition to abortion or support for a pro-life proposal in a straightforward way. Don't be defensive. If the Word of God informs your opinion and motivates you to be involved, share it. The Word of God never returns void.
4. Make your letter relevant to the official by raising a specific question concerning how he or she is going to act on an abortion-related matter, such as a pending bill to stop abortion funding. Computerized replies are sent in response to many letters, but computers cannot answer questions. Letters that pose a relevant question or make a specific proposal are most likely to receive individual attention.

The more personal the correspondence is, the better. Petitions tend to have little effect because the assumption is made that virtually anyone can be persuaded to sign one without feeling strongly about the issue it addresses. Sending in a preprinted, mass-produced postcard that requires only your signature also is lightly regarded.

VISITING LEADERS

State and Federal legislators expect to be visited by constituents. One of the reasons for periodic recesses in a legislature is to provide the members with an opportunity to go to their home states or districts and gather input from citizens on issues they are concerned about. A phone call to a legislative office will quickly yield information on when and where the legislator will be available for meetings in his district.

In meeting with your representatives, you have a valuable educational opportunity. Given the number of issues that demand the attention of leaders, it is unrealistic to expect them to be well versed in many. One hour spent educating a legislator on abortion is time well spent. Meetings can encourage those who oppose abortion to take a more active role in efforts to curb the practice. They can also compel a change of position on the part of leaders who have supported it.

I recommend that a committee of three people attend a meeting with their legislator and that a doctor or a lawyer be among them. The participants should discuss ahead of time what is to be said and who is to lead the various discussions. During the closing minutes of the session, a request for some specific action should be made of the official. Legislators expect this; constituents don't visit them apart from a particular action they would like to see taken. In the request and the response that follows, the benefit of the session is determined.

PUBLIC HEARINGS

When bills or ordinances come before a city council, state assembly, or Congress, public hearings often are called in order to receive citizens' input. Christians should be alert to hearings that are called in regard to the abortion question. Given the opportunity to speak the truth, they should take advantage of it. Their testimony becomes part of the public record and serves as evidence when officials are making their final decision on a matter. Failure to appear at hearings tips the balance of testimony in favor of abortion and serves only to influence officials toward that end.

ELECTIONS

Unfortunately, there are many examples of public officials who are determined to support abortion. This is obvious from debates over the use of federal funds for abortion and fetal experimentation, as well as debates concerning infanticide. It is most obvious from voting records.

Democracy is representative government. The election process was developed to assure that those in authority represent the interests, concerns, and values of the people. Elected officials are directly accountable to voters for the way they have exercised their authority. When leaders fail to act responsibly, they should be replaced.

In recent years a number of organizations have practiced "punishment politics," vigorously working to defeat public officials who refuse to support them. The attitude behind these efforts can be mean and offensive, and that of course is wrong. Even more distressing, however, is the refusal of many Christians to participate in elections and vote their conscience on abortion.

When officials use their authority to support the killing of human beings, whether by abortion, infanticide, or euthanasia, they deny their God-given responsibility to protect the innocent and punish the guilty. They violate the public trust, for as Jefferson put it, "The care of human life and happiness, and not their destruction, is the first and only legitimate object of good government." These officials serve violence and injustice rather than righteousness. We have the opportunity in elections to strip authority from them, and we should take advantage of it.

Newspapers have been flooded with articles in recent years concerning "single issue" voters and their impact on the political process. They are presented as a threat to the nation on the grounds that they lack concern for the overall welfare of the country. What amazes me most is that the charge is leveled only against those opposed to abortion, never against those who work just as diligently to promote the practice.

Anyone who spends much time in Washington, D.C., learns that there is a single issue that dominates virtually all the government's time and attention. It is money. Over 90 percent of votes in Congress deal with budgets, authorize spending, or appropriate funds. The vast majority of lobbies and associations in Washington are there to gain the maximum financial benefit for the groups they represent, regardless of who they are. These include labor, management, industry of all kinds, the arts, agriculture, and foreign nations.

In order to resolve money issues, politicians resort to the simple tactic of compromise. This is easy to do with money, expanding figures in one column and reducing them in the next. No group gets everything it wants, but everyone gets something. This is politics as usual, and it keeps the trains running on time.

Those involved in establishment politics resent "single-issue" voters because their single issue happens to be different. It is abortion, a matter of justice. This does not lend itself to compromise like the "other" single issues. Public officials are forced to take a clear stand on a moral question. There is no room for ambiguity. This kind of exposure threatens many of them.

In addition opponents of abortion are not motivated by the desire for personal gain. Because they are largely selfless in their devotion, the normal means of keeping constituencies under control do not apply to them. This also threatens the political establishment, which has done so much to enshrine the quality-of-life position into law and public policy.

Through their public witness and their participation in the electoral process, Christians can bring public officials to the realization that their main obligation is not to keep the trains running on time, but rather to protect the innocent and punish the guilty. Both these notions are controversial in our day. They rest on a belief that justice exists and must be served. The competing view maintains that no absolute standard of justice exists; therefore inalienable rights do not exist.

In 1975, attorney Harriet Pilpel, chief counsel to Planned Parenthood and Vice-Chairman of the American Civil Liberties Union, testified in Congress against a constitutional amendment to protect unborn children. Her opening remarks were chilling:

> Nowhere in our Constitution or in any amendment adopted to date is there any reference to or any guarantee of a right to life for anyone, born or unborn. All the constitution does in this context is to prohibit the government—federal or state—from depriving anyone of life without due process of law.[2]

We can all agree the phrase "right to life" is not in the Constitution, but to maintain that the principle is not enshrined there is clearly in error. Nevertheless, Ms. Pilpel's views are shared by many. The law does not guarantee the right to life for anyone; it only guarantees that no one can be killed unless it is legal. On this view law becomes a safeguard for lawlessness. This is not the first time such a position has been advocated.

When Adolf Hitler came to power in Germany, he reduced unemployment, brought inflation under control, vastly improved the transportation system, and strengthened the economy. The Volkswagen, the car of the people, was introduced and there was

2. Hearings before the Subcommittee on Civil and Constitutional Rights of the Committee of the Judiciary, 94th Congress, Second Session, on "Proposed Constitutional Amendments on Abortion," Serial No. 46, Part 1, p. 186.

an affluence enjoyed by the German people they had not known for decades. Hitler rebuilt the nation industrially, militarily, and economically, but no reasonable person would say Hitler was a great man. He is not remembered for any of those accomplishments. Hitler is remembered as a tyrant who used the force of law to destroy millions of innocent people and to deny freedom to millions of others.

When Abraham Lincoln came to the White House in 1861, he proved himself a very poor leader in many ways. Inflation was rampant, and the economy suffered tremendously. The government was scandal ridden. Quite literally, the trains did not run on time. More Americans died fighting during his administration than in any other. There was no peace. Nevertheless, reasonable people reflect on Lincoln as a great leader because he addressed himself to the most important issue, justice. Lincoln freed the slaves.

This contrast between Hitler and Lincoln is melodramatic, and I do not wish to insult anyone's intelligence. The point nonetheless must be made that superb performance on secondary issues is no substitute for right performance on fundamental matters of justice.

There are many issues of justice in the United States, and they are all important. With all of these except one, however, opposing parties agree that human beings should be protected from violence, hostility, and prejudice. For example the primary question in the debate over nuclear arms is not whether human beings should be protected, but rather how best to secure their protection.

The abortion issue is different because the question is more fundamental. It is the question of *whether* to protect, not how. Are we obliged to protect the innocent or to approve their destruction if it is deemed socially useful? No issue is more fundamental to justice. The outcome of this controversy more than any other will determine the future of freedom in America. Few citizens have seen this more clearly than President Ronald Reagan.

> Abraham Lincoln recognized that we could not survive as a free land when some men could decide that others were not fit to be free and should therefore be slaves. Likewise, we cannot survive as a free nation when some men decide that others are not fit to live and should be abandoned to abortion or infanticide. My Administration is dedicated to the preservation of America as a free land, and there

is no cause more important for preserving that freedom than affirming the transcendent right to life of all human beings, the right without which no other rights have any meaning.[3]

After all is said and done, I am convinced there really are no single-issue voters. Every voter has a list of issues that concerns him or her. Only one of those, however, can head the list as the most important. Should not abortion be that issue?

Among the various demographic groups within the US, evangelicals have tended to be poor voters. Many are not registered to vote, so they cannot participate in elections. Of those who are registered, many do not exercise the right, which is also a responsibility. The trend currently is toward greater participation by Christians, and this is encouraging. In refusing to vote, we only serve to defeat the truth and assure that our concerns will not receive anything resembling fair treatment.

CHANGE PUBLIC OPINION

Leaders lead only as long as followers follow. This may sound unforgivably trite, but it is true. When authorities resist efforts to protect human life, Christians can still have a tremendous impact by directly appealing to the hearts and minds of the people within their communities. Where abortion and euthanasia are unacceptable, they are not practiced even if they are legal. This local witness in support of life affects elected officials as well. When enough people feel strongly about a particular issue, politicians tend to become supportive, if only for reasons of political survival.

In order to educate and influence people to oppose the violence of abortion, Christians should be wise to those institutions and agencies within the community that largely determine public opinion: the press, libraries, schools. Much can be accomplished through them.

THE PRESS

Virtually every newspaper in the US has an editorial board that determines the editorial policies of their paper. These boards generally welcome presentations from experts and concerned citizens on issues that are relevant to their readers. After more than ten years of abortion on demand, most editorial boards still have not been presented with a pro-life presentation.

3. Ronald W. Reagan, "Abortion and the Conscience of the Nation," *Human Life Review,* 9, no. 2:16.

Substantial literature is now available that can prepare Christians to make clear, forceful presentations to editors. The nation's extensive exposure to abortion demonstrates how destructive the practice is. Specific facts and well-documented evidence are needed to persuade journalists, who are trained to be skeptical. The result of this witness, when followed by periodic contact and additional information, can be a stronger editorial position in support of life or perhaps the gradual reversal of a pro-abortion position.

Other avenues are also available. Whenever an article appears in a local magazine or paper that supports the killing of innocent humans, letters to the editor are in order. Surveys indicate the editorial page of a paper receives more attention than any other, except the front page and the sports page. People are interested in reading the opinions of their friends and neighbors. The opportunity to influence people's thinking is considerable.

It similarly follows that articles in support of human life should trigger letters of approval and appreciation. Editors are interested in knowing whether the content of their papers meets with the approval of their readers. Certainly you can expect those who support abortion or euthanasia to register their disapproval.

Many Christians have grown angry with the press for biased, inaccurate reporting on these matters. As the guardian of freedom, the press has failed to discharge its responsibility. It is important to remember, however, the press is not some monolithic, impersonal force. Journalism is an industry composed of individuals. As we take the time to build relationships with these professionals and supply them with accurate information, our credibility and the credibility of our position increases. This represents necessary groundwork for any change of opinion.

Television and radio newspeople similarly should be approached with information and facts. Steady encouragement is important. Many broadcasting companies air editorial responses from citizens who disagree with them.

PUBLIC LIBRARIES

The typical public library in America carries a lengthy selection of books on abortion and euthanasia. Very often the majority of these support abortion and are unsympathetic toward the sanctity of human life. To remedy the imbalance, Christians can either donate books that uphold the value of life or request that specific books be included. If sufficient inquiries are made after a particular volume, it usually is purchased by the library. When the public record against abortion and euthanasia is established, large numbers of people are influenced, especially students.

PUBLIC SCHOOLS

The sex education programs of our public schools must not be ignored when they contradict the truth. And most do.

In areas where opposition to abortion is strong, parents' groups have succeeded in expelling educational programs that are biased in its favor. In communities where this is not possible, citizens have successfully argued for *additional* educational presentations in order to present the "other side" of the abortion issue.

Public schools will not allow a distinctively Christian presentation on abortion, but many are open to educational efforts that stress the value of human life, the dignity of the individual, and the virtues of self-discipline and personal integrity. Over the last several years a number of workers in our Crisis Pregnancy Centers have been successful in these efforts. They report that students are very attentive when the facts about abortion are presented. After hearing them, many teens feel "ripped off" by presentations that attempted to influence them toward abortion without giving detailed information. They resent being deceived.

PUBLIC EVENTS

Many public events provide good opportunities to educate people to the sanctity of human life. Churches and civic groups are encouraged to set up booths at fairs, enter floats in parades, or provide displays at festivals of various kinds. Taking advantage of these opportunities to share the truth saves lives.

FRIENDS, FAMILY, AND NEIGHBORS

In the midst of our commitment to encourage people to reject violence and protect human life, it is easy to overlook those who are closest to us. Yet we have a greater influence on our family, friends, and neighbors than on anyone else. Where love, friendship, and trust have developed, it is much simpler to deal with matters as controversial as abortion.

The process can begin with an invitation to hear a pro-life speaker or perhaps with the gift of a book or educational pamphlet. The most important factor, however, is your own witness.

People come to oppose abortion through a variety of different experiences. Share with your relatives and friends how your conviction has grown and what you are doing about it.

All the efforts mentioned above can be accomplished with little difficulty. Each of them is an important part of an overall witness to encourage citizens to protect the least among us. More is needed, however, and Christians especially should feel challenged to go this extra mile.

Large-scale educational efforts making use of television, radio, and the print media are necessary to reach the millions of people who have been affected by the press's strong bias toward abortion. The talent exists as do the funds. The only question is one of resolve. Will Christians expend what they have to save human life? Truth rather than propaganda is required, powerful testimonies to the value of life, the violence of abortion, and the better way of alternatives.

Every year Planned Parenthood, the National Abortion Rights Action League, and other organizations that promote abortion spend millions of dollars on campaigns that confuse the issues and play upon people's fears or prejudice. Against these the truth is a powerful weapon. Christians possess it. Their task is to go on the offensive and use it.

EXPOSE THE ABORTION INDUSTRY

The abortion industry shuns public scrutiny. Abortion chieftans want to be left alone to do their job with as little public exposure as possible. Exposés are bad for business. They generally decline debates with articulate advocates of life. The less the public knows, the better. Complacency feeds on ignorance, and clinic owners know it.

Throughout this book, I have referred to women seeking abortions as clients, not patients. When they enter a clinic or surgical ward for "the procedure," they are not coming to receive medical care but to have the life within them destroyed. There is nothing respectable about an abortion clinic. The hospital that provides abortions has compromised its integrity. Unless the air of respectability that surrounds these institutions is stripped away and protests over abortion occur, the acceptance of the community is assured, and we share in the responsibility for this. The following passage from the Torah is relevant.

If a slain person is found lying in the open country in the land which the Lord your God gives you to possess, and it is not known who has struck him, then your elders and your judges shall go out and measure the distance to the cities which are around the slain one. And it shall be that the city which is nearest to the slain man, that is, the elders of that city, shall take a heifer of the herd, which has not been worked and which has not pulled in a yoke; and the elders of that city shall bring the heifer down to a valley with running water, which has not been plowed or sown, and shall break the heifer's neck there in the valley. Then the priests, the sons of Levi, shall come near, for the Lord your God has chosen them to serve Him and to bless in the name of the Lord; and every dispute and every assault shall be settled by them. And all the elders of that city which is nearest to the slain man shall wash their hands over the heifer whose neck was broken in the valley; and they shall answer and say, "Our hands have not shed this blood, nor did our eyes see it. Forgive Thy people Israel whom Thou hast redeemed, O Lord, and do not place the guilt of innocent blood in the midst of Thy people Israel." And the bloodguiltiness shall be forgiven them. So you shall remove the guilt of innocent blood from your midst, when you do what is right in the eyes of the Lord. (Deuteronomy 21:1-9)

When a man was killed and justice could not be served because the murderer was unknown, God required of Israel that the elders of the city nearest the slain man break the neck of a heifer and wash their hands over the animal. In so doing, they publicly acknowledged the violence as an offense against God and dissavowed any association with it. They were not responsible for the crime—"Our hands have not shed this blood." Nor were they responsible for the failure of justice since they were not witnesses who could identify the killer—"nor did our eyes see it."

The elders' response did not end here. In addition they were required to beseech God to forgive His people, for they shared the responsibility for the unsolved crime. Only through these actions could God's people "remove the guilt of innocent blood" from themselves.

We do well to consider the principles behind this law although the particulars of the commandment no longer apply. The principles are both true and relevant. The people of a society bear the responsibility for unresolved crimes of violence. This holds true for Christians as well as for everyone else. As the people of God, Christians—especially leaders—have a duty to denounce publicly such violence and the injustice that accompanies it, to seek justice and protection for the innocent wherever possible, and to intercede in behalf of the church and the society at large that God would be merciful.

certain terms, God declares that spiritual exercise
nothing when injustice is permitted to go unchecked.
ted cries of harm's victims that reach His ears. Their
out to Him from the ground. Petitions from saints
to these sounds that pierce God's heart are hollow by

ast like this which I choose, a day for a man to humble
Is it for bowing one's head like a reed, and for spreading
cloth and ashes as a bed? Will you call this a fast, even an
le day to the Lord? Is this not the fast which I chose, to
e bonds of wickedness, to undo the bonds of the yoke, and
oppressed go free, and break every yoke? Is it not to divide
ad with the hungry, and bring the homeless poor into the
hen you see the naked, to cover him; and not to hide
from your own flesh? Then your light will break out like
, and your recovery will speedily spring forth; and your
ness will go before you; the glory of the Lord will be your
d. Then you will call, and the Lord will answer; you will
He will say, "Here I am." If you remove the yoke from your
e pointing of the finger, and speaking wickedness, and if
yourself to the hungry, and satisfy the desire of the afflict-
your light will rise in darkness, and your gloom will be-
e midday. And the Lord will continually guide you, and
ur desire in scorched places, and give strength to your
d you will be like a watered garden, and like a spring of
ose waters do not fail. (Isaiah 58:5-11)

ises intimate communion with those who "loose the
kedness" and "let the oppressed go free." He prom-
ess in ministry, strength, and His abundant grace in

N NAZI GERMANY

ime Hitler ascended to power in early 1933, the
f Jews became frequent and violent. Dietrich Bon-
enged the German Evangelical church to come to
. The verse he cited was Proverbs 31:8, quoted

mples of courage notwithstanding, the church as a
t respond to Bonhoeffer's challenge. Christian lead-

teridge, *The German Evangelical Church and the Jews, 1879-
ork: Barnes and Noble, 1976), p. 128.

Our current position before God is more precarious than that
envisioned for Israel in Deuteronomy 21. The law addressed the
matter of responsibility and forgiveness when justice *cannot* be
served because a murder cannot be solved. The failure of justice
in that case is completely unintentional. In our society justice is
deliberately set aside so innocent people may be destroyed
through abortion and infanticide. In many instances we know
where the violence occurs and how it is being done. Unborn
children, handicapped newborns, and others are destroyed because the killing is permitted. I am not only speaking of the law
here but of the refusal of citizens—including Christians—to
take steps to curb the violence.

PUBLIC PROTEST

In light of these considerations public protests and demonstrations against abortion facilities not only are morally acceptable
but are morally required. No valid argument exists against efforts to save innocent people from being destroyed, so long as
those efforts are completely nonviolent, harming no one. I know
these conclusions are hard to accept because they are so costly.
They call for acting out our convictions to the full extent possible.

The motivation behind movements comes from any number of
sources. At opposite extremes are hate and love. For any movement to succeed the motivation behind it must be fully expressed. This means that for a movement fueled by hatred, violence is necessary. For a movement fueled by love, self-sacrifice is
required.

Christian efforts to stop abortion are motivated by the love of
God and the love of neighbor. We maintain the newly conceived
human, no matter how small or insignificant in appearance, is a
creature made by God, as valuable as any other human. We maintain the same is true for the handicapped or very sick child, no
matter how burdensome he or she may be. Only when Christians
have determined to sacrifice themselves to protect these people
and to care for them can justice be secured. Only when we say
with our deeds as well as our words, "Their lives are as valuable
as my own," can we seriously expect to see victory.

Without providing an entire plan, several operating principles
for public protest should be kept in mind:
1. The principle of compassion must serve both to motivate and
   instruct. No tactic or protest effort should be undertaken that

violates it. Violence is out of the question. Temptations to rage or vengeance must be shunned.

2. Unlawful activity to save lives should be avoided so long as legal avenues of protest remain. Those who long to be martyrs are welcome to join other movements. It is folly to invite unnecessary grief and suffering upon one's self or family.

3. Any activity to save lives must be the result of careful planning and intensive spiritual preparation. The comfort and peace of the Holy Spirit are needed blessings since confrontations with abortion clinics always are tense occasions. An attorney should be consulted ahead of time so participants know exactly what their rights and the requirements of the law are. In any group effort, there should be one spokesman and one leader. Discipline among the participants is essential. All that is said or done must be done in the name of Christ.

Abortion clinics are businesses that exist only so long as they turn a profit. If economics turn against them, they close down. This provides a major point of leverage.

One form of legal protest that is working well involves a continual witness outside an abortion clinic every hour it is open for business. Christians organize in shifts. They meet to carry signs and pray along public sidewalks outside the facility. At any given time at least two women also are present to gently and respectfully approach those coming to the clinic. The clients are given literature and a word of encouragement. They are briefly told that assistance is available to help them carry their babies to term. Often there is opportunity to witness to the love of God. Day in and day out this lawful witness continues.

Babies are being saved, and women bent toward abortion determine to go elsewhere. Clinic personnel are forced to re-examine what they are doing. Their morale suffers as do clinic profits. Economic concerns become paramount. Pressure builds to close down.

The critical issue for Christians in this kind of effort is perseverance. Unless they resolve from the outset to continue their witness until a clinic shuts down, they should not begin. They must count the cost ahead of time.

___

17

Conclu

"Speak up for those who c
the rights of all who are c

God's commandment that we l
for the victims of human savag
selves. God expects us to be a vo
tion to establish justice in behalf
ed by the cruel passions of men
God delivered us from affliction
our behalf. His grace inspires o

> Preserve justice, and do righteo
> come and My righteousness to

God has demonstrated in our
fatherless. He provides for us a
mercy. Because of that mercy, H
"Vindicate the weak and father
destitute. Rescue the weak and
hand of the wicked" (Psalm 82:
things for us. As His childrer
tradition.

New International Version.

___

In no u
counts for
It is the m
blood cries
indifferent
compariso

Is it a f
himself
out sack
acceptab
loosen t
to let the
your bre
house; v
yourself
the daw
righteou
rear gua
cry, and
midst, t
you give
ed, then
come lik
satisfy y
bones; a
water wh

God prom
bonds of wi
ises fruitful
time of nee

THE CHURCH I

From the
persecution
hoeffer chall
their defense
above.[1]

Isolated ex
whole did no

1. Richard Gu
   1950 (New Y

ers were absorbed in church affairs. When pressure built to retire Jewish pastors from their pulpits and to exclude Jewish believers from Communion, protests were lodged by the "Confessing Church" because the state was intruding into ecclesiastical matters. Few Christians raised objections to the violent persecution of Jews. The voices that did protest focused upon the plight of baptized Jews only.[2]

By 1942, after the Holocaust had commenced, rumors of mass extermination were common. Virtually all the religious leaders knew what was occurring if for no other reason than "half-knowledge" (the Jews were transported out of Germany and were never heard from again).[3] The church had long since lost any opportunity for effective protest against the violence. Those steps that were taken, letters written and sermons preached, required great courage but were inconsequential as exceptions to the silence.

After World War II was over, Martin Niemoeller, considered one of the strongest witnesses against Hitler's tyranny, summed up his own response in the following terms:

> In Germany they came first for the Communists, and I didn't speak up because I wasn't a Communist. Then they came for the Jews, and I didn't speak up because I wasn't a Jew. Then they came for the trade unionists, and I didn't speak up because I was not a trade unionist. Then they came for the Catholics, and I didn't speak up because I was a Protestant. Then they came for me, and by that time no one was left to speak up.[4]

"Too little, too late" became the byword of those who had been involved. Many reasons contributed to the inadequate and shameful response. One of the most significant of these was the prevailing understanding of Luther's doctrine of the "Two Kingdoms."[5] This was understood to imply a separation of church and state that was so absolute that the church surrendered its prophetic role altogether. If the state was going to use the sword to perpetrate violence rather than restrain it, then this was God's will and must be accepted as such.

Barthian theology (neo-orthodoxy) was another factor with its "intolerantly onesided and transcendental faith laden with para-

2. Ibid., pp. 127-28.
3. Ibid., p. 238.
4. *Bartlett's Familiar Quotations* (Boston: Little, Brown, 1980), p. 824.
5. Gutteridge, pp. 268-69.

dox."[6] Although Barth himself came to condemn the persecution and the holocaust that followed, his theology permitted no basis for discourse between church and state. Christian leaders were not clear on their responsibility or how it was to be carried out.

A third major factor was the anti-Semitism that had infested the German Evangelical church by 1930. With few exceptions hatred of the Jews as a race was accepted as a matter of course. In the minds of many Christians, Jews deserved to be persecuted; nonetheless, they felt it wrong to do so.

Bonhoeffer was one of the very few who saw the truth behind the Jewish persecution from the time it began. It represented an attack against Christ, the Son of David after the flesh.[7] It was also an assault against the Word of God, particularly the Old Testament. Its truths were rejected in order to deny the significance of the Jews. Accordingly, Bonhoeffer was the "first to insist that the [Jewish] question was no side issue to be gingerly handled, but was absolutely fundamental in any future controversy between Church and State."[8]

Bonhoeffer prophesied that the church would herself experience the persecution it was permitting the Jews to suffer. After "Crystal Night" in 1938, when thousands of synagogues, Jewish homes, and businesses had been ransacked, Bonhoeffer warned, "If the synagogues burn today, the churches will be on fire tomorrow."[9]

While there were Christian laymen and pastors who were mercilessly destroyed, Bonhoeffer's prediction of widespread persecution for the church did not come to pass. The Nazis' hatred and ambition undoubtedly encompassed this, but the opportunity never came to carry it out. The Nazi sentiment was well expressed on the wall of a canteen in a rail yard in Munich: "When will all mankind be in a state of salvation? When will the world be enlightened? When the last Jew is strangled with the intestines of the last parson."[10]

In spite of the fact that the church was spared in large measure from the Holocaust, it nevertheless was decimated by its own failure to bear witness to the truth. The church in Germany was clothed in shame. To this day the people by and large do not respect the institution or the gospel with which it is entrusted.

6. Ibid., p. 277.
7. Ibid., p. 97.
8. Ibid., p. 92.
9. Ibid., p. 297.
10. Ibid., p. 296.

Luther's homeland has become a mission field.

Will we ignore the command in Proverbs 31:8 in our own day as well? Will we rationalize silence by appealing to the separation of church and state? Will we retreat to a theological refuge where only our personal religious experiences and our churches matter?

We know that human beings by the millions are being exterminated in the abortion clinics and hospitals of America. We also know there remains considerable freedom in this country to overcome the violence and save lives through efforts within our communities and through petitioning the government. We cannot escape the responsibility for this knowledge and for what we do with it.

The fact of freedom in America and the continued enjoyment of material wealth may lead us to the false assumption that God's fury does not hang over this nation. In fact it does, coloring our present course through history. Every day we are spared annihilation, we should thank God for His forbearance and tremble at the same time, for we have drawn one day nearer to the reckoning that must come. Fifteen million unborn infants and thousands of babes have been killed. Their suffering is constantly before Him. He forebears for one reason, that we would repent of our indifference and act on the opportunity He has provided to save lives and restore justice. It is as much an expression of His mercy to us as to the victims of the inhumanities we oppose. One need not be a prophet to heed their warnings and pray their prayers.

> Lord, I have heard the report about Thee and I fear. O Lord, revive Thy work in the midst of the years, in the midst of the years make it known; in wrath remember mercy. (Habakkuk 3:2)

I share with you the response of the German Evangelical church to the "Jewish question" because we face a similar challenge today. Some Christians no doubt will see the question of abortion as a peripheral matter to the "business of the church." They will not recognize that the integrity of the church and its witness for generations is at stake. Nevertheless, the attack on the unborn child and other innocently inconvenient life is an attack against Christ and His Word.

Through the incarnation He became one with them. How men treat the "least of these" is the measure of their regard for Him. In the practice of abortion or euthanasia, they fight God as He creates and sustains life. They reject His law in an attempt to throw Him off as Lord over them. They despise Him as the Savior and embrace instead a god fashioned in the image of man—at once deadly and vain. This god demands the sacrifice of human beings for his pleasure. He is the center of intense religious activity motivated by pride, fear, and despair. Call this devil what you will, he exists and is powerful.

The destruction of human life on such a mass scale as we encounter could not occur were it not for a diabolical power. Only one power exists on earth who can stop it, Jesus. He has been given "as head over all things to the church, which is His body, the fulness of Him who fills all in all" (Ephesians 1:22-23). When the church recoils from confronting abortion in strength, it signals a spiritual poverty that is inexcusable given the riches that are in Christ. Heinrich Gruber's confession in behalf of the German Evangelical church under Hitler is a warning for the church today: "We confess not only that during the twelve years of the Nazis we have been found wanting, but that we had not in the past developed sufficient resources to counter the demonic forces which burst forth and led to this infernissimo."[11] Bonhoeffer's warning belongs to the church in this generation as well as in his. We can fully expect to suffer the violence that we tolerate.

When the Supreme Court legalized abortion on demand, the justices did not require that unborn children be put to death. Their decision, in spite of all the pro-life rhetoric to the contrary, was not in itself a death sentence. Parents are not in the helpless position of watching as their children are singled out for killing.

In reality the High Court's decision both reflected and anticipated the willingness of our society to destroy unwanted people. It rendered this conduct legal and acceptable in the case of abortion. The legal theory behind the decision has implications far beyond abortion and is now used to justify the extermination of human beings other than the unborn.

If the American people were unwilling to kill their offspring, abortions would not be performed. The American people possess the will to kill; they voluntarily participate. Churches by the thousands have approved this. Additional churches by the thousands have remained silent although they know the violence is evil. It is the voluntary nature of the violence more than anything else that creates in me a sense of horror.

I can sympathize with the person who tolerates violence under

11. Ibid., p. 298.

a totalitarian government. If he speaks out, he faces imprisonment or death. His silence is enforced at the point of a gun. But there is nothing restraining people in this country from speaking out and securing protection for innocent human beings.

I have heard voices cry for revival, as though justice will not be secured nor mercy restored unless some great emotional event caused by God comes upon His people. The passage quoted above from Isaiah suggests that in such a season as this, revival comes through our resolve to establish justice in our midst. It comes as a blessing from God to those who "loose the bonds of wickedness." If we cry out, "Dear God," He responds, "Here I am," when we have determined to do His will.

One cannot doubt the ultimate victory of righteousness in light of the prayer that Jesus taught: "Thy will be done on earth as it is in heaven." This comes as a comfort, holding forth a constant promise and a certain hope.

Over the last six years, I have had occasion many times to ask if this struggle is worth the cost of involvement. I have come to realize that this witness against violence is part of discipleship. It is part of serving the Lord Jesus. On those days when I cannot tell if progress is being made or when I feel the sting of defeat, I remember that after all is said and done we Christians look forward to a day unlike any other in history. On that day we will stand before Jesus Himself, the Lord of lords and the King of kings. We shall behold Him in His glory and marvel at His majesty. One look at Jesus, and the works we have done in His name—the sacrifices that were required of us—will seem insignificant. I cannot help but think we shall wish we had done more to exalt Him.

This will not be a time of tears and regrets, however. Jesus tells us through a parable what He intends to do for those who have faithfully served Him (Matthew 25:14-30). He will take us in His loving embrace and pronounce upon us a benediction that will last for all eternity. "Well done, good and faithful [servant]. . . . Enter into the joy of your master."

Appendix

Although most Christians agree substantially with the sanctity of human life and with the fact that abortion is wrong, specific doubts or questions may remain. This appendix is provided to deal with concerns that are most commonly expressed.

Q: *Is abortion ever acceptable?*
A: The willful killing of an innocent human being is never necessary. It is wrong. There are occasions when a pregnancy must be prematurely ended in order to save the life of the mother. In such instances, the doctor should recognize his obligation to care for two patients, both the mother and the unborn child. Tragically, pregnancies that must be ended often require surgery so early (e.g. for a cancerous uterus, an injured uterus, or an ectopic pregnancy) that the baby is incapable of survival outside the womb. On the other hand, the pregnancy-related condition precludes the child's survival *within* the womb as well. The choice facing the physician is not to save the mother *or* to save the child. Rather, it is to save the mother *or* to lose both mother and child. The scope of this problem is gradually being reduced as medical science makes further advances in the care of younger and smaller premature infants.

In 1967, Dr. Alan Guttmacher, a leading advocate of permissive abortion and head of Planned Parenthood, conceded that abortion is virtually never indicated to prevent the death of a woman:

> Today it is possible for almost any patient to be brought through pregnancy alive, unless she suffers from a fatal illness such as cancer or leukemia, and if so, abortion would be unlikely to prolong, much less save life.[1]

In the spring of 1983, I had a unique opportunity while tracking down videotapes of ultrasound examinations. I watched a tiny infant vigorously rotating and exercising within his amniotic sac. He was very much alive and looked to be rather carefree. He was less than ten weeks old from conception. There was an insurmountable problem, however. The baby's placenta was implanted in one of his mother's fallopian tubes rather than in the cavity of her uterus, thus creating an ectopic pregnancy. Had surgery not been performed to remove the tiny infant, his own growth soon would have caused the fallopian tube to rupture resulting in his own death and threatening his mother's life. The little one was removed surgically and died. The mother lived. As the doctor explained the case and gazed at the screen, his eyes welled up with tears. "We've got to come up with a way to save these kids," he whispered. He was a pro-life doctor.

Q: *What about abortion for pregnancies resulting from rape or incest?*
A: Certainly this is the most emotional argument advanced for abortion. It repeatedly was used with success by abortion proponents in the late sixties in order to modify state laws. Once this exception became acceptable, the principle was established that exceptions were permissible so many more followed, and permissive abortion was the result.

This illustrates well the truth of the legal dictum "Hard cases make bad law." It is bad policy to legislate around difficult or extenuating circumstances because in stretching or setting aside a principle of justice for that hard case, a precedent is established for other cases. Having accepted the killing of innocent humans in one circumstance, this may be practiced in other circumstances as well. The right to life is no longer absolute.

1. Alan F. Guttmacher, "Abortion Yesterday, Today, and Tomorrow," *The Case for Legalized Abortion Now* (Berkeley: Diablo, 1967).

In the summer of 1982, President Reagan was asked during a press conference about the rape/incest exception for abortion. In a very candid reply, he pointed out that this exception had led to abortion on demand in California while he was governor (1967), and he was not prepared to see the past mistake repeated. The exception sounded narrow and restrictive, but in practice, it was interpreted broadly.

The explanation for this is fairly simple. If abortion is permissible for pregnancies resulting from sexual assault, presumably assault must be proved. But this requires legal action. Going through the courts takes months. By the time a verdict could be handed down and permission granted for abortion, the baby could already be born. This is totally unworkable. As a result, merely the claim of sexual assault was considered sufficient to justify abortion.

This question must be put in perspective. Pregnancy resulting from rape or incest is extremely rare, for a variety of reasons. In 1977, Vicki Seltzer wrote an article, "Medical Management of the Rape Victim," for *The American Medical Women's Association*. In it she assessed the frequency of pregnancy resulting from sexual assault:

> Perhaps more of a gross exaggeration than a myth is the mistaken and unfortunate belief that pregnancy is a frequent complication of sexual assault. This is emphatically not the case, and there are several medically sound reasons for it.[2]

Granted, such pregnancies are very rare, they still occur. Putting this problem in perspective should not cause us to dismiss it altogether. There are women who face pregnancy after sexual assault; the entire community is obligated to come to their aid. The question of course is how to do this.

Abortion is so often presented as a compassionate and humane alternative to carrying the child to term. My own ministry experience as well as reports from our Crisis Pregnancy Centers has led me to the opposite conclusion. There are two misassumptions that are frequently made in counseling for abortion in this instance.

The first is that abortion eliminates or reduces the trauma of rape for the mother. That is untrue. The emotional trauma of rape is not mitigated by abortion. Regardless of what the woman

2. Vicki Seltzer, "Medical Management of the Rape Victim," *American Medical Women's Association* 32 (1977):141-44.

does once she is pregnant, she must work through her rape experience and her feelings about it in order to resolve the trauma. This does not come easily and may involve professional counseling. There is no shortcut to coming to grips with the pain. From a counseling perspective, abortion is a simplistic and presumptuous suggestion.

Abortion promises only to compound the trauma of rape with yet another experience of violence. In pursuing this course, the victim may assume to herself guilt for the entire episode. In an attempt to overcome the violation of her own person, she does violence to another, submitting to the added humiliation of abortion. This brings no peace of mind and no healing, only more pain and more regret. In the words of one experienced counselor, "Abortion does not unrape a woman."

The second misassumption that is often made in counseling for abortion is that pregnancy is experienced as a nine-month extension of the rape trauma. Pregnancy is traumatic for women regardless of how it occurs; it is highly traumatic when the result of rape. Nonetheless, although affected by rape, the experience of pregnancy is different. In the CPC ministry we have seen how this has led to a new realization that God is sovereign, and He is good. He can provide for the physical, spiritual, and emotional needs of rape victims. He can also bring forth something as precious and redeemable as a new human being through the evil. In the course of choosing life and sacrificing for the child within them, women have regained their self-esteem and acquired a sense of their own worth they never before possessed. In the midst of their pain they have discovered a peace they never imagined was possible.

As with pregnancies that occur under any other circumstances, the main factor in how the victim views herself and her pregnancy is the response and attitudes of those closest to her. If she is supported, encouraged, and honored, she will feel good about her decision and proud of her accomplishment in carrying the child to term. If she is rejected and left unsupported, she may turn against herself as well as the child.

An example is appropriate here. Judy was living in California at the time she was raped. As in most cases of sexual assault, she knew her assailant. She didn't tell anyone about the incident until three-and-one-half weeks later when she suspected she was pregnant. Because of her past convictions about abortion, she dismissed it out of hand.

Judy sought counsel from her church. "The pastors at church

told me they would stand with me and support me and help in any way they could. I received lots of support and encouragement from my friends."

With her family, things were not so easy. "The vote was five to one for abortion, and I was the 'one.' " The entire family was hurt very much by the incident, especially the father.

A week after Judy approached her pastors, she was called in for a meeting. "The head pastor told me to think through my decision once more to make sure I was carrying the baby as a matter of personal conviction, not as a response to any pressure. He never preached at me or demanded that I do anything but directed me to prayer and to the Bible. After a week, my own convictions had been reinforced, and I knew I was doing the right thing."

At the time she was raped, Judy was just leaving her job, and her future was totally uncertain. She had no health insurance, and her finances were low. It was a bad time to be pregnant. It became an occasion for God's faithfulness. An ob/gyn provided free medical care. At one point she needed temporary housing, and this was provided as well. In the middle of her pregnancy Judy received "an extraordinarily good job . . . even though I needed time off." Employment benefits included health insurance, which covered her hospitalization and other medical expenses.

All during this time, Judy says her friends were "extremely supportive." "They'd invite me to the movies or shopping. I was included in activities and treated as a normal person."

Five-and-one-half months into her pregnancy, Judy decided to release her baby for adoption, although this was a difficult decision to make. Through a close friend, she was put in touch with a childless couple in the ministry who were eager to adopt a baby. Judy says with a great deal of satisfaction the child "has made their family life so much richer."

I had the opportunity to explore with Judy how God had worked in her life. Besides meeting all her physical needs, how had He ministered to her? "Even after I was raped," she said, "I had that familiar peace that God would take care of me, but it's important to understand how hard it was to deal with all this."

Judy shared that one of the most dramatic examples of God's grace came after she gave birth. "From the very minute she was born, I've never had a single moment of pain over losing her. I can only explain this by the grace of God."

Judy keeps a list of the lessons God taught her through her

experience. (She says this is so she will remember them and never have to be "re-taught.") "God taught me more about my regular old nonpregnant Christian walk than anything," she explained. Judy learned to accept help from others, and she learned that being vulnerable is not a hindrance to serving Christ. She maintains her belief in the sovereignty of God is now stronger than ever.

Judy also shared that "when you pray that God will help you reach a decision and then you begin to reach it, you have to believe that God is answering your prayer and not second guess yourself." This lesson she learned in deciding to release her baby for adoption.

As I concluded my interview with her, I had to ask Judy one more question. "Judy, have you ever regretted carrying the baby to term?"

"Never," she replied.[3]

When all the arguments have been exhausted, the fact remains that God is sovereign in creating life regardless of the circumstances. In the case of sexual assault, the guilt of the fathers does not rest on the children. Ethel Waters is a remarkable illustration of this.

Ethel was conceived when her twelve-year-old mother was raped. In spite of pressure to abort, Ethel's mother gave birth to her daughter and subsequently raised her. Ethel grew up to become an outstanding gospel singer and a powerful witness for Christ. For many years she was a regular participant in the Billy Graham crusades. Needless to say, in her autobiography Ethel extolled her mother's courage and love in resisting abortion.[4]

Abortion following sexual assault kills an innocent human being and increases the pain and suffering of the rape victim. As we oppose abortion in these hard cases, we must be prepared to extend whatever help and support are necessary to women like Judy as they carry their babies to term. They do not want pity, but they do need respect and love. Their needs are not met by platitudes but through the deeds of people who relate to them as normal human beings and through the knowledge of the living God.

Q: *Why do women have to do all the suffering in pregnancy?*
A: There is no question that women often have suffered the

---

3. Interview on file with the Christian Action Council.
4. Ethel Waters and Charles Samuels, *His Eye Is on the Sparrow* (1951; reprint, Westport, Conn.: Greenwood, 1978).

unfair share of the burden for out-of-wedlock pregnancies. Even within marriage, the unavoidable stress of pregnancy can be intensified through neglect and lack of support by the husband. In both instances, the absence of fatherhood through men's negligence is tragic and the main cause of suffering.

The feminist response, born of grief and hostility, is equally tragic. Rather than confronting men with their responsibilities as fathers, feminists reject men as providers of any sort. They demand the same "freedom," or absence of responsibility, that characterizes bad husbands and poor fathers. The rejection of fatherhood by men becomes the justification for the rejection of motherhood by women. Children inevitably become the victims, whether in abortion or in other forms of abuse and neglect.

The only way to ascend out of very difficult or brutal circumstances is by following Christ, who says, "Come to Me, all who are weary and heavy-laden, and I will give you rest. Take My yoke upon you, and learn from Me, for I am gentle and humble in heart; and you shall find rest for your souls. For My yoke is easy, and My load is light" (Matthew 11:28-30). Trusting Him to work out His kind will and good intention for our lives includes obedience. Even when we are subject to circumstances that are unfair or unjust, He calls us nonetheless to choose life with the promise that as His will is done, we will know unexpected blessing.

Q: *If abortion is again made illegal, would women be subject to prosecution for murder?*
A: This charge has been used with great effect by Planned Parenthood in their campaign to keep abortion legal. In fact they go even further, maintaining that with laws against abortion, "If you have a miscarriage, you could be prosecuted for murder."[5]

Given the role of precedents in the interpretation of law, it is inconceivable that women would be prosecuted for murder in the event of laws or a constitutional amendment prohibiting abortion. This is doubly the case given the bias of the judiciary toward feminist ideals.

Historically, Western society has viewed the willful killing of an unborn child as murder in the moral sense, a violation of God's commandment "Thou shalt not kill." Abortion has *never* been regarded as murder in the legal sense of the term. Accordingly, women have neither been charged with murder nor pros-

5. *Washington Post*, 27 April 1981.

ecuted for murder as a result of their abortions, although abortion was against the law.

In the event of a homicide, the law takes into consideration many factors before assigning the criminal charge of murder. These include the circumstances surrounding the act, the mental state of the individual at the time of the act, the intent or purpose behind the individual's actions, and so on. Accordingly, there are many degrees or categories of homicide, from first-degree murder to involuntary manslaughter.

Abortion has been treated in a category by itself, as "the crime of abortion." Prosecutions have been directed toward abortionists rather than toward the women, who typically have been regarded as victims.

One of the most significant studies published on this issue was produced by attorney Paul Wohlers for the American Center for Bioethics in Washington, D.C., entitled *Women and Abortion, the Prospects for Criminal Charges*. Wohlers investigated virtually every abortion-related case since the mid-1800s that reached the appellate level of state courts. His amazing discovery was that no woman was ever prosecuted for criminal abortion. While granting the woman's role in abortion was "illegal" and "immoral," prosecutions focused solely on the abortionists. The distinction between moral guilt and legal guilt was constantly maintained.

In criminal abortion trials where women were drawn in, the issue at law remained the guilt of the abortionist. Ironically, in over 90 percent of the instances where women were involved in trials, this was due to the abortionists, not to the prosecutors! *Abortionists* attempted to name their clients as accomplices.

> The defense—not the prosecution—sought to have such women named as accomplices because they often were the only eyewitnesses to their abortions. Since most states require that the testimony of an accomplice be corroborated before being admitted into evidence, the abortionist would typically allege that the woman was his accomplice in the performance of the abortion. The defense hoped thereby to make the woman's testimony inadmissable and thus, in the absence of corroborating evidence, to win acquittal.[6]

Of the forty states that confronted this issue, the courts in thirty-nine ruled that women were not accomplices. The excep-

6. Paul D. Wohlers, *Women and Abortion, the Prospects for Criminal Charges* (Washington, D.C.: American Center for Bioethics, 1981), p. 2.

tion was Alabama, but again, no criminal charges were filed against women.

A few states, primarily Iowa and Wisconsin, did name women as co-conspirators. As in the case of naming women as accomplices, the issue was not their guilt but the admissibility of their testimony in convicting abortionists. Prosecutors sought this ruling from judges in order to render women's testimony proper evidence in the trials.

There is absolutely no precedent to support the claim that criminal abortion statutes will result in the charge of murder being leveled against women who have aborted. Prosecution would be directed toward the abortionists. A contemporary analogy is found in the law's vigorous prosecution of dealers in illegal drugs rather than drug users, who are treated more as victims to be rehabilitated.

Q: *Isn't it wrong to bring a child into the world if you can't take care of him?*
A: No. It is never wrong to nurture life throughout pregnancy. It is always wrong to seek the death of an innocent member of the human family.

If a mother can do no more for her child than to carry the baby to term, she should not be condemned for the sacrifice she does make. The inability of birth parents to raise their child does not consign him to a loveless, suffering existence. Very often in these circumstances, family members or relatives fill in the gap and raise the baby as their own. Furthermore, in the US, adoption is a viable option. Estimates place the number of couples willing to adopt a child at 400,000. They are fully prepared to be parents to a child released into their care.

Q: *Does the unborn child have a soul?*
A: A great deal of confusion exists within the Body of Christ concerning this question. Often it is raised out of a misplaced concern that the presence or absence of a soul in the fetus determines whether abortion is acceptable.

Speculations concerning the soul are largely irrelevant and beside the point. Jesus said, "And I say to you, My friends, do not be afraid of those who kill the body, and after that have no more that they can do. But I will warn you whom to fear: fear the One who after He has killed has authority to cast into hell; yes, I tell you, fear Him!" (Luke 12:4-5). Jesus made the point that when men kill another human being, they are not destroying the soul, but rather the body of the individual. In the prohibition against killing, the destruction of the body—not the soul—is in view.

Every abortion destroys the body of a developing human being, robbing him of his life. The obvious evidence of abortion—the mangled corpses of tiny humans—is enough to show that abortion is the moral equivalent of murder. We need not speculate on the relationship between the body and the soul. Some further observations, however, may be helpful.

By the third century A.D., Christian theology was strongly influenced by Hellenistic, or Greek, philosophy. Greek notions colored the theological understanding of the soul and the soul's relationship to the body. From this syncretism, the concept of ensoulment developed in Christian theology, whereby the soul was viewed as the most important part of an individual, trapped within the body and subsequently released at death. Speculation abounded as to when the soul first enters the body.

This viewpoint involved a false dichotomy between the spiritual and physical nature of man. The physical was viewed as defiled and inferior because of its physicalness, while the spiritual part of man was viewed as pure and good because of its spiritualness (generally related to man's reason).

The Bible never teaches this dichotomy. It does teach that people are made up of body, soul, and spirit, frequently interchanging the notion of the soul with that of spirit. In characterizing man in this way, the Bible reveals three aspects of man, not three parts that war against each other.

Unlike the fragmented Greek concept of man as a dichotomy, the Hebrew concept of a man as a fundamental unity pervades the Scriptures. The New Testament's theology of resurrection reinforces this idea. Sin divides and fragments man. This is most evident in death. Through redemption, however, our individual unity is restored. We are not created to be disembodied spirits. (See 1 Corinthians 15:42-49; 2 Corinthians 5:1-5.)

Too often Paul's reference to the spirit's warring against the flesh has been taken to mean that a fundamental division exists within man, between his physical nature and his spiritual nature. In this context the flesh has been understood to mean the physical body when in fact it connotes the propensity we have as sons of Adam to sin, our sin nature. Paul does not present the conflict within man as between the physical and the spiritual, but rather between sin and redemption.

Does the unborn have a soul? If he is a living being, he *is* a soul (Genesis 2:7). The weight of biblical evidence leaves no room to doubt that the unborn child is a human being created by God in His image.

Q: *If abortion is prohibited under the law, won't this result in a return to dangerous "back alley" abortions?*
A: Surprisingly, the legalization of abortion has not eliminated "back alley," criminal abortions. There continue to be in the United States deaths from illegal, botched abortions, although those are few in number. Complications from illegal abortion are periodically reported by the Centers for Disease Control.[7]

In nations where widespread abortion has been legal for longer periods of time, reports confirm that criminal abortions continue. Senator James L. Buckley summed up this phenomenon in testimony before the Senate Subcommittee on Constitutional Amendments during the 93d Congress.

> Data from foreign countries having far longer experience with legalized abortion than we have had in the U.S. suggest that legalization has no effect on the criminal abortion rate. In at least three countries the criminal abortion rate has actually risen since legalization. Legalized abortion moves the back alley abortionists into the front office where their trade can be practiced without fear of criminal prosecution.[8]

The last point Senator Buckley made is especially relevant to understanding the effects of legal abortion. Numerous lawsuits and press reports have confirmed the scandal-ridden nature of the abortion industry, largely because it is unregulated by law. The lengthiest exposé to date appeared in the Chicago *Sun-Times*, from November 12 to 22, 1978. Deplorable practices and abuses within the posh Michigan Avenue clinics of Chicago were uncovered.

1. Twelve women lost their lives as a result of "safe," legal abortions. Many of the deaths had not been reported as abortion-related.
2. Incompetent doctors—including one physician who had lost his license in another state—staffed clinics.
3. Dozens of abortion procedures had been performed on women who were not even pregnant.
4. Women had suffered the loss of all their reproductive organs as a result of complications from botched abortions.

7. See as an example *Morbidity and Morality Weekly Report*, 2 February 1979.
8. Hearings before the Subcommittee on Constitutional Amendments, US Senate Subcommittee on the Constitution, 93d Congress, Appendix F, 81.

5. Women were badly mistreated: "He didn't wait five minutes. He started right in. I was screaming, and squirming all over the table. I asked him to stop until the anesthetic took effect." In some instances abortions were being performed in two minutes without the benefit of pain-killing drugs.
6. One physician had earned nearly $800,000 in Medicaid reimbursements from abortions during a single year.
7. The reporters found one example of doctors who raced each other to see who could perform the most abortions. They kept score by placing hash marks on their surgical gowns.

There is no reason to assume these abuses do not occur in abortion clinics across America. But few major papers have the will of the *Sun-Times* to set aside their pro-abortion bias long enough to sponsor investigative journalism. Abortion may be legal, but it does not at all follow that "back-alley butchers" are no longer in business.

When the Hyde amendment, cutting off Medicaid funds for abortion, was initially passed in Congress, abortion proponents predicted poor women would return to the illegal abortions of the past, and a bloodbath would follow. A year after the Hyde amendment had taken effect, Dr. Willard Cates, spokesman for the Abortion Surveillance Branch of the Centers for Disease Control, reported, "The bloodbath many predicted simply is not happening. . . . Our numbers don't show that there has been any mass migration to illegal procedures."[9]

Since the bloodbath didn't occur, how do we explain reports that as many as 10,000 women were dying each year from illegal abortion prior to *Roe* v. *Wade?* It isn't difficult; they were false. In 1967 the Federal government reported 160 deaths from illegal abortion. In 1972, the number was 39. As cofounder of the National Abortion Rights Action League, Dr. Bernard Nathanson has supplied a very plausible rationale behind the inflated figures.

> In NARAL, we generally emphasized the drama of the individual case, not the mass statistics, but when we spoke of the latter, it was always, "5,000 to 10,000 deaths a year." I confess that I knew the figures were totally false, and I suppose the others did too if they stopped to think of it. But in the "morality" of our revolution, it was a useful figure, widely accepted, so why go out of our way to correct it with honest statistics?[10]

9. *Washington Post,* 16 February 1978.
10. Bernard Nathanson, *Aborting America* (Garden City, N.Y.: Doubleday, 1979), p. 193.

Nathanson further maintains that should abortion be prohibited by law and illegal procedures result, the technology of abortion makes the horrific images painted by abortion proponents very doubtful.

> The practice of abortion was revolutionized at virtually the same moment the laws were revolutionized, through the widespread introduction of suction curettage in 1970 . . . Though it is preferable that this be done by a licensed physician, one can expect that if abortion is ever driven undergound again, even non-physicians will be able to perform this procedure with remarkable safety.[11]

Even with legal abortion, a woman can face an incompetent or sadistic physician. If the abortionist is highly skilled, this means he is proficient at destroying life in the womb without injuring the mother. I am grateful that most abortions do not kill two human beings. Nonetheless, they kill one. This extermination of human life cannot be tolerated by a legal system whose hallmark is freedom.

Q: *Does Planned Parenthood really advocate abortion?*
A: There is no organization in the United States that has done more to promote abortion on demand than Planned Parenthood. The organization has been involved in virtually every abortion-related case that has come before the US Supreme Court. In *Planned Parenthood of Central Missouri* v. *Danforth* and *Planned Parenthood Association of Kansas City, Missouri, Inc.* v. *Ashcroft*, the organization's affiliates were the plaintiffs, or official parties, seeking a change in the law. In those and other cases, Planned Parenthood has argued that parents have no right to be informed of their minor daughter's abortion, that parents have no right to determine through their consent whether their minor daughter should have an abortion, and that a male spouse has no legal right to oppose the aborting of his own child.

According to the 1980 annual report of Planned Parenthood Federation of America, the organization comprises 188 affiliates and more than 700 clinics in 42 states and the District of Columbia. The clinics provided prenatal care to 700 women. They provided abortions to 60,000! One of Planned Parenthood's "services to affiliates" includes a "loan fund to help affiliates initiate surgical services." The organization displays missionary zeal in establishing new abortion clinics.

11. Ibid., p. 194.

Planned Parenthood receives large amounts of money through private donations. And of course, the abortion business is very lucrative. The bulk of the organization's money, however, comes from the United States government. In fact the Planned Parenthood network receives approximately $120 million each year from the Federal government alone. Similarly, large amounts of money are received from local and state governments.

Although PPFA does not declare itself to be a political organization with the IRS, its leaders nonetheless boast of their "Public Impact Program" whose mission is "to safeguard the fundamental right of every individual to full access to reproductive health care." Much of this is propaganda for abortion on demand. You may have seen the full page ads Planned Parenthood ran in major papers from 1981-1983, opposing efforts in Congress to curb abortion. The annual report readily admits active efforts to defeat "restrictive abortion legislation" both in Washington, D.C., and in state capitols across the country.

Planned Parenthood's mission cannot be accurately understood from its slogans. The organization was born of an elitest commitment to population control, not "family planning." There is nothing to indicate any departure from this goal. In Planned Parenthood's Five-Year Plan for 1976-1980, "patient load goals" were established for the numbers of women from various ages or backgrounds PPFA was determined to abort. The commitment to population control at times becomes ludicrous as well as offensive. In 1982, Planned Parenthood Federation of America was the only non-Communist organization to denounce Solidarity, the Polish trade union. Why? Because Solidarity opposed abortion. This led to the dismissal of PPFA from the Combined Federal Campaign, the Federal government's "United Way" among its workers. But alas, the following day a Federal judge ordered that Planned Parenthood must be included as an acceptable charity!

Q: *Does Exodus 21:22-25 justify abortion?*

> And if men struggle with each other and strike a woman with child so that she has a miscarriage, yet there is no further injury, he shall surely be fined as the woman's husband may demand of him; and he shall pay as the judges decide.
> But if there is any further injury, then you shall appoint as a penalty life for life, eye for eye, tooth for tooth, hand for hand, foot for foot, burn for burn, wound for wound, bruise for bruise.

A: Since abortion has become a controversial issue among denominational bodies, attempts have been made to construe this passage as biblical support for abortion. These take advantage of the fact that the meaning of the verses is not absolutely clear. Two possible interpretations exist. Regardless, neither of those remotely suggests that willful abortion is acceptable to God.

One interpretation understands verses 22-25 to refer to accidentally induced miscarriage in which the death of the unborn child is presupposed. The "further injury" phrase refers exclusively to the mother, so that penalties assessed for further injury reflect a concern only for the mother's health and life.

This understanding has been alleged to support abortion. Since the death of the unborn child did not result in the penalty of "life for life," the fetus must be regarded as less than a human being, or creature made in God's image.

This argument is unpersuasive for a variety of reasons. If this passage deals with "abortion," it is accidentally induced abortion that is in view, not abortion on demand. The passage regards the man responsible for the accident as a guilty party who must pay a fine even if no further injury occurs. If verses 22-25 do not exempt from guilt a man who accidentally induces an abortion, how much greater is the Divine condemnation of one who purposefully undertakes the destruction of unborn life?

The fact that a fine rather than capital punishment is prescribed for the guilty party in no way suggests the unborn child is regarded as less than human. For accidental homicide, capital punishment is not as a rule invoked in the Torah. The preceding verse, Exodus 21:20, provides us with an example of this.

The second interpretation of Exodus 21:22-25 holds that it refers to accidentally induced birth, or premature delivery, in which the baby may survive. The "further injury" phrase refers both to the mother and to the child. Thus, if no further injury is done to the mother or child other than the induction of birth, the man responsible is deemed guilty before God and must pay a fine. If further injury to either party does occur, the guilty man must pay according to the law, eye for an eye, and so on.

This interpretation of the passage is the most plausible. The woman is identified in the Hebrew text as literally being "with child." The verb in verse 22 that is translated "has a miscarriage," in every other context clearly refers to live childbirth.

The absence of a named antecedent for the "further injury" phrase is the cause of uncertainty over the meaning of this passage. Nevertheless, Hebrew grammar is inclined to support the rule that if an antecedent to a qualifying phrase is not named, then the phrase most likely refers to the nearest preceding term that could serve as an antecedent or to all preceding terms in the sentence that could qualify as antecedents. In the text, the nearest possible antecedent is a reference to the child, not to the mother. Surely, the mother is in view nonetheless. Thus, both the child and the mother are subject to the "further injury" qualification. This argument is not conclusive, but it is significant.

There is reason to question why this passage is present at all in the Torah if not to lay emphasis on the value of the unborn child. Indeed, accidental homicide is treated in a variety of other passages. What is unique about verses 22-25 in all the Torah is their consideration of the unborn.

One last matter must be addressed, that of the penalty under the second interpretation. This would include capital punishment (life for life) for the guilty party in the event the infant died after birth. How can this be since the incident represented accidental homicide?

There is a principle of mercy and justice clearly taught throughout the Bible. The weaker and more vulnerable an individual is, the greater is our responsibility to care for him. Similarly, the greater is our guilt if we do him harm.

A host of biblical scholars have taken this strong view of the passage. These include John Calvin and the nineteenth-century commentators Keil and Delitzsch. Contemporary Old Testament scholars Gleason Archer and Meredith Kline are also among them. On the strength of exegetical evidence, some scholars have changed their understanding of this passage and adopted the strong view. Jack Cotrell is one example.

One of the most exhaustive treatments of Exodus 21:22-25 may be found in the "Report of the Committee to Study the Matter of Abortion," presented to the 38th General Assembly of the Orthodox Presbyterian Church in May of 1971.

Annotated Bibliography

Bosgra, Tj. *Abortion, the Bible and the Church.* To order write: Hawaii Right to Life Educational Foundation, P.O. Box 10129, Honolulu, HI 96816. This book is an extensive survey of religious institutions and ministries in the United States that documents their positions on abortion.

Brown, Harold O. J. *Death Before Birth.* Nashville: Nelson, 1977. Dr. Brown's book continues to be an excellent introduction to the abortion question from a Christian perspective.

Garton, Jean Staker. *Who Broke the Baby?* Minneapolis: Bethany Fellowship, 1979. This fine book analyzes the slogans used to promote abortion. It is very readable.

Gorman, Michael J. *Abortion and the Early Church.* Downers Grove, Ill.: Inter-Varsity, 1982. Mr. Gorman's contribution to the abortion debate among Christians is considerable. He brings to light the position of the early church on abortion through a study of early Christian literature. He deals as well with prevailing pagan and Jewish views of abortion at the time of Christ.

Grisez, Germain. *Abortion: The Myths, the Realities, and the Arguments.* New York: Corpus, 1970. Although somewhat dated, this remains one of the most exhaustive treatments of the abortion question ever produced.

Grisez, Germain, and Boyle, Joseph M. *Life and Death with*

Liberty and Justice. Notre Dame, Ind.: U. of Notre Dame, 1979. This book covers the abortion controversy generally. It contains a great deal of insight.

Hilgers, Thomas W., and Horan, Dennis J. *Abortion and Social Justice.* New York: Sheed and Ward, 1972. Somewhat dated, this book nonetheless is a very fine treatment of the abortion issue from a variety of perspectives (legal, medical, etc.).

Hilgers, Thomas W.; Horan, Dennis, J.; and Mall, David, eds. *New Perspectives on Human Abortion.* Frederick, Md.: University Publications, 1981. Representing the thoughts of scholars and professionals dedicated to the preservation of human life, this collection of articles represents a very fine reference work on the abortion question.

Horan, Dennis J., and Mall, David. *Death, Dying, and Euthanasia.* Washington, D.C.: University Publications, 1977. This is a very lengthy and technical book on the subject of euthanasia. Its value to the layman is limited.

Horan, Dennis J., and Delahoyde, Melinda, eds. *Infanticide and the Handicapped Newborn.* Provo, Utah: Brigham Young U., 1982. The articles in this book together represent a good survey of issues in infanticide, presented from a sanctity-of-life perspective.

Koop, Dr. C. Everett. *The Right to Live; the Right to Die.* Wheaton, Ill.: Tyndale, 1976. This book represents the thoughts of an impressive and godly man who has given his life to the treatment of children with handicaps.

Mall, David, and Watts, Walter F., eds. *The Psychological Aspects of Abortion.* Washington, D.C.: University Publications, 1979. Produced in part to counter the preponderance of psychological reports sympathetic to abortion, this book is analytical in nature and does not address in any detail counseling approaches.

Nathanson, Bernard. *Aborting America.* Garden City, N.Y.: Doubleday, 1979. As cofounder of the National Abortion Rights Action League, Dr. Nathanson recounts a history of the pro-abortion movement as only an insider can. He also deals with the issue of abortion overall as one who changed his mind and now opposes the practice.

Noonan, John T., Jr. *A Private Choice: Abortion in America in the Seventies.* New York: Free Press, 1979. Dr. Noonan's book is probably the best critique of the abortion issue that has been published. The style is lucid and the arguments concise. It is packed with information as well as anecdotes.

Powell, John. *Abortion: The Silent Holocaust.* Allen, Tex.: Argus, 1981. Father Powell has rendered a tremendous service to the right-to-life movement in bringing his pen to bear on the abortion question. His book is easy to read, very informative, and highly motivating.

Ramsey, Paul. *Ethics at the Edges of Life.* New Haven, Conn.: Yale U., 1978. Professor Ramsey is one of the foremost ethicists writing from a sanctity-of-life perspective. In this book, he considers in some detail court cases, decisions of the Supreme Court, and laws that bear upon abortion, infanticide, and euthanasia.

Schaeffer, Francis A., and Koop, C. Everett. *Whatever Happened to the Human Race?* Old Tappan, N.J.: Revell, 1979. Drs. Koop and Schaeffer teamed up to present an outstanding treatment of abortion, infanticide, and euthanasia. Its peculiar strengths are derived from Dr. Koop's wealth of practical knowledge and experience combined with Dr. Schaeffer's keen ability to frame issues and give perspective.

Thielicke, Helmut. *The Ethics of Sex.* Grand Rapids, Mich.: Baker, 1975. This book addresses human sexuality broadly. A number of issues besides abortion are addressed, including contraception, marriage, and the nature of sexual relations.

The premier pro-life journal is the *Human Life Review,* published by the Human Life Foundation, Inc., Room 540, 150 E. 35th Street, New York, NY 10016.

CHRISTIAN ACTION COUNCIL

The Christian Action Council exists to serve the Body of Christ in its witness against abortion. The organization was established in 1975, following a two-day conference of Christian leaders in the home of Billy Graham. Its numerous sponsors include Harold O. J. Brown, D. Stuart Briscoe, Elisabeth Elliot Gren, Gordon H. Clark, Harold Lindsell, J. Robertson McQuilkin, and Edith Schaeffer.

The Christian Action Council, headquartered in Washington, D.C., has affiliates and Crisis Pregnancy Centers throughout the continental US. The Council has become one of the largest prolife groups in America, uniquely Christian in its commitment. The organization spearheads a number of efforts critical to the protection of human life. These include:

1. Testifying to those who make and enforce our national and state laws that God has His standards that we humans must honor. Beyond testimony, the Council actively works to pass legislation that upholds the sanctity of human life. Since 1979, Doug Badger has served as the Council's legislative director.

2. Educating churches and Christians on issues related to the sanctity of human life. The Council's Speaker's Bureau includes seasoned educators on abortion, infanticide, euthanasia, genetic technologies, and matters related to church and state. In addition CAC literature serves to equip Christians to address these issues. Materials include a series of educational brochures, *Action Line* newsletter, and a worship manual for pastors for a "Sanctity of Human Life Sunday." As of August 1984, a Sunday school curriculum dealing with the sanctity of human life is available for distribution to churches. It features videotaped and written materials.

3. Establishing Christian Action Councils in communities throughout the country. These are community-based efforts to resist abortion and pursue protection for the unborn. The Council has developed a variety of instructive materials and other helps for Christians determined to bear witness in this way. These include periodic nationwide events that are implemented at the community level.

4. Developing Crisis Pregnancy Centers. As a prolife organization the Christian Action Council is comprehensive in its approach to the abortion problem. The development of ministries in alternatives to abortion consumes a major portion of

the organization's resources. Working in the capacity of consultants and instructors with churches, Council staff impart the program of ministry and the training necessary for the ministry.

If you would like to know more about the Christian Action Council and its diverse ministries, please inquire at the following address:

Christian Action Council
422 C St., N.E.
Washington, D.C. 20002

Moody Press, a ministry of the Moody Bible Institute, is designed for education, evangelization, and edification. If we may assist you in knowing more about Christ and the Christian life, please write us without obligation: Moody Press, c/o MLM, Chicago, Illinois 60610.